15/24.

THE
COUNTRY PARSON

Also by Anthony Russell and published by SPCK:

The Country Parish (1986)
The Clerical Profession (1980)
Editor: *Groups and Teams in the Countryside* (1975)
Contributor: *Working for the Kingdom*, edited by
John Fuller and Patrick Vaughan (1986)
The Study of Spirituality, edited by
Cheslyn Jones, Geoffrey Wainwright and E. J. Yarnold SJ
(1986)

THE
COUNTRY PARSON

Anthony Russell

To Sheila

First published in Great Britain 1993
Society for Promoting Christian Knowledge
Holy Trinity Church
Marylebone Road
London NW1 4DU

© Anthony Russell 1993

British Library Cataloguing-in-Publication Data
A catalogue record for this book is available from the British Library

ISBN 0-281-04695-6

Typeset by Pioneer Associates Ltd, Perthshire
Printed in Great Britain by
Biddles Ltd, Guildford and King's Lynn

Contents

Preface

This book is published in the year in which the four-hundredth anniversary of George Herbert's birth is celebrated. During its preparation the author has been aware that to write about George Herbert is to tread on holy ground, for such is the regard in which both he and his poetry are held by so many people. Although this book has its roots in the life and work of George Herbert, it is not directly concerned with his poetry but with a lesser-known work, *The Country Parson*, and the implications of what he wrote for those who minister in rural communities today.

Many of the chapters of this book were first given as talks or addresses to clergy groups in this country and abroad and I am grateful for the comments and suggestions that were made on these occasions. Many of the ideas in this book were first developed in the discussions of the Archbishops' Commission on Rural Areas (ACORA), whose report *Faith in the Countryside* was published in 1990. To the members of the Commission I owe a considerable debt for their friendship and stimulation.

Undoubtedly this book has suffered from the piecemeal fashion in which it has been written, amidst many other concerns; it would not have been written at all without the patience and skill of Mrs Caroline Long, who typed the manuscript and to whom I owe a deep debt of gratitude.

I would like to thank in particular Miss K. M. Lea (formerly Vice-Principal of Lady Margaret Hall) for kindly lending me Professor F. E. Hutchinson's own copy of his definitive edition of George Herbert's works, published in 1941. During the rest of his life Hutchinson added, in his microscopic handwriting, points of elucidation and new references as he discovered them. I am also grateful to the Reverend Ben de la Mare for his assistance in the final stages of the preparation of this book, and for the help of the Reverend Alan Archer (priest-in-charge of Bemerton).

This book has been completed at the time when the Church of England has taken the decision to ordain women to the priesthood. The words *clergyman* and *he* have been used throughout this book, partly for reasons of stylistic simplicity and partly because they correspond with George Herbert's own usage. In a relatively short time, it is likely that many women will serve in rural areas where their contribution will be greatly appreciated, as they take their place in the tradition of rural pastoral ministry which goes back to George Herbert's book *The Country Parson*.

Finally, to the clergy and people of Oxfordshire I owe a considerable debt of gratitude for their stimulation and encouragement in recent years which is reflected at many points in this book.

Holmby House   Anthony Russell
September 1992

1

The Country Parson
and the
Anglican Pastoral Tradition:
An Introduction

It might be said that it is already too late to write a book about the country clergyman and the Church's ministry in rural communities. Declining congregations, the problems of maintaining the many church buildings, the financial crisis of the Church and the difficulties of meeting traditional expectations are all regarded as symptoms of an institution in terminal decline. In 1985, reviewing a report on the Church in Suffolk, the Religious Affairs correspondent of *The Times* wrote (7 June): 'The Church of England faces extinction in the countryside in the next twenty years . . . it is a picture of unmitigated hopelessness.'

Two years later, the anonymous author of the *Crockford's* Preface (later identified as Dr Gareth Bennett) wrote: 'Perhaps the most serious problem of all is the future of the Church of England in the countryside . . . at a time when there is so much discussion of ministry in the inner cities, there is an urgent need for new thinking about the rural ministry and new encouragement for the clergy.' Such thinking led to the establishment of the Archbishops' Commission for Rural Areas which took evidence from many people and whose report *Faith in the Countryside* was published in 1990. Two bishops advised the Commission that the Church should prepare itself to carry out what would be in effect a strategic withdrawal from the countryside and should concentrate such resources as remained in the market towns. One bishop specifically said that under no circumstances should a clergyman under the age of 55 be appointed to a rural parish. The Rural Church Project (a research project partly funded by the Archbishops' Commission) reported:

> Our basic conclusion is that the content and meaning of clergy work remains firmly within traditional understandings of the parochial ministry and of the parson as the focus of that ministry. The clergy are hard working, they perceive their task in fairly traditional terms and exhibit relatively high levels of job satisfaction. It is at that point that we run up against the thrust of much recent theology of ministry which not only questions the efficacy of a clerically based ministry but does so, in some cases, on the assumption that the traditional role of the clergyman has largely broken down.

In recent decades no part of the Church, not even in the inner city, has experienced such dramatic change as the Church in the countryside. Almost exactly a hundred years ago, Dean Church wrote of the country clergyman:

> He was often much, very much, to the society around him. When communication was so difficult and infrequent he filled a place in the country life of England which no-one else could fill. He was often the patriarch of his parish, its ruler, its doctor, its lawyer, its magistrate, as well as its teacher, before whom vice trembled and rebellion dared not show itself. (R. W. Church, *The Oxford Movement* (London 1891), p. 3)

By contrast, today, rural ministry and the life of the rural clergyman can seem peripheral both to rural society and to the Church as a whole; those who serve in country parishes are sometimes made to feel that they are members of the Church's 'second eleven'. Certainly, within the living memory of the older members of the congregation, the church had an acknowledged place in the life of the village, of which its resident clergyman was a conspicuous and respected member; well-attended services were held every Sunday; there was a Sunday school; a youth fellowship; uniformed organizations and a Mothers' Union. Much of village life seemed to focus naturally around the church and its annual programme of activities. Today, in many places, the clergyman responsible for the church lives as many as five miles away and is rarely seen in the village; services are held at fortnightly intervals and the small congregation is oppressed by the financial burden of maintaining an ancient building and contributing to the diocese for its services. Of the annual programme of activities there is now almost no trace.

Conventionally, this process is known as 'the breakdown of the parochial system', a process which has been discerned by contemporary observers at almost all stages of the history of the Church of England. In 1927 the author of the Preface to *Crockford's Clerical Directory* commented that 'a crisis of the first magnitude draws nearer every year'. Then, as now, this crisis was attributed to the gradual decline in the number of stipendiary clergy but, as later chapters will show, if the parochial system is breaking down, the causes of that may be found in the changing patterns of rural society at the end of the twentieth century. In reality, the 'parochial system' like 'the Establishment' has proved to be an enduring part of the life of the Church because it stands for certain understandings about the nature of the Church and because of its inherent flexibility. If the parochial system is thought of only in terms of the form it took in the twelfth and thirteenth centuries (when clericalism was at its peak), in which there was one clergyman for one church within a single community, then the Church of England has never at any stage in its history been able to operate this model (though it came close to it in the last quarter of the nineteenth century). Clergy numbers, relative to the number of churches and congregations, have never been high enough for this to be possible and Herbert himself served two communities. In every generation the organization of the Church in the countryside has had to be adapted to a number of constraints, as is described in Chapter 5. Perhaps what is termed 'the breakdown of the parochial system' in the contemporary Church is but one more stage in the long history of its development and change.

Whilst Jane Austen (the daughter and sister of country clergy) wrote that 'a clergyman has nothing to do but to be slovenly and selfish, read the newspapers, watch the weather and quarrel with his wife', the modern country clergyman finds himself with a great deal to do as he attempts to spread his time over five or six parishes, and, in extreme cases, as many as seventeen. Charles Forder, in an influential book on the work of the clergyman (*The Parish Priest at Work*, 1947) turns to rural ministry in the penultimate of his twenty-nine chapters. The overriding sense that he conveys is that the country clergyman possesses leisure, in a low-key and un-demanding occupation; a pipe smoking, tweed-jacketed existence, well away from the demands and activity of urban ministry. Andrew Bowden has written of his experience as a member of the Archbishops' Commission: 'Time and again we met clergy who were bewildered, frustrated, unclear about what they should be doing.' It is this observation, shared by other members of the Commission, which provides the spur for this book, for nothing undermines the dedication, energy and effectiveness of many country clergy so much as this lack of a clear vision of the nature of their task. At such a time, it may be helpful to look back to that formative era in which many of the central ideas about the Anglican pastoral ministry were first shaped and set down by George Herbert in his book of pastoral guidance, *The Country Parson*.

This is the third in a sequence of separate but related books which have been concerned both with the Church and with the countryside. The first, *The Clerical Profession* (SPCK 1980), was concerned with the historical development of the clergyman's role, particularly in the late eighteenth and early nineteenth century when that role took on many of the conventions of a professional occupation. The second, *The Country Parish* (SPCK 1986), was concerned with the context of the Church's ministry and the way in which changes in the countryside and the village have had a significant impact on the development and modern outlooks of rural ministry. This book seeks to describe the nature and content of the clergyman's role today and does so by reference to that period in which the English pastoral tradition was established in its recognizably modern form. Although the context has changed so significantly, the insights and vision set out by George

Herbert still form the heart of Anglican rural ministry and, for this reason, George Herbert remains in some ways our contemporary because the values and understandings which he enunciated remain of contemporary significance. A further similarity with the present situation may be found in the fact that Herbert was aware of writing at a time when the country parson was held in low esteem and when country clergy lacked confidence in the task that was before them.

T. S. Eliot was once asked why he drew so heavily from the past, since 'we know so much more than they did'. 'Precisely', he replied, 'they are what we know.' It sometimes seems, particularly to country clergy, that the Church of England is imprisoned by its history, yet the events of the sixteenth and seventeenth centuries will always be of profound significance for the Church ('The Caroline period' is an inaccurate phrase, variously interpreted, but it often refers to the period between 1594 and 1728; that is, from the publication of Hooker's first volume of *The Laws of Ecclesiastical Polity* to William Law's *A Serious Call to the Devout and Holy Life*). Many of the problems which face the Church today can be traced back to this period. The tension between views of the Church as an open institution 'an inn in which all those who come are welcome' and as a gathered institution with a strong sense of its own membership is present in the Church today and was among the causes of the English Civil War. As Hensley Henson wrote, this is 'the ancient controversy between the parish church and the gathered congregation which played such a prominent role in the seventeenth century'.

The Church of England is an enigmatic institution and scarcely less so is the role of its clergy, and neither can be understood or explained without reference to their historic development. To some, the lack of appreciation and understanding of the Church's history and the failure of confidence within the Church in recent years seem not unconnected, for an ignorance of history robs us of the perspectives with which to judge and evaluate the present problems which face the Church. For some, the history of the Church imprisons and confines; but to neglect the Church's history is, by implication, to deny the truth that the Church is the product of a process of historical development and that its present is built out of its past. Certainly, in the country church the past is never dead, and to ignore the way it has shaped the present is to have only an incomplete understanding of the contemporary situation. In the late 1970s those responsible for the examinations taken by candidates for ordination removed church history from the list of required subjects. Yet all the evidence is that the Church of England needs to take a firmer hold on its own tradition: that chain of belief and practice that stretches across the generations and of which we are the heirs. Certainly, it is impossible to be unaware, in a country church, of the former generations who have knelt where we kneel, whose lips have repeated these prayers and whose feet have worn these stones. They are part of the testimony that authenticates our faith and gives quiet assurance to our tradition. The forty years between the accession of James I and the onset of the Civil War saw the flowering of the Anglican tradition, which firmly rejected the notion that it was a sixteenth-century creation, and was aware of its lineage and inheritance from the early Church and the patristic period. Herbert, Ferrar, Andrewes, Donne and Laud, to record only some of the principal names, belong to what Izaak Walton came to regard as the high noon of Caroline Anglicanism. The oldest of these men, Lancelot Andrewes, passed on to the next generation an understanding of the Church not as a schismatic body but as an integral part of Catholic Christendom. If Anglicanism, the *via media*, had something of value, and particularly its own, to merit its survival, it must show itself not only in controversy, but in prayer, worship and Christian living, to be a worthy member of the Holy Catholic Church. It was on the quality of life of such men as Andrewes and Herbert that that claim came to rest.

   Those who serve in rural parishes are aware of entering into the tradition of Anglican country ministry which has existed in its recognizably modern form at least since the birth of George Herbert four hundred years ago. On the night of an institution in a country parish in Oxfordshire the new incumbent may glance at the row of photographs and pictures in the vestry which record at least some of the long line of clergy that have served in that parish. He will kneel where they have knelt, as the Archdeacon inducts him into the 'real and actual possession of the church and benefice'. He will be aware of entering into a tradition of country ministry which can be traced back to the pages of *The Country Parson*. In Oxfordshire, the seventeenth century seems present in an almost tangible way; close to the house where this book was written is the lane which Charles I used when he left his army on the main Banbury to Chipping Norton road to visit his friends at Great Tew. At Northmoor church are the altar rails originally given by Archbishop Laud as a gift to his college, St John's; it is hard not to be aware of the significance of those altar rails and the consequence of Laud's insistence in this and other matters. A little further away is the small country church at Finstock, where, in 1927, T. S. Eliot was baptized. Eliot did much to reawaken the Church to the significance of its seventeenth-century heritage and in particular the lives of Andrewes and Herbert.

Conventional solutions offered to the problems of the contemporary rural church often take the form of advocating the extension of non-stipendiary and local ministry and the involvement of the laity in every aspect of the church's life and ministry. While such developments are, without doubt, the route along which the rural church in the future must progress, little is said about the future role of the country clergyman. Indeed, it is suggested by some that in the future he will either be unneeded or simply will have disappeared. This book, by returning to that formative period, seeks to restate the central Anglican understanding about the clergyman's role in the countryside and his life in the country parish. It is offered in the belief that God still calls ordinary men to this extraordinary task, as he called George Herbert to serve in the parish of Bemerton. The reason that what George Herbert wrote has the capacity to stretch across a gulf of four hundred years lies in the fact that he touched upon the essential features of parish ministry which remain unchanged by the passage of time. In every age, George Herbert has been appreciated as a profound analyst of the mind and soul. During his ministry he may have seemed an obscure country clergyman, but through his life, and through *The Country Parson*, he is perceived as a man who, in many ways, is our contemporary. Still, God is using the gifts which, in his lifetime, George Herbert feared were wasted. In any age, the mark that a priest should aim at is that his life should reflect Christ and that others should see, and share a glimpse of, the hidden glory in and through him. In Herbert, his parishioners and friends saw in this tall, gracious man something of the hidden Christ.

2

The Role of the Clergyman

It is not necessary to search far to find in church newspapers and ecclesiastical journals articles with such titles as 'Parish priests in search of a role' (Leighton Thomas, *Church Times*, 14 April 1989) or books with such titles as *Priesthood and Ministry in Crisis* (Terence Card, SCM Press 1988). The theological and ecclesiological upheaval of the 1970s and 1980s has left many clergy uncertain about their role and their function. Many find themselves adrift in a society which they do not understand and which gives little evidence of either understanding or valuing them. Some continue to obey their traditional instincts but others have begun to doubt whether there is a specifically priestly task still to be performed. For some, the only solution to these dilemmas has been quietly to withdraw from the ministry; the vast majority have continued, but have found themselves increasingly troubled as hard questions are asked with more confidence than answers can be found. Few could claim to be unaffected by these uncertainties and not a few have found themselves giving way to cynicism, despair or aggressive self-justification.

If clergymen today are apologetic about their role, reasons may be sought, both in the general changes that have affected the place of religion in society and the more specific changes which have affected the situation of the clergyman, particularly in rural areas. In what has been called a post-Christian society, the Church, as an organization, has become increasingly marginal and has lost the precedency which, as a social institution, it once possessed. At the same time, personal and social situations are no longer diagnosed, or remedies sought, in terms of religion, in a society where to think and act in secular terms has become conventional. Thus, the Church has ceased to be the arbiter of moral values, and, at the local level,

9

as will be shown in Chapter 5, social welfare and many other matters passed out of the hands of the Church in the nineteenth century to other professional agencies. In many ways, the tolerant pluralistic character of English society, particularly in the village, has disguised the extent to which the Church's position has declined and the legacy of the Church's former importance in all aspects of local life continues to cast a long shadow.

But the reasons for the apparent crisis in the identity of the clergyman's role must be sought in more specific and immediate factors. All occupational roles depend upon that role being understood and supported within the wider society; a part of the weakening of the self-confidence of the clergy results from the declining public understanding and appreciation of the clergyman's role. In a sense, society no longer sees the significance, nor has any expectation of, what the clergyman has to offer, and, as a consequence, the clergyman's role has lost social support and understanding, and the clergy themselves perceive that their role has lost status and significance. When George Herbert went visiting in the afternoon in Bemerton he could find people 'religiously employed'. Today, the majority of people the clergyman meets no longer appreciate the nature of his role nor do they understand why he should be visiting in his parish during the afternoon. Many seem to think he must either be selling something or collecting for charity. The fact that the clergy role eludes easy definition and is not widely understood in society has led to assumptions that there are no duties to be performed other than those that are highly visible, such as the leadership of worship on Sunday. Clergy constantly experience comments which imply that they have little to do during the week and that Sunday is their busiest day. In reality, for most country clergy the pastoral and other demands made upon them during the week constitute a much greater burden than the taking of services on Sunday. The perception that whatever the clergy do cannot reasonably be defined as work lingers on, and in rural Warwickshire, if people wish to denote scarcity, they still speak of something as being 'as rare as sweat on a parson's brow'. Within the Church itself there has been a marked reaction to views of Christian ministry which, in any way, could be described as authoritarian or hierarchical. In its extreme form this is represented by a view that the mission of the Church no longer requires the type of institutional church structure and professional clergy which belonged to a former era.

Among the clergy themselves the changes that have taken place in their self-understanding are partly the consequence of theological changes and partly the result of changes in the more practical aspects of the clergyman's role. Recent decades have seen a recovery of a theological understanding of the Church and its ministry which places emphasis upon the call and participation of all Christians in the Church's tasks of ministry and mission, as a consequence of their baptism. This theological understanding which sees the Church (the company of all Christian men and women) rather than the clergy as the principal vehicle of Christian ministry and mission implies that understandings discernible in the earliest period of the Church's life, and in the New Testament, have been subsequently distorted by the rise of clericalism from the fourth century onwards. In effect, tasks which once belonged to the whole Church have become the responsibility of a single person and are now being reclaimed by the Church as a whole. The phrase 'the priesthood of all believers' is for the few an anti-clerical protest, but for the many it is a statement about the corporate nature of the Church's vocation to ministry and mission. The widespread acceptance of assumptions implicit in this understanding leaves unanswered the question: 'What is distinctive about the clergyman's role?' The fact that many clergy find it increasingly difficult to provide answers to this question which satisfy both them and their parishioners, is perhaps the central cause of the present level of anxiety and uncertainty.

Furthermore, two recent changes in the pattern of ministerial recruitment have also had a far-reaching effect on the clergy in their occupational role, though their significance has been largely unacknowledged. In recent years, the proportion of clergy whose decision to seek ordination as a second career choice has risen significantly; in 1989, 57% of clergy ordained in that year were over thirty. Whilst in many ways this is seen as a desirable development (that the ministry of clergy should be enriched by some experience of non-clerical life and of lay membership of a congregation) the fact remains that the number of people seeking ordination as a first career choice has significantly diminished. At the same time, the increase in non-stipendiary ministry (those who are ordained and assist in parishes on a part-time, unpaid basis) has risen significantly in recent years; since 1972, approximately 150 clergy have been ordained to non-stipendiary ministry in the Oxford diocese. The development of non-stipendiary ministry was initially regarded as a new form of ministry which would lead to a radical reshaping of the Church and to its indigenization in working class areas and its penetration of areas of society, particularly those associated with work, from which the Church increasingly realized itself to be alienated. However, in the main, as their original name, auxiliary pastoral ministry, implies, most non-stipendiary ministers have provided much needed assistance to hard-pressed clergy both in urban and rural areas. Whilst this has been welcomed, the clergy, like other professional groups, have been concerned about the possibility of the development of a sub-professional group which could encroach on and take over their role. Like other professions, the clergy have insisted on the highest standards of qualification, but, at the same time, have limited those areas in which the sub-professional can work. Like all professions, the clergy have been sensitive to the implication that their role can be performed adequately by those working in their leisure time without remuneration. The fact that an increasing number of parishes, particularly in rural areas, indicate that they would be happy to be served by a non-stipendiary clergyman, has obvious implications both for the status and the future of the role of the country clergyman.

However, of greater significance to the morale of the clergy than either of these two factors has been what is sometimes called 'the psychology of institutional contraction'. The clergy are aware of working within an organization which is widely believed to be contracting in size and significance. It seems that every year there are fewer clergy, less money (and as a consequence painful, cost-cutting decisions have to be made) and fewer churches. The fact that in reality some parishes and dioceses are recording steady growth in numbers, that relatively few churches have been closed, and many new ones have been built (in 1991, twenty-four new churches were consecrated; twenty-one were declared redundant), and that the number of ordinations in the Church of England has not been affected by the sharp decline in recent years in almost all other European Churches, does not detract from the fact that most media presentations of the Church describe it as an organization in decline, whose future cannot be guaranteed. Certainly, total clergy numbers and the proportion of clergy working in rural areas has been declining since the First World War and this decline has accelerated significantly in recent decades. The Paul Report (1964) recorded that there were 15,437 full-time clergy in the Church of England; in 1987 there were 10,624 and today there are 10,315 (see page 125). The local impact of this has been much greater; in one deanery in Oxfordshire, in 1967, there were twenty-three clergy – today there are ten. It is as a response to this challenge, particularly as it is experienced in rural areas, that the Bishop of Norwich wrote in a recent report: it is 'most important that we should move away from our dependency on the full time stipendiary clergy and focus in a new way on the central place and role of the laity'. Whilst this is clearly an appropriate response to the present situation, particularly as it is experienced in the countryside, it does by implication raise questions about the nature and the future of the role of the stipendiary clergyman in rural areas, and it is these questions that this book seeks to address.

In order to understand the background to this situation it is necessary to look at the clergyman's role both from the point of view of a historico-sociological and a theological understanding. The Church of England is a notoriously enigmatic institution and scarcely less so is the role of the clergyman. 'Clergyman', 'minister', 'parson', 'clerk in holy orders', 'priest' and 'vicar'; this range of designations indicates the variety of ways in which the religious functionary of the Church of England may be regarded. However, a basic and fundamental distinction can be maintained between theologically derived and historico-sociologically derived definitions; that is to say, between the terms 'priest' and 'clergyman'. To call the religious functionary of the Church of England a 'priest' is to use a theological definition grounded in the writings of the New Testament and in the subsequent development of the doctrine of ministry and priesthood within the Church. The term 'priest' denotes a theological status within the Church and the criteria for testing the adequacy of such statements are theological criteria. However, the term 'clergyman' denotes an occupational role among many occupational roles in society. In this case, the role of the religious functionary, like other roles, may be examined and subjected to investigation according to other methods and principles. The fact that the terms 'priest' and 'clergyman' afford a double definition of the religious functionary of the Church of England can create much confusion, particularly when statements based on different sets of criteria are too readily juxtaposed. Analytically, at least, it is possible to hold apart this double definition and to conduct separate examinations of each part.

After the Reformation, in the Ordinal appended to the Book of Common Prayer in 1550, the title 'priest' was retained, though subsequently this was one of the central subjects of debate between the Presbyterians and the Arminian party within the Church of England. However, if the word 'priest' was retained, it was shorn of many of its pre-Reformation resonances and was no longer understood in the cultic manner against which much of the Reformation protest had been directed. The Anglican understanding of priesthood placed the emphasis upon the preaching and pastoral aspects of ministry in addition to the sacramental functions. Hooker, for instance, saw the priest as a man commissioned by Christ in the Church to a ministry that was principally sacramental and pastoral, though he rejected any idea of sacrifice in the Eucharist. For Cranmer the priest was to be a watchman, a steward, a pastor, a preacher and a teacher, a view which placed him in the tradition of Luther, who wrote: 'Whoever comes out of the water of baptism can boast that he is already a consecrated priest, Bishop and Pope, although, of course, it is not seemly that just anybody should exercise such an office . . . but a priest in Christendom is nothing but an office holder.'

Thus, the Church of England is the inheritor of two theological understandings of priesthood and the views of an individual clergyman will lie somewhere along the continuum between these two poles. At one end of the spectrum is the ontological view of priesthood, by which ordination confers upon a priest an order of being different from that of the laity as a consequence of his vocation and his ordination. By his very presence he contributes a sacramental dimension to the ministry of the whole people of God, regardless of any particular functions he performs, which receives its fullest expression in his presidency of the Eucharist. At the other end of the spectrum the functional view of ordained ministry proceeds from the belief that any ministerial role within the Body of Christ can, theologically speaking, be carried out by any member. The ordained minister is the one in whom the gifts of leadership have been discerned and tested by the wider Church, who believes himself to be called by God to this task, who has received appropriate training and is then duly authorized to exercise gifts of teaching and ministry. The presidency of the Eucharist, at present restricted to the ordained, is an appropriate liturgical expression of this leadership role.

More recently, Anglicans have come to see the priestly role as representing and symbolizing the total ministerial calling of the Church. The priest is set apart within the common priesthood of the whole Church to exercise a representative priesthood on behalf of the Church. The ordained clergy are a focus of leadership and unity: to use words from the ARCIC statement on Ministry and Ordination, a 'focus of apostolicity and catholicity for the whole church'. A well-known statement of this Anglican understanding of priesthood identifies three aspects of its representative nature. First, he *displays* the total response demanded by Christ of his disciples as they respond to his call to follow and obey. By this is meant that certain Christians, publicly and unambiguously, stand for that total dedication to Christ which should characterize the life of every Christian. As a consequence, they accept responsibilities to make explicit the functions and nature of the Church's ministry. They are beacons of pastoral, prophetic and priestly concern and activity; they are signs of the ministry of the whole Church.

Second, he *enables* other members of the Church to see more clearly the implications of Christian discipleship and to pursue this more purposefully. The ordained priesthood does not dominate or inhibit the Church, but, by personal example and by the clergyman's teaching and leadership, is able to encourage and enable others to fulfil their own vocation and calling.

Third, he *involves* the whole Church in all that he does because he is its representative; when he visits, when he says his prayers; when he teaches; when he offers worship; it is not a personal act but one which he does visibly and on behalf of the whole Church. Thus, to summarize: 'The ordained minister gathers, builds up, enables, equips and leads a church community. He represents or personifies or embodies the whole Church in Christ in the things that he does; he links in his person the local church to the great Church; he acts with representative authority in both the Church and the world. He preaches, teaches, interprets the gospel, administers the sacraments, takes responsibility for the ordering of worship. He exercises some degree of oversight, responsibility, care and rule' (see G. R. Dunstan, *The Sacred Ministry*, 1970). In the Anglican tradition, represented by its Ordinal, the words of which Herbert would have heard when he was ordained as a priest in Salisbury Cathedral, the priest is called to celebrate the sacraments, to preach and teach the word of God, to be a pastor to the people in his care and to be their spiritual leader. It is to this that Herbert eventually came to dedicate his life, and to write a manual which lies at the centre of the Anglican pastoral tradition.

There is an extensive literature on the theology of priesthood and ministry to which this book is not an addition, for it is concerned primarily with the tasks and duties of a clergyman in the contemporary countryside. It can be seen that the role of the religious functionary has a double definition and that the term 'priesthood' is defined by theological criteria, whilst the term 'clergyman' is an occupational role in contemporary society that responds to change in a way not dissimilar to other occupational roles. It is held by social anthropologists that, in the evolution of society, as separate occupational roles began to emerge, the role of the religious functionary was probably the first, or at least one of the first, and thus retained a certain degree of primitiveness. All roles in society can be divided between those that are *ascribed* and those that are *achievement-orientated*. *Ascribed* roles are the consequence of a person's place in the kinship structure of a society. In the main, these are the biological roles, and the surrogate terminology of ecclesiastical roles (father, sister, brother) indicate their ascribed nature. By contrast, *achievement-orientated* roles are those gained by a person as a result of preparation, training and certification; all occupational roles in modern society fall into this category. It can be seen that the role of the clergyman as an occupational role has both ascribed and achievement-orientated dimensions. At one level it is close to biological roles, and the 'totality' or 'character' of the priestly role is a manifestation of this. At the same time, it is an achievement-orientated role in the sense that a person is ordained only after he has been selected and trained and can demonstrate that he has understood the particular knowledge which is the basis of the authority and legitimation of the clergyman's.

As the Church of England emerged from the Reformation, the dominant understanding of its ministry underwent a profound change. The pre-Reformation clergy were mostly poor men of modest education, much concerned about their rights and standing in society. The records of the church courts at the time indicate that there was much anti-clericalism, providing a receptive climate, particularly in urban areas, for people to hear readily the preaching of the reformers. However, there was little ambiguity about the role of the priest. His primary duty was to celebrate the sacraments and this was the vital function that he performed at the centre of the medieval village community. In the post-Reformation period, when printing had made the Scriptures more widely available, the principal role of the clergyman was that of expounding, teaching and guiding his flock, as they themselves read the words of Scripture. The dominant functions of the clergyman's role became those of preaching and teaching (in fact the clergyman became referred to as 'the preacher' at this time). To exercise a preaching and teaching ministry required different skills and understandings, and, thus, the clergy of the Church of England became a learned profession. It is in religious usage that the word 'profession' retains the original meaning of the Latin *profiteri* – 'to declare publicly'. In post-Augustan Latin the term *professor* was applied to the occupant of a teaching post. In contemporary usage the term professional bears a whole range of meanings, usually as an antonym of unpaid, amateur or part-time; and this variety of meanings indicates something of the imprecision in the use of the concept of the profession in contemporary society. Carr-Saunders and Wilson, in the first analytical study of professions, found it impossible to better the Oxford English Dictionary definition: 'A vocation in which a professed knowledge of some department of learning or science is used in its application to the affairs of others or in the practice of an art founded on it'.

Thus, the clergyman's role emerged in the post-Reformation period as that of a learned profession; like the doctor or the lawyer, he was the person who controlled access to a body of information of considerable social significance and utility. By 1620, half the clergy were graduates and the proportion of graduates continued to increase in the eighteenth and nineteenth centuries. Theological colleges (which date from the founding of St Bees in Cumbria in 1816) were a response to the shortage of clergy, particularly in the remoter rural areas, in the early nineteenth century. The early colleges trained men who possessed neither the qualifications nor the means to matriculate at Oxford or Cambridge. In the middle of the century the clergy became a professional body in the full sense of the term, as an occupational group based on access to an area of socially useful knowledge, with a measure of internal government and organization and with their own culture and ethos. As professions developed, so the notion of the professional 'character' became important, for the professional man was a person of a certain and distinctive type. By his training, by the rules of his professional body, and by the particular nature of his relations with his patients, the doctor became a professional man in a distinctive and acknowledged manner. This was an important feature of Victorian professionalization which particularly affected the clergy and allows us to speak of a typical Victorian country clergyman and of the 'rectory culture'.

However, professions are not static entities and many professions have been significantly changed in recent years by the impact of technological standardization. Professions are also affected by the way in which the wider society regards the body of knowledge to which they control access. The characteristic knowledge of the clerical profession is that of theology, biblical understanding and pastoral practice. As society has become disposed to regard this body of knowledge as no longer having the social significance and utility which it once possessed, so this has had a corresponding impact upon the clergyman's role.

It is an appropriate response at a time of confusion and crisis to look back to the formative period in which the clergyman's role took on its recognizably modern form. It is possible that no profession has more readily available published and manuscript material on the performance of the role of its members than the clerical profession. In a previous book *The Clerical Profession* (SPCK 1980), the author sought to chart the development of the clergyman's role and the impact of professionalization on that development, particularly in the nineteenth century. Before theological college training was widely available, the only instruction which a clergyman received was from books specially written for the purpose, and, in the late eighteenth century and early nineteenth century, many of these 'handbooks' were published with such titles as *Hints for a Minister to his Curate for the Management of his Parish*; *A Clergyman's Instructor*; *The Clergyman's Obligations Considered*; and *Practical Advice to the Young Parish Priest*. These books provide a valuable source of information for they chart the changes which the clerical profession underwent during this crucial period in which it was moulded into its recognizably modern form. If *The Clerical Profession* has any claim to originality it lies in the use of approximately one hundred 'handbooks', found in the Bodleian Library, which were published between 1750 and

1875. Most of them were written by busy parish priests whose names are not familiar from the standard histories of the Church. Indeed, so predominant has been the tendency to write the history of the Church as if it were the history of its upper echelons, the bishops, cathedral dignitaries, and Oxford dons, that there are few published works on the parochial clergy, and such as there are tend to be anecdotal rather than analytical.

During the analysis of the handbooks it was noticeable that the overwhelming majority referred at some stage to George Herbert's book, *The Country Parson*. Very frequently both the shape and substance of what Herbert wrote were used as the starting-point for such handbooks. The references start in Richard Baxter's *The Reformed Pastor* (1656) in which he speaks of 'the divine poet Herbert', for it was as a poet that Herbert was first and has remained most widely known. Lord David Cecil, in his introduction to *The Oxford Book of Christian Verse*, speaks of Herbert as having an exquisitely Christian disposition, 'all humility and spontaneous trusting love', which was cultivated in a lifetime of devotion. Herbert's religious vision was narrower than that of Donne but of a purer quality. His spiritual vision is unusually sunlit, and Cecil wrote elsewhere that Herbert would have agreed with Dr Johnson that 'the only end of writing is to enable the reader better to enjoy life or better to endure it'. Herbert's was not an inhuman spirituality but one that was sociable and full of appreciation of the attractiveness of the world. He had experienced the dark night of the soul when he felt he was cut off from any contact with God, but the very beauty of his character prevented his spiritual struggle from achieving the tension so evident in John Donne.

His piety is an eminently Anglican piety, refined, dignified, with a delicate appreciation of the value of style and ceremony, but subdued and restrained: its pure outline and quiet tints are the product of a quiet existence in the countryside, a profound understanding of the human heart, calm good sense and a deep capacity for self-understanding.

(David Cecil, ed., *The Oxford Book of Christian Verse* (Oxford, 1940), pp. xvii – xviii. See also Hannah Cranborne, *David Cecil: A Portrait by his Friends* (London, 1990), p. 84)

It is sometimes said that, whilst the French developed a civilization (and bequeathed it to their colonies), the English developed a way of life, of which Anglicanism was an integral part. What is sometimes called 'the domesticity of Anglicanism' can be clearly seen in Herbert's writing. Having turned his back on the life at court, Herbert became a country parson living the life of his calling in an atmosphere of peaceful seclusion. At the time that he wrote, though a few dissenters had already broken away to form their own congregations, and the Pilgrim Fathers has established themselves in New England, the majority of Puritans remained officially within the Church of England. They were constantly voicing their disapproval of its theology, ritual and administration, and arguing about predestination and election; but of this contentious background there is scarcely a hint in the reasonable, courteous and quiet disquisitions of his book. Herbert is principally concerned with the Christian faith as a way of life for all, believing that true Christianity was a response, in worship and in personal conduct, to God's love as manifest in Christ. '*It is a good strife to go as far as we can in pleasing of him who hath done so much for us.*' The characteristic Anglican attitude was a tolerant and temperate one, whether of other institutions, dogmatic difficulties or human frailties.

Whilst in the poems Herbert lays bare the long story of his inner life, with all its faults and ardours, and the inner conflict which he experienced lends such poignancy to the poems he wrote in a period of indecision and inaction, *The Country Parson* shows George Herbert with his doubts resolved and unhampered by misgivings. He writes with such authority that it is easy to forget that the book is not a distillation of years of experience. Now, at last, he has found the haven where he would remain, and his later poems and *The Country Parson* speak with an air of simplicity and gravity and the eternal beauty of holiness. Here is a man whose goodness speaks through his poems and his writings, and the reader feels himself to be in touch with a man of personal charm, gentleness, devotion to his family and deep religious faith.

Though the poems are so well known, Herbert's handbook on the life of a clergyman, *The Country Parson*, is now virtually unknown. *The Country Parson* has the same intimacy and richness as are expressed in the poetry, but it is concerned with the outward practical application of the Christian faith. At one level it can be read as a simple guide as to how the clergyman should perform his duties, but it is also a description of a saintly life lived among ordinary people in the countryside. Through the book it is possible to see the cottages and the muddy streets, the livestock and the labourers and to glimpse the plain, clean church and the rectory with its simple furniture and garden filled with flowers and herbs. Through the village Herbert moved with faithfulness and joy, soberly dressed, visiting the sick and the elderly, talking to farmers and labourers and walking with his family to the daily offices in the morning and the afternoon in church. Herbert was no detached mystical aristocrat nor kindly welfare worker but a father in God upon whom every person in the parish might depend. T. S. Eliot wrote about the spiritual stamina of the author of *The Country Parson*, who cared for his people 'as if he had begotten a whole parish'. Through the book one comes face to face with Herbert's good sense and tender sensibility, his moderation and gentleness, his courtesy and stubborn honesty which make an amalgam that is conspicuously English; his language, too, defies translation in its colloquial richness and ease.

Izaak Walton appreciated the value of the book: 'a book so full of plain, prudent and useful rules that that country parson that can spare 12*d* and yet wants it is scarce excusable; because it will both direct him what he ought to do and convince him for not having done it'. Yet if this book is hardly known, does it mean it no longer speaks to our time? Herbert is a profoundly attractive person to the country clergyman today, not just because by his asides and his comments he reveals that he stood where we stand, and suffered what we suffer, but because he reveals himself so fully. He does not disguise the struggle, the spiritual conflict, and the difficulties which he suffered, and yet his glorious triumph over them was so spectacular and so complete. As with any clergyman, what ultimately matters is not what he writes or speaks but who he is as a person. Herbert himself and his manual, *The Country Parson*, have implanted a lasting pattern at the back of the Anglican mind, whether this is consciously acknowledged or not. At a time of uncertainty and confusion there is much to be said for looking again at what might be regarded as the rootstock of the Anglican pastoral tradition, to be found in the life and the writings of George Herbert; to be recalled amidst the confusion and contradictions of contemporary church life to the riches of prayer and his only aim of making Christ, crucified and risen, known to his parishioners. As John Keble (another Anglican country parson, whose life and practice bear some similarity to that of Herbert) wrote to one of his friends: 'Do not forget George Herbert's *Country Parson*'. George Herbert is our contemporary because the things that he stood for and the guidance he gives are of continuing significance to the clergyman seeking to serve his Lord and his people in a country parish.

3

George Herbert, the Author of
The Country Parson

The personal nature of George Herbert's book, *The Country Parson*, demands some account both of the author and the times in which he lived. It is likely that *The Country Parson* was written towards the end of Herbert's brief period as incumbent of Bemerton, between 1630 and 1633. What Herbert wrote as he reflected on his own ministry was not just the consequences of those brief years, but was the upshot of a life which formed a preparation for that ministry. The path along which Herbert was led to ordination and to Bemerton provide the background from which *The Country Parson* was written. With one exception, this is a journey of which there remains a fairly full record, partly to be found in Herbert's poetry and partly from contemporary references.

Herbert's poetry has been the subject of much detailed analysis in recent years, and it is for his poetry that Herbert is chiefly known. Many of the poems were written (or revised) in the later stages of Herbert's life and the one hundred and sixty poems of *The Temple* were sent from Herbert's deathbed to Nicholas Ferrar, who later wrote of them as being 'inspired by divine breath'. It is clear that the poems of *The Temple* were copied at Little Gidding (two copies exist: that in the Bodleian Library and that in Dr Williams' Library in London). Not without some difficulty, Nicholas Ferrar obtained the signatures of the five licensees in Cambridge necessary for publication, and these signatures can be seen in the Bodleian copy. The first edition was published in 1633 and five more editions were produced before 1641. Sir Thomas Herbert, who was a personal attendant to the King during his last months, in his *Memoirs of the Last Two Years of the Reign of Charles I* wrote that Herbert's divine poems were among the few books which the King read often during his captivity. Richard Baxter ended *The Saints Everlasting Rest* (1650) with Herbert's long poem *Home* in full. By the end of the 1670s ten editions had been published and seventy thousand copies had been sold.

In 1709 the last of the early editions was published, but already Herbert's poetry was losing its former popularity, for Herbert's was a voice that did not speak to a different age, and it was nearly a century before the next edition appeared. However, during that period John Wesley's devotion to Herbert is remarkable. He included forty-seven poems from *The Temple* in his various collections of hymns and sacred poems. Many of them have dropped out of use but 'Let all the world in every corner sing' was alone admitted into the first edition of *Hymns Ancient and Modern* (No 548) in 1861. William Cowper tells of the relief he found in *The Temple* when he was first 'overtaken with a dejection of spirits', and many have written of the debt they owe to George Herbert's poetry. When Lord David Cecil edited *The Oxford Book of Christian Verse*, his criterion for admission was whether a poem could possibly be included within the same covers as those of George Herbert. With many others, Cecil regarded Herbert as the supreme Christian poet. 'Herbert's religious vision is narrower [than that of Donne's] but of a purer quality. Born with an exquisitely Christian disposition, all humility and spontaneous trusting love, he cultivated it by a lifetime of devotion. Christ was to him as real a personality as any human being. His life story is the history of his relation to Him.' It is with this life story that this chapter is concerned, as, like the poems themselves, it discloses much about Herbert that was eventually to flower in the three brief years at Bemerton and in *The Country Parson*.

There are three contemporary or nearly contemporary accounts of George Herbert's life. Nicholas Ferrar wrote a prefatory address to the readers of the first edition of *The Temple* (1633). He spoke of him as a person and also of his priesthood 'wherein his faithful discharge was such as may make him justly a companion to the primitive saints and a pattern or more for the age he lived in'. The first edition of *The*

Country Parson was included in Barnabas Oley's publication, *Herbert's Remains* (1652), to which he contributed an unsigned biographical introduction. The first biography of Herbert was written by Izaak Walton, whose *Life* was published in 1670. In many ways these three accounts are very similar, but it is Walton's *Life* which is by far the most detailed and which has become the definitive biography. Izaak Walton and George Herbert were exact contemporaries, for both were born in 1593, though Walton lived until 1683, reaching his ninetieth year. Born in Stafford, much of Walton's life was lived in London; he became a prosperous ironmonger in the parish of St Dunstan's, where he was a friend of the vicar, John Donne. After the King's defeat at Marston Moor in 1644, Walton abandoned his business and retired to spend the rest of his life as a guest 'mostly in the families of the eminent clergymen of England, of whom he was much beloved'. His second wife was Bishop Ken's half-sister and he spent the last twenty years of his life as a guest of George Morley, Bishop of Winchester, at Farnham Castle. Morley had been a member of Lord Falkland's convivium at Great Tew and, when he lost his Oxford fellowship in 1649, joined Prince Charles in Antwerp; in 1662 he was appointed Bishop of Winchester and was said to have 'a lively mind' with a generous, if hot, temper.

Izaak Walton was a Royalist high churchman who favoured priests who were devout, contemplative and learned, and who called all Puritans 'schismaticks'. As the Puritan ascendancy gathered pace Walton found himself increasingly out of temper with the changing times. He retreated to the countryside, where he took up fishing and writing, and combined his two hobbies to produce the book for which he is best known, *The Compleat Angler*. This was published in 1653 and, with the exception of the Bible and The Book of Common Prayer, to which he was devoted, has been reprinted more times than any other book. *The Compleat Angler* enjoyed immediate popularity and from its fifth edition was printed with his friend Charles Cotton's *Treatise on Fishing for Trout and Grayling*. Cotton (whose memorial is in St James's, Piccadilly) was a Derbyshire squire of similar tastes, a French scholar whose translation of Michel de Montaigne's three books of

Essays, in 1684, became for many years the standard English translation. Walton's book combines a lyric picture of the English countryside with a practical manual on fishing; a book born of quiet days on the riverside, and written in a style which already had an old world Jacobean flavour. It ends with the quotation from the Epistle to the Thessalonians, 'Study to be quiet', which may have been Walton's own personal motto. Many of the early editions show evidence of having spent time in the bottom of a boat and having shared a creel with tackle and catch.

During his time in London, Walton wrote a biography of his former parish priest, John Donne, which was published in 1640. Walton was drawn to men who, like himself, had found themselves out of sympathy with the times and, in some measure, had retreated from the world of affairs and public life. In leisurely succession he produced a series of biographies of Anglicans who shared his preference for a life of learning, devotion and quiet retirement. The thread that binds them together is that they all in some way refused the offer or the prospect of high office, preferring the life of retirement for which Walton showed such a marked preference. To his life of John Donne, Izaak Walton added that of Sir Henry Wotton in 1651. Wotton had been ambassador in Venice and The Hague and returned to England as Provost of Eton, refusing higher appointment. He was a noted connoisseur of Italian painting. In 1665 Walton published the life of Richard Hooker, a man who preferred to remain quietly in his parish in Kent, writing his monumental work of ecclesiology and theology. Walton's life of George Herbert was published in 1670 and his life of Bishop Sanderson in 1678. Sanderson had been ejected from Oxford as Regius Professor of Divinity by the Parliamentary Commission, and was consecrated Bishop of Lincoln after the Restoration. He was the author of the Preface to the 1662 edition of the Book of Common Prayer containing the famous phrase which described the Church of England as keeping 'the mean between the two extremes'. These biographical sketches were not simply the old age rememberings of a squire with a taste for literature, who treasured his close connections with senior churchmen, but were a modest attempt to place on record the lives of men who had lived in the high noon of Caroline Anglicanism and whose witness to a quieter and more orderly form of church life Walton wished to put before a rising generation of clergymen, men who had known only the disturbed and disjointed times that had followed the beginning of the Civil War. There is a sense in which Walton's work became propaganda for the practices of the Church of England before the Civil War, which were to be so firmly re-established after the Restoration of the monarchy.

These biographies may be regarded as a particular literary form known as 'exemplary biography', a form well developed in the sixteenth and seventeenth centuries. Just as in earlier generations Sir Philip Sidney represented the ideal courtier in the biographies of Thomas Moffet and Fulke Greville, so Herbert became the ideal country priest. Just as Walton's treatment of John Donne is that of a sinner turned saint, so his treatment of George Herbert is that of the refined scholar and sophisticated man of the world turned simple country parson, a man who had been seduced from his early intentions of ordination by secular ambition and who, having passed through a period of great trial, achieved the crown for which he was destined. Walton is critical of Herbert in his earlier years, against which his last years at Bemerton shine with a special brightness. At times the book comes close to hagiography of a more conventional form, and instances such as the occasion when Herbert helped a man unload a fallen animal are intended to remind the reader of the Good Samaritan.

Recent writing on Herbert's life has sought to demonstrate that Herbert was a much more complex character than that revealed by Walton's biography. Certainly, there are aspects of his life which Walton did not know about, or chose to ignore, particularly his time in Parliament and his connections with the Virginia Company. Walton freely constructed conversations and, it seems, occasionally invented incidents or accepted them on the basis of unreliable reports. The attempt to portray George Herbert as a man of uncomplicated and simplistic faith must be reconciled with the close friendship which he maintained with Francis Bacon, a man not regarded as an orthodox believer, but who, in 1625, had dedicated a verse rendering of seven psalms 'to his very good friend Mr. George Herbert', and in whose honour Herbert contributed to a memorial book. Bacon's death in 1626, from bronchitis contracted in Highgate, profoundly affected Herbert. (It seems that at the time Bacon was experimenting with ways of preserving chickens in snow.)

At the same time, Herbert's elder brother, Edward, Lord Herbert of Cherbury, a 'man of great learning and reason', wrote in protest against what he regarded as the intolerant orthodoxy in England and Europe. Throughout his life Herbert remained on good terms with his brother, who came to be regarded as 'the father of English deism'. Edward's book *De Veritate* (first published in Paris in 1624 as it was considered too unorthodox to be published in England) was dedicated to his brother, and the fact that both he and Francis Bacon dedicated works to George Herbert shows that Herbert was in contact with trends in theological thought that were to prefigure developments in the next century. Herbert was neither simple nor ignorant, and through association with friends, family and Cambridge was well aware of various currents and counter-currents in religion, politics and literature. The fact that *The Country Parson* shows so few borrowings from such sources must be the result of conscious choice rather than the consequence of limited knowledge.

Nor were all Herbert's close friends as totally dedicated to the Royalist cause as it might have seemed prudent to portray them in 1670. Herbert's own stepfather, with whom he was clearly on good terms and whom he appointed as the overseer of his will, was Sir John Danvers, one of the regicides who in 1649 condemned Charles I to death. Edward Herbert surrendered Montgomery Castle to the Parliamentarian forces (in exchange for his library seized in London) and declared in many letters to Sir Robert Harley, one of the most extreme Protestant iconoclasts, his loyalty to the King's opponents. Nor did it suit Walton's purposes to remember that Bishop Williams, who was Herbert's chief ecclesiastical patron, disliked William Laud and much of what he stood for. Thus it is not possible to identify Herbert with a specific ecclesiastical party, despite Walton's attempts to link him so closely to Laud (who became Archbishop of Canterbury five months after Herbert's death). Herbert belonged to the Anglican tradition of 'thoughtful holiness', which combined a love of tradition with intellectual enquiry, in which prayer and study are held close together. It may be that Herbert was closer in spirit to those in the Great Tew circle than customarily has been portrayed. However, in an age of religious controversy, often conducted with violent bitterness, Herbert remained a quiet defender of his beliefs rather than a protagonist within the current theological debate. In George Herbert can be seen that union of a conservative heart and an inquiring mind, which has stamped itself upon the Church of England over the centuries.

If Herbert was a more complex man that Walton's *Life* portrays, nevertheless the final picture which emerges accords not only with Herbert's own writings but with contemporary and early accounts, such as those of Ferrar and Oley. 'Thus he lived', concludes Izaak Walton, 'and thus he died like a saint, unspotted from the world, full of alms-deeds, full of humility and all the examples of a virtuous life.' But 'holy Mr. Herbert' was not the creation of Izaak Walton, as a study of *The Country Parson* will demonstrate, for in this book can be seen his 'thoughtful holiness' and the beguiling gentleness of his life.

George Herbert was born on 3 April 1593, nearly sixty years after the passing of the Act of Supremacy (1534), which effectively marked the secession of the Church of England from the Church of Rome. Throughout the intervening years, interrelated religious and political questions had caused continuing tension and trouble; yet the Church of England had managed, in a comparatively brief period, to consolidate its position, so that few people regarded it merely as an expedient, set up by Parliament and the desire and will of a Tudor sovereign. The growth that took place in the intervening years; the emergence of Anglicanism as a living way; the skill of Cranmer in reducing the medieval service books to one English prayer book; the statesmanship and scholarship of Archbishop Matthew Parker; the theological and legal foundation given to the Church of England by Richard Hooker; the example of Lancelot Andrewes as a pastor and preacher; these were some of the factors which established the Church of England as a living reality with its own understanding and ethos by the time of George Herbert's birth.

Herbert's ancestors were made Earls of Pembroke for supporting Edward IV in the Wars of the Roses, and the first Earl's grandson married Anne Parr and so became brother-in-law to Henry VIII, who gave him Wilton Abbey, one of the most magnificent properties confiscated by the Crown during the dissolution of the monasteries. In all likelihood, George Herbert was born at Black Hall, which stood below the family castle at Montgomery. The date of his birth is given by Izaak Walton though no record of his baptism has survived. Of Herbert's father little is known; he was described by his son Edward as 'black haired and bearded . . . of a manly and somewhat stern look, but with all very handsome and well compact in his limbs and of great courage'. Richard Herbert was a landowner who died when George was only three, but it is clear that he inherited some of the passion and ambition for which his family was renowned. John Aubrey records that Black-Will Herbert (later Earl of Pembroke) was involved in an affray between Welshmen and the King's Watch in Bristol at midsummer 1527. On the second day, Will Herbert killed a mercer, Richard Orme, for 'a want of some respect in compliment'. George Herbert speaks of his 'fierce youth' in one poem, and in another he coupled youth with fierceness. In an otherwise admiring description of his younger brother, Edward notes that George 'was not exempt from passion and choler being infirmities to which all our race is subject'.

Richard and Magdalen Herbert had ten children, of whom George was the fifth of their seven sons. Magdalen was carrying her last son when her husband died in October 1596. It would seem that he died suddenly (certainly he died intestate) and was buried in the parish church of St Nicholas, Montgomery at the foot of the castle. Magdalen Herbert raised a magnificent tomb in the south transept, with her husband's image lying in full armour. With his father dying at such a young age, Herbert's mother Magdalen became the most important influence in his life. She was the daughter of the Newports of Eyton in Shropshire, who were rich landowners, and Lady Newport was well known for her piety and liberality. Magdalen married Richard Herbert in 1581, and was fond of pointing out that she had the same number of children as the patriarch Job, and, like Job, she took their upbringing with the utmost seriousness. The purposefulness and serenity of her character can be seen in her portrait at Weston Park. Her friendship with John Donne was close and for a period he was writing to her almost daily. Donne, who always stood close to poverty, needed the kindness of his friends to support his wife and many children. He wrote flattering letters to many but his letters to Magdalen Herbert reflect a genuine admiration and friendship. When Queen Elizabeth died, George Herbert was ten and by this time his mother had moved to London, where, on 29 June 1605, Herbert was elected a scholar of Westminster School. As a King's Scholar, he attended the Abbey regularly and part of the Westminster curriculum demanded of him a detailed synopsis of the sermon (small boys in English; older boys in Latin; advanced students in Latin verse).

At Westminster Abbey the Dean was Lancelot Andrewes, who already had been there for four years. With Richard Hooker, Lancelot Andrewes can be claimed as one of those who established the Anglican *via media* by his rejection of the doctrine of transubstantiation on the one hand and his critique of predestination on the other. It was for the holiness of his life and for his learning that Lancelot Andrewes is chiefly remembered. It is said that he learnt a new language every year, and the historian Thomas Fuller wrote of him: 'The world wanted learning to know how learned this man was, so skilled in all [languages], that some conceive he might almost have served as an interpreter-general at the confusion of tongues.' Though he became a bishop in an age when bishops were required to play a significant role in the life of the court and government, he spent five hours a day in prayer and refused any disturbance before noon. His *Preces Privatae*, a collection of his devotions compiled for his personal use, revealed the breadth of his learning, for, in addition to extensive quotations from the Old and New Testament, he draws upon a range of other sources, including the Roman Breviary, Irenaeus, Tertullian, Cyprian, Jerome, Ambrose, Gregory Nazianzen and Gregory of Nyssa, John Chrysostom, Cassian, Augustine, Cyril of Alexandria, Bede, Anselm, Bernard, Aquinas and many others. The manuscript, which was stained with his penitential tears, was sent to Laud just before his death on 25 September 1626, and was not published until 1648. Deeply learned and widely read, Andrewes' spirituality was rooted in his awareness of the place of the Church of England in the historic continuity of Christ's Church. His was a spirituality which was personal but never private, never detached from his sense of the wholeness of the Catholic Church in all time. It was within this tradition that Herbert's own understanding eventually grew.

During his lifetime Andrewes' fame rested on his preaching and his *Ninety Six Sermons* were edited by Laud and published in 1629. James I (it seems likely that Lancelot Andrewes was his confessor) was enthralled by his preaching and after one sermon declared that no one had spoken so well 'since the days of the Apostles', and another sermon delighted him so much that he slept with a copy under his pillow. Charles I, when he received his daughter Princess Elizabeth at Whitehall on the eve of his execution, commended Lancelot Andrewes' sermons to her. Herbert would have heard the man universally regarded as the most accomplished preacher of his generation, whose sober piety and love of ordered beauty transformed the services at Westminster Abbey. Lancelot Andrewes directed the committee charged with the translation of the first twelve books of the Old Testament (Genesis to 2 Kings), which formed the first section in the new translation of the Bible authorized by James I and published in 1611. In later years, when George Herbert read these parts of the Old Testament he would have heard the echo of the voice of the Dean preaching in the Abbey. It is recorded that Lancelot Andrewes was particularly interested in the school and fond of walking, often accompanied by scholars. Walton was anxious to place Herbert within the 'succession' of Anglican divines whom he so greatly admired, and recorded Herbert's indebtedness to the guidance and example of Lancelot Andrewes, 'the ointment of whose name is sweeter than any spice', and he wrote to him as 'sanctissime pater'. Certainly, Herbert's own spirituality owes more to the tradition in which Lancelot Andrewes stood than to many contemporary influences, though later he came to criticize Andrewes' style of preaching. Something of Lancelot Andrewes' character is revealed in the articles of enquiry which he sent out before his first visitation in the Diocese of Winchester (1619); from these it is clear that he was anxious to learn about the character of the clergy as well as concerned about the cleanliness, order and furniture of the churches, the frequency with which Holy Communion was administered, the care of the sick and the poor and the morals of the people under the parish clergyman's charge. It is hard not to believe that Herbert's later life in Bemerton was in some measure, consciously or unconsciously, influenced by the example of the sober piety, ordered beauty, humble but vigorous attention to his duties, disciplined life of prayer and worship, and the sense of order and tranquillity which he saw in Lancelot Andrewes.

There is no record of Herbert's childhood, nor of his time at Westminster School, but Walton, perhaps over-conscious that he was writing the life of a saint, declared that 'the beauties of his pretty behaviour and wit shined and became so eminent and lovely in this his innocent age, that he seemed to be marked out for piety and to become the care of heaven'. One of Herbert's school friends at Westminster was John Hacket, seven months his senior, who would later share many of Herbert's years at Cambridge, would become chaplain to Bishop Williams (later Herbert's patron) and would himself later become Bishop of Lichfield and Coventry. On 5 May 1609 George Herbert was named as one of the three King's Scholars who were to proceed to Trinity College, Cambridge. For the next twenty years Herbert's life revolved around Cambridge, and on 18 December George Herbert matriculated at Trinity College as a pensioner and thus began the middle years of his life. At this point the close supervision of his life, which his mother had previously exercised, slackened, though her influence remained considerable. The previous spring she had married Sir John Danvers, a man only half her age, who was the younger brother of Baron Danvers of Dauntsey, a 'magnificent and munificent' bachelor, much interested in gardening, whose patronage included the founding of the

Botanical Gardens at Oxford.

Cambridge in the second decade of the seventeenth century was much influenced by Reformed theology from the Continent, and had established itself as the heart of the Reformation in England. When Queen Mary ascended the throne, English Protestants felt that this was itself a judgement on the lack of thoroughness displayed by the Reformers in the previous decades, and the University was influenced by the Presbyterianism of such men as Thomas Cartwright. Of Herbert, Walton (quoting from Dr Nevil, Master of Trinity) paints a picture of a conceited and self-concerned young man: 'He kept himself too much retired and at too great a distance with all his inferiors.' He was fond of fine clothing, conscious of his birth, breeding and rank and of the name that he carried, and it seems that his natural instincts led him to bright colours rather than to the dark gown of an academic life. He was a man whose friends were among the aristocratic and intelligent and who found themselves at ease in the learned, lively and cultivated atmosphere of the University. He dressed carefully, it seems over-carefully, for Walton says that his 'clothes seemed to prove that he put too great a value on his parts and parentage'.

There is little doubt that Herbert soon formed a close relationship with his new stepfather, a relationship which was to have a considerable influence on his future. Like many students, he appears to have been short of money, and his only source of income was an annuity allowed by his elder brother of £2 10s per month. He found it necessary on 18 March 1618 to write to Sir John Danvers suggesting that his poor financial situation inhibited the purchase of books and thus hampered him just when he was 'setting foot into divinity', a direction in which his mother, Sir John's new wife, had constantly encouraged him. Some authorities have suggested that Herbert found academic work tedious, but it seems he made an early success of his time in Cambridge, taking his BA in February 1613. On 3 October 1614 Herbert was elected as a minor Fellow, and his signature in the Fellows' Admissions Book is immediately above that of his friend John Hacket. On

15 March 1616 he became a major Fellow, and in the following year he was elected Sub-Lector of Trinity College and, in 1618 Praelector in Rhetoric of the University. At this stage there is no reason to believe that Herbert had set aside ideas of ordination, for the acceptance of such appointments were, for many, a preliminary to ordination, and Fellows of Trinity College were required to be ordained after a period of years. However, it is clear that Herbert's health was already causing him and others concern. In two sonnets sent to Lady Danvers in the second year of his time at Cambridge he mentions 'my late ague'. The damp, cold climate of Cambridge played its part in the deterioration of Herbert's already fragile health and it may well be that in this period lie the origins of the tuberculosis from which eventually he would die.

In the early seventeenth century the universities were more closely linked to the centres of power and authority in the country than was the case in later centuries. The amount of royal patronage in the universities was one reflection of their importance both to the monarchy and to the government. The close relationship between Cambridge and the centres of power was reinforced in James I's reign by his genuine interest in theology and in intellectual discussion. His passion for hunting meant that the King was frequently at Royston, and thus Cambridge and the court circle became closely acquainted; those who made themselves conspicuous in the one could easily aspire to appointments in the other.

In 1618 Herbert's recent appointment required him to give the four Barnaby Lectures in Rhetoric, and he chose as his subject a recent book by King James I, which took the form of instruction to his son Charles. Herbert subjected the book, chosen in place of one of the customary classical texts, to modest analysis and much adulation. Whether the reaction of his hearers was one of amusement or shock is not recorded, but such treatment would not have been uncharacteristic of the time. (In Oxford the book was subjected to similar flattery). Clearly, Herbert was becoming a public figure in the University and it was not surprising that, when the post of deputy University Orator fell vacant in the following year, Herbert was appointed. In 1620 the University Orator, Sir Francis Nethersole, a man of strong Presbyterian opinion, resigned, and there is little doubt that Herbert set about acquiring this vacant office (of which he was already the deputy) with some determination. In effect, Herbert ran his own campaign for election as Orator of Cambridge University. It appears that he found it necessary to reassure his family that this did not constitute a departure from his intention to pursue a priestly vocation, and in this connection wrote: *This dignity hath no such earthiness in it but it may very well be joined with Heaven, or, if it had to others yet to me it should not, for ought I yet knew.*

Thus Herbert set about energetically to 'work the heads'; that is, to promote his candidature among the heads of the Cambridge colleges whose support and vote he had to gain. Herbert's actions at this time are of particular interest when contrasted with his later years. It may be suggested that humility, like calmness of temper, was not one of Herbert's family characteristics. He wrote to his brother Henry on the subject of pride with all the force of family conviction: 'Be proud, not with a foolish vaunting of yourself when there is no cause, but by setting a just price on your qualities . . . it is the part of a poor spirit to undervalue himself and blush.' Herbert's campaign culminated in his appointment in 1620 as University Orator, a post which, in the eyes of many, was but a stepping-stone to greater honours and offices, but which was to prove the zenith of Herbert's university career. A predecessor had been appointed as Secretary of State concerned with the King's foreign policy, and the fact that Herbert was learning Italian, Spanish and French at this time may be taken as some indication that he harboured similar expectations. Herbert's duties were to speak in the name of the university whenever occasion demanded. One such occasion required Herbert to act as the university spokesman in opposition to the proposed drainage of the fens to the north and east of Cambridge. At that time, half a million acres of swamp surrounded Cambridge and stretched into Lincolnshire, Suffolk and Norfolk. Opposition in the University was based on the belief that, if

Parliament granted a patent to the Corporation of Bedford Level, the effect of the drainage work would be the disappearance of the River Cam.

The evidence of Herbert's desire to seek higher office is at best contradictory. If his attitude to James I's book had been marked by the sycophancy for which the period was renowned, it is clear that Herbert took no care to win the favour of Buckingham and the Prince of Wales, whose opinions were of increasing consequence. In the summer of 1623 the Prince of Wales and Buckingham had travelled to Spain on a journey which they hoped would culminate in the Prince of Wales' marriage to the Spanish Infanta. Charles' attempt to wed the princess of a country which for decades had been England's chief enemy never enjoyed popular support, but was part of his father's foreign policy aimed at avoiding any future conflict. James' love of peace was based on the experiences of his youth, which had been spent amid scenes of violence and disorder. When Charles returned in the summer of 1623, believing himself to have been slighted by Spain, popular opinion called for war. Only three days after Charles' return, the Prince visited Cambridge, and, on 8 October 1623, Herbert delivered the official oration. Herbert's impassioned plea for peace could hardly have found favour with a slighted Prince bent on war. It seems unlikely that Herbert at this stage cherished the ambitions Walton ascribed to him, for he would have known that the realization of such ambitions was the reward for compliments and deference. Herbert was a much more complicated man than that portrayed by Walton's biography, and it is hard to believe that he was bent on a steady course of self-advancement.

It is clear that 1623 marked the onset of a period of change for George Herbert. His links with Cambridge were all but broken, and he took up residence in London for reasons that are nowhere made explicit. After the death of his brother Richard in the previous year, and with Edward and Henry in France, George was the oldest (and possibly the only) son remaining in England. As a consequence he may have regarded it as his duty to enter Parliament for what was in effect the family seat, and Herbert was elected as the member for

Montgomery in November 1623. He may also have felt that he
could care for his mother, now declining in health, and
discharge his responsibility as guardian to his two young nieces
(daughters of Margaret Herbert Vaughan) better from London
than from Cambridge. Some have suggested that he entered
Parliament specifically to support the anti-war policies of the
King, who was now seriously ill, confused and dispirited. For
whatever reason, Herbert attended the parliamentary sessions
from 19 February to 29 May 1624 and on 11 June 1624 was
granted six months' leave away from his office as Orator 'on
account of many buisinesses away'. Herbert never resumed his
office and his deputy, Herbert Thorndike, delivered the
oration at the death of James I. Unlike his elder brother
Edward, George was not an active parliamentarian. It appears
he only attended the February–May 1624 session and was a
member of one committee (Edward sat on ten), concerned
with considering accusations made against schoolmasters and
members of colleges. During this session a schoolmaster was
accused of popery and unspecified charges were laid against
John Richardson, Master of Herbert's own college; these were
dismissed.

However, during this period it is certain that Herbert was
involved, together with Nicholas Ferrar, in the activities of the
Virginia Company. He regarded this (as one poem suggests) as
a religious as well as a commercial enterprise. For some time
the Company had been the object of royal disfavour, for the
King regarded its activities as an open provocation to Spain
and therefore likely to lead to the hostilities he was so keen to
avoid. Herbert's anxiety in this matter must have been
considerable, because he supported the King's anti-war policy
and yet many of those involved in the Virginia Company were
his family and friends, all of whom shared a strong sense of
religious purposefulness as they approached the affairs of the
Company. The desire to protect the Company's interests may
be another reason why Herbert was persuaded to enter
Parliament. It was partly because of his opposition to the
Virginia Company, that Nicholas Ferrar helped draw up, and
spoke out on, the charges of impeachment (for bribery) brought
against the Earl of Middlesex; an action which Ferrar deeply

repented in later years. With the rumour that the Crown intended to seize the records of the Company, Herbert's stepfather, Sir John Danvers, had them copied and sent to the Earl of Southampton for safekeeping. On 28 April 1624 Danvers and Nicholas Ferrar were among those who presented their compliments to a committee of the whole House; but on the following morning a message came from the King, forbidding Parliament to concern itself with this matter. The session ended disastrously on 29 May and on 24 July the Court of the King's Bench declared that the charter of the Virginia Company was null and void. These events deeply affected many of those who played a leading role. Sir John Danvers was transformed from a loyal courtier to one who was increasingly hostile to the Crown and was eventually to join the Parliamentary cause and sign the warrant for the execution of the King's son. In the following year Nicholas Ferrar, distressed by his part in the Middlesex affair, left London at the time of the plague for Little Gidding, and signalled his abandonment of civil affairs by his ordination as a deacon in 1626.

It may well be that George Herbert became a Member of Parliament, and accordingly placed himself at the centre of civil affairs, in a last attempt to discover whether the nation had need or use of him or he had any taste for spending his life in this employment. By this time he may have already been subject to that change of mood which became so evident in the mid 1620s. For the court had become increasingly worldly, pleasure-loving, vicious and profane; the dark clouds which were eventually to break in the next decade were already forming. Men like Herbert and Ferrar came to believe that there was no longer a place for them at the centre of the nation's life or rather that, if they stayed, they did so at their soul's peril. The conclusion was forcing itself upon their minds that a life dedicated to God and also placed at the service of civil affairs was no longer a position that could be held with integrity. Earlier, at the time of his campaign for the oratorship at Cambridge, Herbert had written in a letter quoted above, that *this dignity hath no such earthiness but it may very well be joined with Heaven.* The older theories, based on the joining of the religious and civil dimensions, came under increasing stress, and both Herbert and Ferrar eventually came to see that the essentially medieval idea of a courtier, as one who served his God and his prince, and, by serving one, served the other, was no longer sustainable. By coincidence, Andrewes, as well as Bacon, died in 1626, and they represented the last of those who, from the previous reign, had clung to the older theories.

Both George Herbert and Nicholas Ferrar felt themselves drawn into actions and activities that compromised their ideals; Ferrar, for the rest of his life, was haunted by remorse for the part that he played in the Middlesex affair. Though Charles I espoused and died for the highest ideals of monarchy, yet the court and government over which he presided were corrupt and their inner contradictions were plainly apparent, not only to such as Herbert and Ferrar. Events were already moving towards their climax at Edgehill in 1643. Whilst the nation addressed this problem in subsequent decades, both Herbert and Ferrar had to resolve it for themselves as best they could; for them and for others the only satisfactory resolution was to acknowledge that they were faced with a choice, and having made that choice, to leave London.

Izaak Walton only hints at the deep anxieties with which Herbert had to wrestle at this time, but seeks to account for his departure from London in more straightforward and simple terms. For him, Herbert, at this stage in his life, was an ambitious young man whose ambitions were thwarted by the untimely death of the three patrons from whom he might have expected preferment and position. On 27 March 1625 King James I died at Theobalds (his palace, later demolished by order of Parliament), and a few days before the Marquis of Hamilton had died. In the previous year the Duke of Richmond had died and thus, in Walton's simple explanation, all Herbert's 'court-hopes' came to an end.

Effectively, Herbert disappeared from view for a period of four years, during which only occasional references give any indication either of his life or his whereabouts. It seems that Herbert passed through a crisis (possibly a depressive illness) of which increasing physical ill-health may have been either part of the cause or the effect. He spent Christmas 1625 in London and there is a record of him and John Donne being at the Danvers' home in Chelsea on 23 December. Certainly, in early 1626, he spent a long period in Essex with his brother, Sir Henry Herbert. Of this period Walton wrote:

> So that he presently took himself to a retreat from London ... where he lived very privately and was such a lover of solitariness as was judged to impair his health, more than his study had done. In this time of retirement he had many conflicts with himself, whether he should return to the painted pleasures of a court life or he take himself to a study of divinity and enter into sacred orders, to which his dear mother had often persuaded him. These were such conflicts, as they only can know, that have endured them; for ambitious desires, and the outward glory of this world are not easily laid aside; but, at last, God inclined him to put on a resolution to serve at his altar.

On 3 November 1624, the Archbishop of Canterbury signed a dispensation permitting Bishop Williams of Lincoln (whose chaplain was now John Hacket) to ordain George Herbert as a deacon. That Herbert was considering offering himself for ordination is clear, but when he was ordained is not known. It must have been between 1624 and 1626, for, on 5 July 1626, he was described as a deacon when he was instituted *in absentia* as Prebend of Leighton Eulesia at Lincoln Cathedral, a gift which he received from the bishop. However, at that period, being made a deacon did not commit him to parochial life but merely barred him from some forms of civil employment. It is clear from later references that Herbert did not adopt clerical dress, though anything that is said about Herbert at this period must be approached with caution, as he almost completely disappears from view for a period of nearly eighteen months. Herbert may well have been deeply disappointed that the hopes that he and others had for his public career had come to nothing; the only preferment he ever received came to him in December 1624, when he was named by the King as comportioner at Llandinam in Montgomery, from which he derived a small income. This, coupled with his disappointment at the turn of events in the country, as he could deduce them from the eclipse of the anti-war party and the disgrace and death of his friend Bacon, may have caused this prolonged period of ill-health. It is most likely that Herbert's health suffered a nearly total breakdown, and it is clear that it was to recover from illness that he went, in 1626, to stay with his brother Sir Henry in Essex, where he found the damp climate of Essex as uncongenial as that of Cambridge. Walton referred to his illness as 'a sharp Quotidian Ague'.

The only reference to Herbert's movements that can be substantiated is the visit to London in December 1625 to his mother's house in Chelsea. Here he saw John Donne, by now Dean of St Paul's, who had succeeded Lancelot Andrewes as the most admired preacher in the country. It may have been Donne's counsel and his example that prompted Herbert to become a deacon. Certainly, this would have been in accord with his mother's steady encouragement, and it may well have been a decision influenced by conversations with his friend Nicholas Ferrar, who was himself preparing to be ordained deacon in Westminster Abbey on Trinity Sunday of the next year.

Among those who had lost power in this turbulent period was Bishop Williams of Lincoln, who, though he retained his extensive ecclesiastical patronage, had lost his former influence at court. Williams had already ensured that Herbert received the sinecure rectory of Llandinam on 6 December 1624, and, in July 1626, made him a Prebend of Lincoln Cathedral, to which he was installed by proxy. Though the appointment carried no obligations beyond that of preaching (either personally or by the agency of a deputy) on Whit Sunday, Herbert would have known of the ancient duty of the Cathedral Chapter to recite the whole of the psalter every day. This was done by allocating the psalms among the prebends, and over the carved choir stall that belonged to the Prebend of Leighton Ecclesia are the Latin titles of the two psalms he was expected to recite: 'In thee, O Lord, do I put my trust' (Psalm 31) and 'Blessed is he whose transgression is forgiven' (Psalm 32). It is likely that Herbert had a strong sense of the undeserved nature of this gift and the revenue supporting it (from which he now benefited) that came from the parish of Leighton Bromswold only a few miles from the manor house at Little Gidding where Nicholas Ferrar now lived. It seems that Herbert initially decided that the prebend should go to Ferrar, but he refused and perhaps it was Ferrar who made the suggestion that Herbert should restore the church at Leighton Bromswold. When Lady Danvers heard that her son was planning to do this, she commented that it was not fitting for a man with his 'weak body and empty purse to undertake to build churches'. The influence of Herbert's mother over her son was clearly still strong but, on this occasion, he replied, 'that she would, at the age of 33 years, allow him to become an undutiful son'. Thus Herbert set about what came to be one of his life's achievements, the restoration of Leighton Bromswold church.

By now the direction of Herbert's life was firmly established, but, in June 1627, his mother died and was buried in the parish church of St Luke's, Chelsea. In July the delayed funeral sermon was delivered by John Donne, who had known and admired her for a quarter of a century. Among the congregation on that day was Izaak Walton, who saw John Donne openly weeping as he prepared to preach, and, probably, for the only time in his life, saw the tall emaciated figure of George Herbert himself. Herbert, like many bachelors, was close to his mother, and was deeply affected by her death, the consequences of which were that he cut loose some of his ties with his family and with Cambridge. For some time Robert Creighton had been deputizing for Herbert as Public Orator at Cambridge, and, on 29 January 1628, he took over this office. Walton says that Herbert had only retained the post so long because it had been his mother's express wish. On 21 July 1627, Herbert suddenly benefited from a grant of crown land at Ribbesford in Worcestershire which was made to him, his brother Sir Edward, and his cousin Thomas Lawley; almost immediately this land was sold to his brother Henry for £3,000, and, at last, Herbert had an independent income. It is not known exactly when, but during 1628 Herbert moved to Dauntsey House, Wiltshire, the home of his stepfather's elder brother, the Earl of Danby. It appears that the change of air, the consciousness of the opening of a new chapter in his life after his mother's death and the final severance of his ties with Cambridge had a bracing effect on him. However, Herbert's whereabouts during this four-year period cannot be firmly established. It is clear that he suffered from severe ill-health and spent some time recuperating in Essex and Wiltshire; many of the poems in *The Temple* were written during this period.

In Wiltshire he met Jane Danvers, who, according to Walton's account, had admired him for some time, and they married in Edington Priory on 5 March 1629 and lived for a while in her mother's house, Baynton House. According to Aubrey, Herbert 'when he was married lived a year or better at Dauntsey House'. But, according to Walton, they were at Baynton when Arthur Woodnoth visited them a year after their wedding. At the time of his wedding Herbert still dressed as a layman, having not changed his sword and silk clothes for those of a clergyman. This was against the rubric but it seems that Herbert was inclined to be over-concerned about his clothes. His wife, according to Walton, did not at all demur at the change of status when he became a priest. According to Walton he lost no time in admonishing her that she must now forget her father's house so as not to claim a precedence over any of her parishioners and to this she cheerfully assented. A natural and happy humility 'begot her an unfeigned love and a serviceable respect from all that conversed with her; and this love followed her in all places as inseparably as shadows follow substances in sunshine'.

It was at this time that the living of Fugglestone-with-Bemerton fell vacant on the appointment of its incumbent, Dr Curle, as the Bishop of Bath and Wells, approximately three months after Herbert's wedding. As a consequence, the presentation of the living lay with the Crown, and according to Walton, William Herbert, the fourth Earl of Pembroke, commended his kinsman to the King. Charles I, according to Walton's account, was surprised that a man of such a family should want so modest an appointment, but consented to William Herbert's wish and George was presented to the living on 16 April 1630.

According to Izaak Walton's account, Laud (then Bishop of

London) was staying with the Earl of Pembroke and helped to persuade George Herbert to accept this offer of royal patronage by giving his opinion that a refusal would constitute a sin. A tailor was sent for with all speed to take measurements for Herbert's clerical dress so that he could be presented to Dr Davenant, Bishop of Salisbury, on 26 April. It is almost certain that this is a case of historical reconstruction at the hands of Izaak Walton, for there is no record of Laud staying at Wilton at that time. Furthermore, the Earl of Pembroke, the candidate of the anti-Laudian faction, had just lost to Laud the bitter election for the Chancellorship of Oxford University on 12 April, four days before he asked the King for the small favour of Herbert's appointment. It seems most unlikely that his victorious opponent would have been a guest at Wilton. However, Walton was anxious to associate Herbert with Laud, the martyred hero of the restored Church at the time when the *Life* was published, but Walton failed to recognize that many of Herbert's associates and his patrons were not in sympathy with the views or policies of the man who was shortly to become Archbishop of Canterbury. Thus, although Herbert had long treasured hopes of receiving patronage and preferment from the King that would lead to a career at the heart of civil affairs, he now received from his sovereign this modest gift, in which he was to find the satisfaction and joy which at one time he sought in other and greater appointments.

On 26 April 1630, George Herbert was instituted as rector of Bemerton by Bishop Davenant and later that day was inducted at St Andrew's Bemerton into the 'real and actual possession' of the living. At last his many conflicts were resolved and he surrendered his whole life and being to God in his service as a country clergyman; and as a consequence was transformed, for Herbert learned the unteachable lesson that the more freedom a man surrenders the more freedom he receives. What in former years appeared to be vacillation and reluctance to commit himself to any course of action was swept away as hesitations and fears were resolved. He embarked on his task with all the energy of a man long kept waiting, and united all his intellectual and spiritual powers, all the gifts of grace and gentleness, which have been attested to by so many, to the single end of serving God in a country parish. It is the intensity with which he pursued this end that made such a profound impression both on his friends and upon those among whom he ministered. It seems as if suddenly a dam burst, the infirmity of purpose fell away and all the years described in this chapter seemed to act as a time of preparation for that brief period of incandescent brightness when Herbert shone in his small parish. Then, as now, country people find holiness of life a quality both difficult to understand and hard to acknowledge, yet, within a short time, those who knew the rector of Bemerton regarded him as 'little less than a saint'.

This intensity of purpose radiated from Herbert from the very beginning. Walton's story of the day of his induction must come from Arthur Woodnoth, a cousin of Nicholas Ferrar. The bell at Bemerton was an old one (of the type sometimes called an alphabet bell), and Herbert's friends waited outside for a long time to hear the new incumbent toll the bell to signify that he had taken possession of his living. Once more, it seemed, Herbert was hesitating. Finally, Woodnoth, concerned by the delay, looked through a window to see Herbert lying at full length before the altar. Walton records this incident:

> When at his induction he was shut into Bemerton church, being left there alone to toll the bell (as the law requires him) he stayed so much longer than an ordinary time, before he returned to those friends that stayed expecting him at the church door, that his friend Mr. Woodnoth looked in at the church window and saw him lie prostrate on the ground before the altar; at which time and place (as he afterward told Mr. Woodnoth) he set some rules for himself, for the future manage of his life; and then and there made a vow to labour to keep them.

Thus Herbert lay in abasement and consecration before the altar of the church in which God had called him to serve, at what may be regarded as the very crux of his life. The journey had been long, and the surrender had been much delayed; but, when it came, it was absolute and transforming. It is reasonable to consider that the origins of *The Country Parson* lie in those rules which Herbert set himself at the beginning of his ministry at Bemerton for the future management of his life. The benefice into which George Herbert was inducted comprised the village of Fugglestone with St Peter's church (this is now in the parish of Wilton and is not to be confused with the modern housing estate of Fugglestone Red, which takes its name from some isolated farm buildings); the village of Bemerton with St Andrew's church and the rectory; and the hamlet of Quidhampton which lies between the two but does not have a church. The Herberts were not able to move immediately into the rectory, and for a while Jane remained at home; the house Herbert knew was smaller than the present Bemerton rectory, which was enlarged in later centuries. The Herberts had no children of their own, but before long they had taken into their house the three orphaned children of his sister Margaret, of whom Herbert was a guardian. Of Herbert's time in Bemerton almost all we know is that which can be inferred from *The Country Parson* and from Izaak Walton. From other evidence it is known that Herbert and his wife continued to live according to their standing and station in life, and Herbert's will revealed that he had six servants at the time of his death, as well as two curates.

When Herbert was inducted into the living he was still in deacon's orders. This, and Herbert's declining health, accounts for the need for two curates in such a small living of three hundred persons. Nathaniel Bostock was a priest and lived at St Peter's Fugglestone and looked after that parish. John Hays assisted Herbert at Bemerton in the little church of St Andrew's, which John Aubrey described as a 'pittiful little chappell'. However, although the church may have been unpretentious, the living of Bemerton was a good one, being nearly double the value of the neighbouring parish of Wilton. It was regarded as a significant parish and Herbert's predecessor had been active in the Chapter of Salisbury Cathedral.

It might be assumed that Herbert would have sought ordination to the priesthood as soon as possible, but here again Herbert seemed to hesitate and it is not easy to account for this. Perhaps it was the example of Ferrar who remained all his life a deacon, and had said before his ordination that 'he would never take priest's order' for 'he durst not advance one step higher'; or it may have been Herbert's continuing sense of deep personal unworthiness. However, Herbert was not ordained at the Trinity ordination on 23 May 1630 at Salisbury Cathedral, when twelve other men were ordained priests, including Herbert's own curate, Nathaniel Bostock. The answer may lie in Herbert's inclination to delay, or in the fact that he was not well enough to present himself as a candidate on that occasion. However, as George Herbert waited to be ordained as a priest by Bishop Davenant, he would have heard the words of the exhortation from the 1550 Ordinal:

> And now we exhorte you, in the name of our Lorde Jesus Chryste, to have in remembrance, unto how hygh a dignitie, and to how chargeable an offyce ye be called, that is to saye, to bee the messengers, the watchemen, the Pastours and the stewardes of the Lorde, to teach, to premonishe, to feede and provide for the Lordes familye: to seeke for Christes shepe that be dispersed abrode and for his children, which be in the middest of this naughtye world, to be saved through Christ for ever. Have always therefore printed in your remembrance, how great a treasure is committed to youre charge: for they be the shepe of Christ which he boughte with his death, and for whom he shed his blood. The churche and congregation whom you muste serve, is his spouse and hys bodye.

The final three years of Herbert's life were extraordinarily fruitful. Initially, much of Herbert's energy must have been channelled into the restoration of St Andrew's Bemerton and the refurbishing of the rectory. At the same time, work was proceeding at Leighton Bromswold, and one of his most autobiographical poems, *The Cross*, almost certainly refers to that church, where services had previously been held in the manor house belonging to the Duke of Lennox. At Herbert's death the work was not yet completed and it was through the diligence of Arthur Woodnoth, Sir Henry Herbert and John Ferrar that the church of St Mary's Leighton Bromswold was restored with the beauty and dignity that are such an eloquent testimony to Herbert's sense of what was fitting and proper for the worship of God. At the same time, he was responsible for the care and education of his three orphaned nieces; he engaged in considerable correspondence not least with his friends at Little Gidding, and this was a period of considerable literary activity: he translated two Latin texts, revised many of his earlier poems, added to *The Temple* and wrote *The Country Parson*.

It is not known what Herbert's relations were with Wilton House (formerly a Benedictine Abbey). Just before his induction, William, Earl of Pembroke, was succeeded by his brother Philip, a man of very different temperament. Philip married Lady Ann Clifford, widow of the Earl of Dorset, a gifted and well-read woman who it is recorded he neglected and ill-treated. It may well have been part of William's original intention that Herbert should have acted as a family chaplain whilst he was at Bemerton. Certainly Herbert was on good terms with Lady Ann and there exists a sympathetic letter, dated 10 December 1632, in which he sends her *a priest's blessing* while she is at Court.

Clearly, poetry and music had been part of Herbert's life since his childhood, and his proximity to Salisbury allowed him to arrange his time so that he could regularly enjoy the music of the Cathedral. Walton writes: 'Though he was a lover of retiredness, yet his love to music was such that he went usually twice every week on certain appointed days to the Cathedral church in Salisbury; and at his return would say that his time spent in prayer and Cathedral music elevated his soul and was his heaven upon earth.'

By the winter of 1632 (only two years after he had been ordained priest), Herbert must have been seriously ill. Early in the next year he despatched his poems to Nicholas Ferrar by the hand of Edmund Duncon, and, on 22 February 1633, dictated his will to Nathaniel Bostock. He left both his curates six months' wages, and to Bostock his copy of St Augustine, and to Hayes his *Comment of Lucas Brugensis*. In the fatal final stages of consumption, Herbert died on 1 March 1633, just before his fortieth birthday. Two days later, 3 March 1633, Quinquagesima Sunday (on which day the epistle from 1 Corinthians Chapter 13 provided the theme for one of Herbert's most famous poems: 'A man that looks on glass . . .'),

Herbert's body was buried under the chancel floor and some of the cathedral choir, whose music had meant so much to him, came to sing at his funeral. According to John Aubrey, whose uncle Thomas Danvers was at the funeral, 'he was buried (according to his own desire) with the singing service for the burial of the dead, by the singing men of Salisbury . . . he lies in the chancel under no large nor yet very good marble gravestone without any inscription.' To this day there is only a small tablet let into the chancel wall with the initials G.H.

George Herbert died as an almost unknown country clergyman, but his poems were already in the hands of Nicholas Ferrar, who knew immediately the value of this manuscript book, for he recognized that 'there was the picture of a divine soul in every page'. The publication of *The Temple* in 1633, with four more editions within the next three years, gave Herbert, in death, the reputation and the distinction for which, in the earlier years of his life, he appeared to long. Herbert's papers and sermons were taken by Jane to the house of her second husband, Sir Robert Loke of Highnam in Gloucestershire, and were lost when the house was sacked by Parliamentary forces. But the manuscript of *The Country Parson* was in safe hands and, in 1652, Barnabas Oley, a Fellow of Clare Hall, Cambridge, arranged for the publication of *Herbert's Remains*, to which he contributed an unsigned biographical introduction. It is in this book that the first published edition of *The Country Parson* may be found.

4

The Country Parson

As with the poems, the precise circumstances under which George Herbert wrote *The Country Parson* are not known. It is thought that the poems were largely written in his hidden period immediately prior to his marriage and move to Bemerton, but they subsequently underwent considerable revision, as the manuscripts indicate. All authorities have assumed that *The Country Parson* was written at Bemerton, and it is possible to connect it with Herbert's desire to draw up some rules for his future life at the time of his induction. Certainly, 1632, the last full year of Herbert's life, is the date appended to the author's short introductory notice to the reader.

A Priest to the Temple, or *The Country Parson, his Character and Rule of Life*, is a short book with only a hundred and sixty-eight pages in the first edition; sixty-six pages in the definitive edition, *The Works of George Herbert*, edited by F. E. Hutchinson in 1941, from which all references in this chapter are taken. *The Country Parson* appears to have no scheme, and in some ways seems random and incomplete; as if Herbert had set down sections as they occurred to him and kept it by him, like a commonplace book, to be added to periodically. The book comprises an introductory note from the author to the reader; two prayers and thirty-seven chapters (chapter numbers are given after the quotations in this book). The chapters vary in length; some are of three or four pages, others a single paragraph; thirty-three of the chapters commence with the words, *The Country Parson . . .* In places one theme leads to another; in other places the organization seems more random. In striking contrast to the poems, the book has a straightforward and businesslike tone and a number of chapters are clearly constructed with a sequence of points as if they had originated as parochial sermons. As there is no early manuscript, it is impossible to know anything of the manner in which the book was written, nor the extent to which it was revised or corrected. The earlier manuscript of Herbert's poems, corrected by him, provides a means of following the development of his ideas and the working of his mind. The lack of order and the repetition in *The Country Parson* suggest that it was not subject to subsequent revision in the way that Herbert later edited his poetry.

The book first appeared at a time when, under Cromwell, the Anglican Church had been almost eclipsed and its ministers were forced to practise, preach and conduct the services according to The Book of Common Prayer in secret. In the preface to the second edition, which appeared after the Restoration, Barnabas Oley congratulated himself on his courage in having emulated Ezra, Nehemiah and Daniel in publishing such a book at a time 'when violence was at the height'. If, in the earlier period, Oley had seen the triumph of the Commonwealth as a just punishment for the sins of the clergy, whose fortunes would be restored if only they emulated George Herbert's life, he clearly sees this later edition as making a special appeal to the younger clergy 'not born before the troubles broke forth'. He was able to remind them 'what a halcyon calm, a blessed time of peace, this Church of England had for many years, above all the churches in the world besides'. The book was reprinted in 1675 and a fourth edition appeared in 1701, and although there are a number of references to *The Country Parson* (recorded by Hutchinson in manuscript additions to his own copy, mentioned above) it was not reprinted again for over a hundred years.

Herbert states the purpose for which the book was written in the prefatory note, 'The Author to the Reader'.

Being desirous, through the Mercy of God, to please Him, for whom I am, and live, and who giveth me my Desires and Performances; and considering with myself, that the way to please him, is to feed my Flock diligently and faithfully, since our Saviour hath made that the argument of a Pastor's love, I have resolved to set down the Form and Character of

*a true Pastor that I may have a Mark to aim at: which also I
will set as high as I can, since he shoots higher that threatens
the Moon, then* [than] *he that aims at a Tree.*

Hutchinson suggested that the original manuscript may have
come into the possession of Arthur Woodnoth, who was at
Bemerton at the time of George Herbert's death and who may
have left it when he died (in about 1650) to Edmund Duncon,
who lived until 1673. In any event, the manuscript was in
Edmund Duncon's possession when it was first sent to the
printers in 1652 by Barnabas Oley. As this manuscript has
never been found, all editions date back to that of 1652.
However, Izaak Walton's account in his *Life* is somewhat
different: 'At the death of Mr. Herbert, this book fell into the
hands of his friend Mr. Woodnoth; and he commended it into
the trusty hands of Mr. Barnabas Oley, who published it with
a conscientious and excellent preface.' In 1671 Oley published
a second impression in which his prefatory view of the life of
George Herbert was displaced by a new preface, and the old
preface was included at the end of the book. In this edition
Oley corrected Walton's story 'to do a piece of right, an office
of justice to the good man that was the possessor of the
manuscript of this book and transmitted it freely to the
stationer who first printed it . . . he was Mr Edmund Duncon,
rector of Fryarn Barnet.' It seems that when Duncon came, at
Ferrar's request, to visit Herbert in his last sickness, he received
The Country Parson from its dying author.

In the 1652 edition the title was given as *A Priest to the
Temple, or The Country Parson, His Character and Rule of
Holy Life.* It is clear that the first part of the double title, *A
Priest to the Temple*, represented an attempt by the publishers
to link the book to the author's poetry, published under the
title *The Temple*, which was already widely known and read.
(It was first printed with a text from Psalm 29 on the title page,
'In his Temple doth every man speak of his honour'.) In
Herbert's Remains, a further subtitle was given: *Sundry Pieces
of that Sweet Singer of the Temple, Mr. George Herbert, now
exposed to public light.* However, it is by its second title that
the book has come to be known, *The Country Parson*, and it

seems that this was the title that George Herbert intended for it as he began almost all his chapters with these words. The book is a personal collection of Herbert's thoughts and aspirations; his notes for the regulation and guidance of his new life. The idea of writing such a book may have been put into his mind by Nicholas Ferrar who, at the time of his ordination, is known to have written some guidelines for himself. Walton records that after his induction at Bemerton church, Herbert 'set down some rules to himself for the management of his life'. It may reasonably be assumed that either *The Country Parson* is that volume or else that it contains the rules to which Herbert refers. However, it is clear that Herbert had a wider audience in mind, for he concludes: *The Lord prosper the intention to myself and others, who may not despise my poor labours, but add to these points which I have observed, until the book grow to a compleat pastorall.* No doubt the audience Herbert had in mind was the generality of clergy in the fourth decade of the seventeenth century, the majority of whom, it appears, came nowhere near the standards to which he aspired. To them and to their successors in every generation Herbert's *compleat pastorall* became a model and example. Its good sense and simple language; its practical advice based on personal experience; the goodness of the author and his dedication to the highest ideals of parochial ministry; his faithfulness in prayer and study; his constancy in visiting and his care for his people have inspired clergy in every generation. As a consequence, the book lies at the heart of the Anglican tradition of pastoral ministry and when that ministry was revivified in the mid-nineteenth century many authors turned back to *The Country Parson* as their guide. Above all, it is a practical book written by a man who knew at first hand the difficulties and the demanding nature of the country parson's life. Herbert was neither a mystic nor a scholarly recluse but a man who sought, by prayer and by compassion, to draw people to God and to show them through his life something of God's nature and his love. Of the country clergyman he wrote: *Love is his business and his aim* (XXXV); in this lies the continuing task of the country parson.

The Country Parson was written against a background of a

Church, the majority of whose clergy came nowhere near
sharing Herbert's vision of the pastoral ministry. The reforms
of Henry VIII had not addressed the low standards of many
clergy and the poverty of their livings, widely held to be the
principal problem which faced the Church. The crisis continued under Elizabeth I with the widespread impropriation of
livings and the practice of keeping livings and bishoprics
vacant so that the Crown could benefit from their accumulating
revenues (a practice against which Lancelot Andrewes objected
by refusing two bishoprics). At a time of growing wealth in the
nation as a whole and rising standards in many areas of public
life, the poverty of the clergy became more conspicuous, as did
their ignorance, their modest attention to their duties and
their occasional misconduct.

One solution to the problem of providing sufficient clergy in
rural areas was to lower the standards of ordination below the
ideal of an educated ministry held by all Reformed Churches.
There were constant complaints during the years of Elizabeth's
reign that incompetent persons occupied the pulpit, but the
practice was defended and continued, because it was held that
it was better for a man of only limited education to preach
than for the pulpit to be empty. Archbishop Matthew Parker
sanctioned the ordination of those whose competence in any
other age would have been questioned, though he later came
to change this policy. For a variety of reasons it was considered
right to limit those who preached to the reasonably qualified
and thus many country parishes had to be content with the
services either of a clergyman not licensed to preach or of a
reader (both of whom read out published homilies). By 1620,
the village of Eaton Constantine in Shropshire had been served
by four readers in succession; each of them was the village
schoolmaster and all four were judged to be 'ignorant'. They
read Morning Prayer on Sundays and holy days but were not
allowed to preach sermons. In the villages round about there
were a dozen elderly clergy, none of whom possessed a licence
to preach. A visitation of the Archdeaconry of Norwich in
1597 revealed that the majority of churches had only four
sermons in the year, eight having no sermons at all.

When William James was appointed Bishop of Durham in

1608, the diocese contained only thirty-six preachers, who served one hundred and thirty-five parishes in County Durham. In Northumberland, there were only four licensed preachers in 1601, and only twenty-eight per cent of the clergy were university graduates, in a diocese which had the highest proportion of impropriated livings. When Samuel Crooke arrived at Wrington, Somerset in 1602, he found that the parish had never had a preaching incumbent; it appears that their new incumbent made amends for this omission by preaching seven thousand sermons in the next forty-seven years. A Hereford magistrate noted in 1610 that none of the twenty-four parishes in his local hundred possessed a preaching minister. Across the country as a whole fewer than four thousand clergy possessed a licence to preach; the remainder were described as 'dumb mouths' by their Puritan critics. It was widely agreed that this situation could not be remedied without increasing the income of the Church, and that the miserable pittance that awaited the average priest served as a severe deterrent to the recruitment of abler men and the attainment of higher standards.

At the beginning of James I's reign Archbishop Whitgift estimated that £30 per annum could be regarded as an appropriate stipend for an incumbent. At that time the majority of livings were not valued at half that amount. Archbishop Bancroft determined to raise clerical incomes, and under his influence the revived diocesan courts began the long process of rescinding various agreements which in effect had reduced the Elizabethan clergy to the economic status of servants. Many payments had simply been waived and the agricultural tithes had been commuted for cash at low values or alienated to laymen. Bancroft fought against all these injustices as, at the same time, adjacent parishes, too small to support an incumbent, were merged. There were still many pluralities and much non-residence, for both of which a clergyman was officially required to receive the permission of his bishop.

In 1610, Bancroft put forward a scheme in the House of Lords for a national fund to buy out all the lay rectors' rights and restore the tithe to the clergy, but it did not succeed. Lack of income was often the indirect cause of the indiscipline and ignorance of which so many complained. The Jacobean bishops did much to raise standards and encourage the clergy. Bishop Lake of Bath and Wells increased the number of preachers in his diocese by introducing a system of 'reading exercises', and at one period there were one hundred and six clergy writing theological exercises, the majority of these being poorly educated ministers who had not acquired the habit of regular study. Typical of these was Thomas Webber, curate of Rushford; when Lake enquired 'in what divinity he hath busied himself in study', Webber admitted that he had not read any text or commentary. Despite the work of such men and particularly Abbott and Andrewes, the standards of parochial ministry during the reign of James I remained extremely low. When William Laud became Bishop of London in 1628 he wrote in the flyleaf of his diary a list of things that he intended to do; these included, 'to find a way to increase the stipends of poor vicars'.

It is against this background that George Herbert called the clergy to a higher vision and understanding of their duties at a time when the country parson, in many remoter parts of England, was living in ignorance and destitution, held in contempt by all sections of society. Thus Herbert wrote *The Country Parson* in part to remind his contemporaries of the higher standards to which they should aspire and of the deeper importance and significance of their calling.

The Country Parson can be seen as a manual of instruction and a distillation of George Herbert's ideas about the life and duties of a country clergyman; these he summarized at the beginning of the first chapter:

> A pastor is the Deputy of Christ for the reducing [leading back] of man to the Obedience of God. This definition is evident and contains the direct steps of pastoral duty and authority for first, man fell from God by disobedience. Secondly, Christ is the glorious instrument of God for the revoking [recalling] of man. Thirdly, Christ being not to continue on earth, but after he had fulfilled the work of

reconciliation, to be received up into heaven, he constituted
Deputies in his place and these are priests . . . Out of this
charter of the priesthood may be plainly gathered both the
dignity thereof, and the duty: The dignity, in that a priest
may do that which Christ did, and by his authority, and as
his vicegerent. The duty, in that a priest is to do that which
Christ did, and after his manner, both for doctrine and life. (I)

Herbert's aim and the aim of every priest is that his parishioners
should see in and through him something of Christ's hidden
glory. Herbert knew himself to be *in God's stead*, that is to say
that his ministry was a sharing in Christ's ministry, through
whom he hoped others would see something of the divine
nature revealed. 'It is not I who lives but Christ in me'
(Galatians 2.20). In a later chapter he wrote:

The country parson is in God's stead to his parish and
dischargeth God what he can of his promises. (XX)

The intention of the book was to remind himself and others of
the duties and obligations of his calling, but Herbert tran-
scended the practical and homely advice which filled many of
his chapters with a deeper meaning and understanding. All
the duties he must perform for his parishioners are essentially
subordinate to this central consideration, that the priest must
imitate Christ in his life as well as in his preaching of his word
and the celebration of his mysteries. There is equal emphasis
on the dignity of the office and the humility of the office-
bearer. Whatever the parson is engaged in, it is his constant
obligation to reveal the love and the justice of God towards
mankind. The book is not autobiographical, nor is it a
description of Herbert's own ministry, though it is the pattern
and the model to which he aspired. It is an example of an
earlier form of popular literature, an attempt to set down the
true character of a particular occupation or calling. Herbert
writes with simplicity of language in his introduction: *I have*
resolved to set down the form and character of a true pastor.

The country parson hath a special care of his church, that all
things there be decent, and befitting his Name by which it is

called. Therefore first he takes order, that all things be in good repair. (XIII)

At the centre of Herbert's understanding of the parish ministry lies his desire to see the parish as a praying community, centred on the regular daily worship of God in the parish church. His day was given its shape and focus by the regular offices of Morning and Evening Prayer. As a consequence, Herbert's first concern was with the state of the church building itself; he sets out an inventory of the work that needs to be undertaken:

> *As walls plastered, windows glazed, floor paved, seats whole, firm and uniform, especially that the pulpit and desk and communion table and font be as they ought for those great duties that are performed in them. Secondly, that the church be swept and kept clean without dust, or cobwebs and at great festivals strawed and stuck with boughs and perfumed with incense.* (XIII)

Herbert recommends that texts be painted on the walls *not with light colours or foolish antics.* There then follows a list of fittings and furnishings that are required: *A fitting and sightly communion cloth of fine linen with a handsome and seemly carpet of good and costly stuff or cloth and all kept sweet and clean in a strong and decent chest, with a chalice and cover, and a stoop or flagon; and a basin for alms and offerings; besides which he hath a Poor-Man's box conveniently seated to receive the charity of well-minded people.* (XIII) It may have been the example of Nicholas Ferrar, who sought to make his own parish church and his own family the centre of a praying community, for, like Ferrar, and following the example of Lancelot Andrewes, Herbert sought to make the church a place where *all things be done decently and in order.* (XIII)

At Leighton Bromswold it is still possible to see the ordering of the church undertaken at Herbert's direction, though completed after his death. In this church may be found some of the finest church furniture of its period, and its solid beauty reflects Herbert's view that only the best could be used in the service of God. The layout of the church demonstrates the way in which Herbert drew from both Puritan and high church

understandings of worship. The particular feature of the
church is its twin pulpits; the one on the left being the pulpit
itself and the one on the right being the reading desk. The
exact similarity of these two structures articulated Herbert's
desire to make prayer and preaching of equal importance and
not to give superiority to one above the other. It is clear from
the layout of the church that Herbert accepted the Puritan
style of celebrating Holy Communion and the benches in the
chancel are communion benches, not choir stalls. On a
sacrament Sunday the portable altar would have been placed
in the aisle, and, after the reading of Morning Prayer and the
Litany, communicants would have been invited to take their
place in the chancel. The simplicity and beauty of Leighton
Bromswold church is an eloquent testimony to Herbert's desire
for a fitting place in which God's worship could be offered in
the spirit of dignity and holiness.

After the changes and disruptions of the previous century,
the early decades of the seventeenth century saw the full
development of an ordered and liturgical form of worship
according to The Book of Common Prayer. The emphasis on
'the beauty of holiness' was found in the reordering and in the
ceremonial of such as Lancelot Andrewes, in his chapel at Ely
Palace in Holborn (in which one contemporary said he wished
to die, as it was the nearest place to heaven), and in the
reforms of William Laud and John Cosin. Herbert's exact stance
towards these innovations is not easy to establish, though he
favoured the reception of communion kneeling and the use of
the cross in baptism, which might have marked him out as an
Arminian rather than a Puritan. As in other matters, Herbert
sought to arrive at a moderate course between the two
extremes. He states that *in the time of popery* outward signs
were *over highly valued and now we are fallen to the clean
contrary.* (XXXVI)

On the Sunday after Ascension, 2 June 1549, for the last
time, congregations in English churches worshipped according
to the medieval Latin service books. Seven days later they
were introduced to The Book of Common Prayer, the product
of Cranmer's liturgical skill and wide scholarship. The liturgical
readings and the psalms came from the 'Great Bible', the work

of Miles Coverdale and first issued in 1539. In April 1540, after extensive revision by Coverdale, the Great Bible was reissued with a preface by Cranmer, and this version is sometimes known as 'Cranmer's Bible'. Cranmer himself was part of a European movement of reform which sought to reorder and simplify the extensive medieval service books. Prominent in this movement was the Spanish cardinal Quiñonez, whose reformed *Breviary* was first issued in 1535 and passed through a hundred editions before it was suppressed in 1568. It is this book that gave Cranmer guidance for his revision of the Hour Services of the Sarum Breviary which resulted in the Order of Morning and Evening Prayer. A part of the Preface to the 1549 Prayer Book is a direct translation of the Preface to the first edition of Quinonez's work (and is found in the 1662 Prayer Book under the title 'Concerning the service of the church').

The Prayer Book with which George Herbert would have been familiar as a young child was the 1552 edition, reissued after the reign of Mary by Elizabeth I in 1559 with few alterations. The 1552 edition had resulted from determined opposition by the Puritan party to many aspects of the earlier edition. Although the book was scheduled to be published on 1 November, printing of the Prayer Book had to be stopped by an Order of Council on 27 September, as the Puritan party made a last effort to remove the rubric requiring kneeling at the reception of holy communion. The Council added the notorious black rubric, 'that it is not thereby that any adoration is done . . .' as the only means by which a compromise could be achieved. Throughout much of his life Herbert would have used the Prayer Book as revised in 1604 (sometimes called the Hampton Court Prayer Book). Puritan objections to certain aspects of the Prayer Book, which had continued during Elizabeth's reign, were focused in the Millenary Petition presented to James I as he travelled south to London. Initially they hoped both for the sympathy of the new King and for an extensive revision of the Prayer Book. But it seems that at the Hampton Court Conference in 1604 the King preferred the opinions of the bishops, and refused to delete the use of the sign of the cross at baptism, kneeling at the reception of holy communion and the wearing of a surplice. The most significant of the few alterations was the insistence that baptism be administered by 'the lawful minister' and the addition of the second part of the catechism; a service to which George Herbert later attached considerable significance. It is likely that Herbert used the Great Bible in the earlier part of his life and then the Authorised Version. However, it seems that Miles Coverdale's version of the psalms from the Great Bible soon became well loved and, even after the publication of the Authorised Version (the more significant consequence of the Hampton Court Conference) continued to be widely used. When, in 1662, the Psalter eventually came to be printed with The Book of Common Prayer (which was not the case in the earlier editions) it was printed in the Coverdale version. Thus Herbert used the three books that have formed the foundation of Anglican worship: Cranmer's Prayer Book, Coverdale's Psalter and the Authorised Version of the Bible.

Following Quinonez, Cranmer was able to condense the richness and complexity of the monastic offices into the two services of Morning and Evening Prayer. By so doing he preserved much of the monastic tradition in a new form; a tradition that went back to the earliest days of the Church. But the Prayer Book was not the breviary in translation, but rather a lay manual of common prayer for the use of the whole Church. It is often said that the Anglican tradition of daily liturgical prayer is indebted to the inheritance of the Benedictine tradition, which shaped so much of medieval church life, and was possibly more influential in England than in any other European country. There is much in Herbert's life and in *The Country Parson* which may be regarded as an unconscious rediscovery of the life and truths that lay in the Benedictine tradition and in Benedict's Rule. Benedict, himself a layman, made the *opus dei*, the saying of the daily offices, the centre of the life of his community. (There is no eucharistic teaching in the Rule in which the psalms are quoted more frequently than the New Testament.) Though unacknowledged, this tradition of the prayerful ordering of time, study and activity centred on the offices, with its emphasis on stability and its willingness to accept constraint, is at many points similar to Herbert's understanding.

Nicholas Ferrar, who had travelled in Europe, was probably more conscious of his indebtedness to this tradition, for he had been impressed in Padua by the followers of St Philip Neri and had read St Francis de Sales. At Little Gidding, Nicholas Ferrar and his family maintained a pattern of three services a day, Morning Prayer, the Litany at midday and Evening Prayer (immediately prior to the three main meals). Herbert would have known of Lancelot Andrewes' practice of spending five hours daily in prayer and may have had a copy of John Cosin's collection of private devotions, published in 1627; it had been compiled at the instigation of Charles for the use of his Roman Catholic Queen Henrietta Maria's Anglican maids of honour. It contains the lesser hours in addition to services of Morning and Evening prayer (called Lauds and Vespers) and much additional material. John Cosin had spent a large part of his life writing on liturgical subjects: his works included commentaries and annotations on The Book of Common Prayer, with hardly a rubric or punctuation mark regarded as insignificant.

Above all else, it was Herbert's principal aim to create a community of prayer. This worshipping community started with his own household, but it seems clear that he soon attracted others either to attend the services with him or at least to mark with some simple act of devotion the canonical hours of 10 a.m. and 4 p.m., as they heard the bell toll. If Cranmer's aim was to put the old services into the hands of the people, this came to fruition in the ministries of George Herbert and Nicholas Ferrar. Izaak Walton records that Herbert

> brought most of his parishioners and many gentlemen in the neighbourhood, constantly to make a part of his congregation twice a day; and some of the meaner sort of his parish did so love and reverence Mr. Herbert, that they would let their plough rest when Mr. Herbert's Saints Bell rang to prayers, that they might also offer their devotions to God with him; and would then return back to their plough.

Despite the fact that Herbert's ministry took place nearly a hundred years after its initial introduction, it is clear that the Prayer Book was not yet wholly established in the popular devotion of country people and Walton devotes several pages of his *Life* to quoting in detail Herbert's rationale for Morning and Evening Prayer.

It is necessary that all Christians should pray twice a day, every day of the week, and four times on a Sunday, if they be well. This is so necessary and essential to a Christian, that he cannot without this maintain himself in a Christian state. (XXXI)

The country parson, when he is to read divine services, composeth himself to all possible reverence ... (VI)

Herbert required orderly and decent behaviour in church both from the priest and the congregation. He writes:

No sermon moves them so much to a reverence ... as a devout behaviour in the very act of praying. (VI)

Thus Herbert gave precise instructions:

Accordingly his voice is humble, his words treatable and slow; yet not so slow neither, as to let the fervency of the supplicant hang and die between speaking, but with a grave liveliness, between fear and zeal, pausing yet pressing, he performs his duty. (VI)

He is concerned to instruct the clergyman not only in the conduct of the services but also with the behaviour of the congregation. The clergyman is to instruct

his people how to carry themselves in divine service, exacts of them all possible reverence, by no means enduring either talking or sleeping or gazing or leaning or half kneeling or any undutiful behaviour in them, but causing them, when they sit or stand or kneel, to do all in a straight and steady posture, as attending to what is done in the church and everyone, man and child, answering aloud both Amen and all other answers ... which answers also are to be done not

in a huddling or slubbering fashion, gaping or scratching the
head, or spitting, even in the midst of their answer, but
gently and pausably, thinking what they say. (VI)

In another chapter (XIII), Herbert cites two scriptural rules
which should govern these matters.

Let all things be done decently, and in order, and
Let all things be done to edification. (1 Corinthians 14.26, 40)

These were clearly Herbert's rules, that order and beauty
should be the governing principles in the determining of
worship. It is clear that Herbert placed great emphasis on the
importance of music. He was in the habit of joining some
members of the cathedral choir in Salisbury for a musical
evening and 'the singing men' of Sarum sang at his burial
service at Bemerton. For Herbert, as for many others, music
provided one of the principal avenues along which he
approached the glory and infinite majesty of God.

From one reference it is clear that Herbert also observed the
other hours of prayer:

besides this, the Godly have ever added some hours of
prayer, as at nine, or at three, or at midnight . . . (XXXI)

A number of Caroline writers composed prayers for every
occasion, waking, dressing, grace before meals, starting a
journey, and it may be supposed that this formed part of
Herbert's spiritual practice. But The Book of Common Prayer
and its offices were the centre of Herbert's prayers and of his
pastoral understanding as he sought to make his parish a
praying community. For him the offices were not part of the
private discipline of the clergyman, to be said in his study
alone, but were the centre of the life of the parish. He and his
household were seen as they made their way to church, the
services were public occasions at which all might join, and
even those prevented from doing so were reminded that the
prayers of the Church were being said by the tolling of the
bell. The Prayer Book, in the hands of Ferrar and Herbert,
became the lay manual of common public prayer that Cranmer
had intended, and gave shape to their lives, centred round the

rhythmic pattern of alternate periods of prayer and work and study through which Herbert sought to make the whole parish aware of the presence of God.

Herbert showed his esteem of Sunday in one of his poems which contains the lines:

> Sundays the pillars are,
> On which heav'ns palace arched lies:
> The other dayes fill up the spare
> And hollow room with vanities.

In Chapter VIII he gives details of his practice on a Sunday; it is a full and demanding day:

> The country parson, as soon as he awakes on Sunday morning, presently falls to work . . . as a market-man is, when the market day comes or a shopkeeper when customers use to come in. (VIII)

Herbert's practice was to read divine service twice fully; in the morning he preached and in the afternoon he catechized. It is possible to catch a glimpse of Herbert as he enters the church,

> humbly adoring and worshipping the invisible majesty and presence of Almighty God and blessing the people. (VIII)

Having conducted the two services,

> The rest of the day he spends either in reconciling neighbours that are at variance or in visiting the sick, or in exhortations to some of his flock by themselves whom his sermon cannot or do not reach. (VIII)

And to complete a full day; at night . . . [it was his custom] to entertain some of his neighbours or to be entertained of them. (VIII)

It was to the Church's loss that what The Book of Common Prayer had sought to indicate as a minimum soon became the norm, and, in many churches, Holy Communion was celebrated only four times a year. The weekly practice of a celebration of Holy Communion on Sunday as the focus of the parish's worship was not sustained. Whilst in some places,

such as cathedrals, there were celebrations every Sunday, the
normal practice in most parishes was for Morning Prayer,
Litany and Ante-Communion to form the morning worship
and in the afternoon Evening Prayer with or without
catechizing. A celebration of Holy Communion was added
either monthly or at more distant intervals and was for many
no longer a part of popular devotion.

George Herbert's views about the sacraments of Holy
Communion and baptism are contained in Chapter XXII and
he begins from the sense of his own unworthiness and the
awesome responsibility of administering the sacrament. Thus
he considers

> *what behaviour to assume for so holy things. Especially at
> Communion times he is in a great confusion, as being not
> only to receive God, but to break, and administer him.
> Neither finds he any issue in this, but to throw himself down
> at the throne of grace, saying 'Lord, thou knowest what thou
> didst, when thou appointedst it to be done this. Therefore,
> do thou fulfil what thou didst appoint; for thou art not only
> the feast, but the way to it.'* (XXII)

In order to prepare for Holy Communion,

> *He first takes order with the churchwardens, that the
> elements be of the best, not cheap, or coarse, much less ill
> tasted or unwholesome.* (XXII)

Second, he considers the state of his flock and their need for
instruction, catechizing (the subject of a long previous chapter)
and lively exhortation, not only on a sacrament Sunday but on
the Sundays before and on the eve of the day. He makes the
point that,

> *the time of every-one's first receiving is not so much by years
> as by understanding; particularly, the rule may be this:
> when anyone can distinguish the sacramental from common
> bread, knowing the institution and the difference, he ought
> to receive, of what age soever. Children and youths are
> usually deferred too long, under pretence of devotion to the
> sacrament, but it is for want of instruction; their under-*

standings being ripe enough for ill things, and why not then for better? (XXII)

The service may be regarded as a feast and therefore, Herbert comments, sitting might seem the appropriate position to adopt but *man's unpreparedness asks kneeling.* Kneeling to receive the sacrament at the altar rail surrounding the altar at the east end of the church was a controversial matter at that time, advocated by those who followed Arminian practice (and the example of such as William Laud who became Archbishop of Canterbury in 1633, the year of Herbert's death, and who presented the set of altar rails to St John's College, Oxford, mentioned above), but strongly disapproved of by the Puritans. While at Leighton Bromswold the altar was in the middle of the chancel, it seems that the practices advocated by Laud, with the altar against the east wall and an altar rail, and the sacrament received kneeling, were followed at Bemerton. With regard to the frequency of communion, it is clear that at this time practices differed considerably; for instance, in Ireland in 1638, Strafford wrote to Laud expressing his surprise that in Archbishop Ussher's chapel there was a pulpit but no altar. Herbert recommends that

> *the parson celebrates it if not duly once a month, yet at least five or six times in the year; as at Easter, Christmas, Whitsuntide, afore and after Harvest, and the beginning of Lent.* (XXII)

He makes the point that it is of importance not only in itself but also for the churchwardens, who are required to present all those who do not receive three times a year:

> *if there be but three communions, neither can all the people so order their affairs as to receive just at those times, nor the churchwardens so well take notice who receive thrice and who not.* (XXII)

With regard to baptism, it is likely that Herbert was recording his own practice:

> *. . . being himself in white he requires the presence of all, and baptizeth not willingly, but on Sundays or great days. He admits no vain or idle names but such as are usual and*

accustomed. He says that prayer with great devotion, where God is thanked for calling us to the knowledge of his grace, baptism being a blessing, that the world hath not the like. He willingly and cheerfully crosseth the child and thinketh the ceremony not only innocent but reverend. He instructeth the Godfathers and Godmothers, that it is no complemental or light thing to sustain that place, but a great honour . . . (XXII)

Thus Herbert would only baptize on Sundays and great festivals, and by his attitudes and actions convey to the families of the newly baptized the importance and eternal significance of this sacrament.

In the post-Reformation period the home and the parish church replaced the convent and the seminary as the centres of spiritual life, and there is about Herbert's writing and about his practice a gentle domesticity, a subdued joyfulness. Such characteristics were to be found later in the life of that other Anglican parish priest who was regarded by his contemporaries as a saint, John Keble. While Christian spirituality is apt to veer between a cold formal intellectualism and undisciplined emotion, Caroline spirituality, as represented by George Herbert, achieved a balance between these two extremes, based on the ideal of 'true piety with sound learning'. What Puritanism lacked, and what is conspicuous in Herbert's life and ministry, is the quality of godly joyfulness that is the essence of true devotion. This devotion itself rests in the knowledge of God's infinite mercy, in utter simplicity of heart, and lives in the consciousness of his innumerable benefits: a deep joy, serene, peaceable and untroubled, unaffected by the trials and troubles of life. The God with whom Herbert had struggled in an earlier period had become a friend, and bore no resemblance to the stern deity whose laws Calvin had codified. He had found, as he wrote in one of his poems, *such a Truth as ends all strife.* He had found that the power of love and the power of God were ultimately the same reality.

The country parson preacheth constantly, the pulpit is his joy and his throne. (VII)

If the prayers of the Church formed the centre of Herbert's life, then he saw preaching, the communicating to his parishioners of the knowledge of salvation in Christ, as his central task. At his ordination Bishop Davenant said to those about to be ordained: 'Have always therefore printed upon your remembrance how great a treasure is committed to your charge.' Though none of Herbert's sermons remain, there can be no doubt as to how important he regarded this duty. He goes so far as to warn that

> *sermons are dangerous things, that none goes out of church as he came in.* (VII)

While vast congregations flocked to hear John Donne preach at St Paul's, Herbert preached in a church that would scarcely hold a hundred people, the majority of whom must have been villagers of very modest, or no, education. In one of his longest chapters, *The Parson Preaching* (VII), Herbert lays down the principles which guided his preaching; it is among his most practical chapters. Walton recalls that on his first Sunday Herbert, the former university Orator, had preached a sermon which bore the marks of the university disputations with which he was so familiar. Then, as now, the sermons of those who preach for the first time often bear the burden of much learning recently acquired. No doubt Herbert immediately saw the inappropriateness of such a style of preaching to a village congregation, and from then on he was concerned with only one thing – that his words should move his hearers to goodness by means of unadorned sincerity.

The early part of the seventeenth century had been noted for 'witty' preachers, who summoned up all their 'wit', their knowledge, ingenuity and learning to demonstrate, by frequent quotations from Scripture, history, classical and patristic sources, that in everything God's wisdom and power was revealed. Such sermons were more often a demonstration of the preacher's 'wit' rather than of God's wisdom. The coiled thought-webs and verbal splendours which characterized Jacobean preaching were rejected by Herbert for a simple desire to communicate that sense of a yearning for God and a knowledge of his salvation. As in the poems, Herbert strove for a style of simple sincerity:

> *The character of his sermon is holiness. He is not witty or learned or eloquent but holy.* (VII)

> *The parson's method in handling of a text consists of two parts; first, a plain and evident declaration of the meaning of the text, and secondly some choice observations drawn out of the whole text, as it lies entire and unbroken in the Scripture it self . . . Whereas the other way of crumbling a text into small parts . . .* (VII)

In effect, Herbert was one of the earliest critics of the Jacobean style of preaching, which had its origins in medieval practices. Such preachers as Lancelot Andrewes, who enjoyed great popularity and royal patronage, subjected his text to the most minute word by word analysis, leaving no syllable or punctuation mark unexamined. Herbert was critical of this *crumbling of the text* and wrote that *the words apart are not Scripture but a dictionary*. This earlier style of preaching, which reached its zenith in the sermons of Andrewes and Donne, gave way to a more lucid and accessible style, as can be seen in the sermons of Jeremy Taylor. Nevertheless, the skills and experience which Herbert had acquired as university orator he deployed in the parish; he advises the preacher:

> *When he preacheth, he procures attention by all possible art, both by earnestness of speech, it being natural to men to think that where is much earnestness, there is somewhat worth hearing; and by a diligent and busy cast of his eye on his auditors, with letting them know, that he observes who marks and who not; and with particularizing of his speech, now to the younger sort, then to the elder, now to the poor, now to the rich . . . Sometimes he tells them stories and sayings of others . . . for them also men heed and remember better than exhortations which though earnest, yet often die with the sermon, especially with country people; which are thick and heavy and hard to raise to a point of zeal and fervency and need a mountain of fire to kindle them; but stories and sayings they will well remember.* (VII)

It may well be that the collection of proverbs which Herbert
made was an aid to his preaching; it was published as
Outlandish Proverbs Selected in *Witts Recreations*, 1640.
Certainly, it is possible to find some of these proverbs in *The
Country Parson*, as . . . *He* [God] *sees hearts as we see faces*
(VII); *prayers and provender never hinder a journey* (XVII).

Some sermons at this time were of considerable length (an
hour and half-hour glasses were available to aid the preacher).
Herbert advised:

> *The parson exceeds not an hour in preaching, because all
> ages have thought that a competency, and he that profits
> not in that time will less afterwards.* (VII)

In order to preach, the country parson must study:

> *The country parson is full of all knowledge . . . but the chief
> and top of his knowledge consists in the book of books, the
> storehouse and magazine of life and comfort, the holy
> Scriptures. There he sucks and lives.* (IV)

In the study of the Bible, the preacher finds four things:

> *precepts for life, doctrines for knowledge, examples for
> illustration and promises for comfort.* (IV)

But the secret of the Scriptures can only be opened to those
who follow a holy life.

> *But for the understanding of these, the means he useth are
> first a holy life . . . assuring himself that wicked men,
> however learned, do not know the Scriptures, because they
> feel them not and because they are not understood but with
> the same Spirit that writ them. The second means is prayer
> . . . the third means is a diligent collation of Scripture with
> Scripture. For all truth being consonant to itself, and all
> being penn'd by one and the self-same Spirit, it cannot be,
> but that an industrious and judicious comparing of place
> with place must be a singular help.* (IV)

Here George Herbert commends a common practice, such
as can be found in Lancelot Andrewes' devotions: *The fourth*

means are commenters and Fathers; here he adds a caution that . . .

> *he doth not so study others as to neglect the grace of God in himself and what the Holy Spirit teacheth him.* (IV)

These points he reinforces elsewhere:

> *The country parson hath read the Fathers also and the schoolmen and the later writers or a good proportion of all, out of all which he hath compiled a book and body of Divinity, which is the storehouse of his sermons and which he preacheth all his life, but diversely clothed, illustrated and enlarged. For though the world is full of such composures, yet every man's own is fittest, readiest and most savoury to him.* (V)

Preaching, if it is to contain a living, life-giving message which the congregation will both hear and understand, must proceed from the preacher's own deep sense of conviction, as Herbert wrote:

> *that the auditors may plainly perceive that every word is heart deep.* (VII)

Herbert was concerned that his sermons should be understood and should help his congregation and he came to know, both as a poet and as a preacher, the importance of the personal and of self-disclosure.

> *For the temptations with which a good man is beset, and the ways which he used to overcome them, being told to another, whether in private conference, or in the church, are a sermon. He that hath considered how to carry himself at table about his appetite, if he tell this to another, preacheth; and much more feelingly and judiciously, then* [than] *he writes his rules of temperance out of bookes.* (XXXIII)

The country parson's library is a holy life (XXXIII) and it is clear that Herbert understood at a deep level that it is the preacher's person that is exposed in a sermon, and if that person does not communicate a desire to love and serve God then no amount of words will make good that deficiency. But what would Herbert's congregations have heard, as, Sunday after Sunday, he addressed them from the pulpit? Certainly, Herbert was a child of the Reformation with a deep sense of the radical emptiness of all human claims in relationship to God. *He is a great God and terrible, as great in mercy, so great in judgement* (VII); and of the all-sufficiency of Christ's atoning death . . . *the great shepherd of the fold, who first shed tears over Jerusalem, and afterwards blood* (VII). He combined a deep sense of the divine majesty and glory with an acute realization of man's enslavement to sin. Some of the poems indicate a belief in predestination and the doctrine of the covenant of grace, and his emphasis on the importance of calling and of hard work indicate his indebtedness to Protestant theology. But, at its centre, lies a picture of a loving God calling his erring children back to himself. In places it is possible to catch the authentic voice of Herbert the preacher in the pulpit at Bemerton:

> *With some of these heads enlarged, and woven into his discourse, at several times and occasions, the parson setleth wavering minds. But if he sees them nearer desperation, then* [than] *atheism, not so much doubting a God as that he is theirs; then he dives into the boundless ocean of God's love and the unspeakable riches of his loving-kindness. He hath one argument unanswerable. If God hate them, either he doth it as they are creatures, dust and ashes; or as they are sinful. As creatures he must needs love them; for no perfect artist ever yet hated his own work. As sinful, he must much more love them; because notwithstanding his infinite hate of sin, his love overcame that hate; and with an exceeding great victory, which in the Creation needed not, gave them love for love, even the Son of his love out of his bosom of love. So that man, which way soever he turns, hath two pledges of God's love.* (XXXIV)

This may come directly from one of Herbert's sermons, for it is the kernel of Herbert's gospel of love, of which one commentator has written: 'For broken and contrite hearts he has some of the most consoling words which were ever uttered by mortal lips.' At the end of Herbert's book there are two prayers, one of which contains the passage:

> *Thou hast exalted thy mercy above all things; and hast made our salvation, not our punishment, thy glory; so that then where sin abounded, not death, but grace super abounded; accordingly, when we had sinned beyond any help in heaven or earth, then thou sayest, 'Lo, I come . . .'*

This is the gospel of Christ's redemptive love that the parishioners must have heard from the pulpit of Bemerton and that they saw portrayed in the life of their parish priest.

Herbert records that during the afternoon service he catechized the congregation:

> *Now catechizing being a work of singular, and admirable benefit to the Church of God, and a thing required under canonical obedience, the expounding of our catechism must needs be the most useful form. Yet hath the parson, besides this laborious work, a slighter form of catechizing, fitter for country people; according as his audience is, so he useth one or other; or sometimes both, if his audience be intermixed.* (V)

So Herbert records that during the afternoon service he catechized the congregation, a work to which he attached considerable importance:

> *The country parson values catechizing highly: for there being three points of his duty, the one, to infuse a competent knowledge of salvation in every one of his flock; the other to multiply and build up this knowledge to a spiritual temple; the third to inflame this knowledge, to press and drive it to practice, turning it to reformation of life, by pithy and lively exhortations.* (XXI)

It was his opinion that *whereas in sermons there is a kind of state, in catechism there is a humbleness very suitable to Christian regeneration* (XXI). His practice was to catechize the children but to do this in the hearing of the adults, both because the children paid greater attention under these circumstances, and the adults too benefited from this accessible and easy instruction. He commended the Socratic method of question and answer and makes connections between the Bible and the everyday lives of country people:

> *This is the skill and doubtless the Holy Scripture intends thus much, when it condescends to the naming of a plough, a hatchet, a bushel, leaven, boys piping and dancing; showing that things of ordinary use are not only to serve in the way of drudgery but to be washed and cleansed and serve for lights even of heavenly truths.* (XXI)

As a form of teaching he believes it exceeds even sermons, for which he has such a high regard: *at sermons and prayers men may sleep or wander; but when one is asked a question he must discover what he is* (XXI). Sermons, according to Herbert, are for informing and for inflaming, but for solid instruction and teaching Herbert commends the catechism and the practice of catechetical instruction during the afternoon, *catechizing being a work of singular and admirable benefit to the Church of God, and a thing required under canonical obedience* (V).

As in the Great Commandment, the two points of reference in Herbert's life were his love of God and his love of his fellow men. Owen Chadwick draws a distinction between George Herbert and Charles Borromeo, in whose *Instructions to Pastors*, a pastoral treatise written in Milan soon after 1565, a different character can be perceived. Borromeo instructed the pastor to refuse every possible invitation from the laity to dine or sup at their table, in contrast to Herbert's easy fellowship with his neighbours, both as a friend and as a spiritual guide. While Borromeo's pastoral is characterized by ardour, vehemence and fervour, and the social distance required for such a style of leadership, in Herbert's book there emerges a picture of a man, vigorous and lively, human and gentle, and at ease with his neighbours. In Chapter XXXV he commends the practice of inviting his parishioners into his home for a meal, and comments: *There is much preaching in this friendliness.* *The Country Parson* is full of shrewd comments about those to whom he ministered, which can only be the result of a genuine interest and concern in his neighbours' welfare and the product of careful visiting. When it comes to such matters as the dispensation of charity, it is clear that Herbert remained a man of his age and class, but, as he moves among his neighbours, there is about him an easy friendliness that characterizes the best of Anglican rural ministry in any age.

Despite the fact that much of the middle part of Herbert's life had been spent in Cambridge and London, a lifetime's experience seems to lie behind some of his comments on country people and how the clergyman should seek to relate to them:

> *Country people are full of these petty injustices, being cunning to make use of another and spare themselves . . . scholars ought to be diligent in the observation of these and driving of their general school rules ever to the smallest actions of life, which, while they dwell in their books, they will never find; but being seated in the country and doing their duty faithfully, they will soon discover; especially if they carry their eyes ever open and fix them on their charge.* (XXVI)

Some of those who have written about Bemerton have portrayed its people as meek, devoutly religious villagers, but there can be no doubt about the unsentimental realities of rural England in the seventeenth century, and Herbert was addressing the same squires and villagers who were about to take up arms in the Civil War. It is clear that Herbert's eye was *ever open* and what has commended his pastoral to subsequent generations has been his mixture of piety and common sense born of a genuine feeling for country people. Though from an aristocratic family and a man of highly refined spiritual and aesthetic sensibilities, he shows himself to have a deep understanding of the countryside and its people. In a sense, Bemerton was an unsuitable parish for a sickly patrician man of letters, but he portrays a profound understanding of the ways of country people.

To begin with, Herbert commends to the priest a knowledge of the way of life of his people:

The country parson is full of all knowledge ... He conde-
scends even to the knowledge of tillage and pasturage and
makes great use of them in teaching, because people by
what they understand are best led to what they understand
not. (IV)

The people of the countryside in any age may appear to an
outsider as simple people but Herbert observes:

Country people live hardly and therefore as feeling their
own sweat and consequently knowing the price of money ...
because country people do much esteem their word, it being
the life of buying and selling and dealing in the world.
Therefore the parson is very strict ... The parson's yea is yea
and nay, nay. (III)

Clearly, Herbert used his knowledge of farming and of the
village in his preaching:

The country parson, considering the great aptness country
people have to think that all things come by a kind of
natural course, and that if they sow and soyle [manure] their
ground they must have corn; if they keep and fodder well
their cattle they must have milk and calves, labours to
reduce them to see God's hand in all things. (XXX)

So that if a farmer should depend upon God all the year and
being ready to put hand to sickle shall then secure himself
and think all cock-sure; then God sends such weather as lays
the corn and destroys it: or if he depend on God further,
even till he imbarn his corn, and then think all sure, God
sends a fire and consumes all that he hath: For that he ought
not to break off but to continue his dependence on God, not
only before the corn is inned but after also; and indeed, to
depend, and fear continually. (XXX)

In Herbert's writing can be found references to his view of
village people: they *are thick and heavy, and hard to raise to a*
point of zeal and fervency and need a mountain of fire to
kindle them (VII). He refers in different places to the smell of
the unventilated village homes and their unwashed inhabitants

and makes constant reference to drunkenness and to idleness, as well as to the vagaries of the seasons *summer and winter, earing* [ploughing] *and harvest* (XXXIV) and in many places indicates his knowledge of farming and the countryside.

The country parson is a lover of old customs, if they be good and harmless . . . because country people are much addicted to them (XXXV). In particular Herbert mentions the Rogation procession around the fields and farms of the parish to bless the crops at the beginning of the new season. No doubt this would have been frowned upon by many of Herbert's Puritan contemporaries but he saw it as part of the continuity of rural life, so much of which had been dislocated in the previous century, and to be regarded as *good and harmless . . . Another old custom there is of saying, when light is brought in, God send us the light of heaven. And the parson likes this very well; neither is he afraid of praising or praying to God at all times* (XXXV). These ancient words (which can be found in some of the oldest services of Vespers) indicate the way in which the pre-Reformation world continued to linger in the rural England of the mid seventeenth century. Though Herbert may not have known their long liturgical history, these continuities with the past, like the sign of the cross at baptism, were of great significance to him. He also commends grace at meals as well as the importance of the public saying of the offices if he should be staying in a country house or in an inn (XVII).

But some of Herbert's most extensive guidance he offers to his own peers, those of noble birth.

If there be any of the gentry or nobility of the parish who sometimes make it a piece of state not to come at the beginning of service with their poor neighbours but at mid prayers, both to their own loss and of those also who gaze upon them when they come in, and neglect the present service of God, he by no means suffers it but after divers gentle admonitions, if they persevere, he causes them to be presented; or if the poor churchwardens be affrighted with their greatness . . . he presents them himself . . . [his duty] being to obey God rather than men. (VI)

Much the same tone can be discerned in his guidance to those clergy who serve as chaplains to the nobility, a position which he may well have held informally at Wilton. He directs them

> not to be oversubmissive and base ... but to ... preserve a boldness with them ... even so far as reproof to their very face when occasion calls, but seasonably and discreetly. They who do not thus, while they remember their earthly Lord, do much forget their heavenly. They wrong the priesthood, neglect their duty ... with their over-submissiveness and cringings. (II)

In the mid seventeenth century society was rigidly divided between the leisured and the labouring. Herbert expressed through his charities his concern for the labouring, but, with the leisured, he was particularly concerned that they did not live frivolous, vicious and idle lives, of which he had seen much, at close quarters, in London and at court. He wrote in one of his poems, O England full of sin but most of sloth.

> The great and national sin of this land he esteems to be idleness, ... for when men have nothing to do then they fall to drink, to steal, to whore, to scoff, to revile, to all sorts of gamings. Come, say they, we have nothing to do, let's go to the tavern ... (XXXII)

His concern for the gentry, and particularly for the education of their sons, emerges at several points. Here, as elsewhere, Herbert does not question the social order—riches are the blessing of God and the great instrument of doing admirable good (XXXII). As England increased in wealth and outgrew the constraints of medieval feudalism, contemporary commentators believed that many of its social problems derived from the preferences of the newly wealthy to live in London rather than on their country estates. Charles I was so concerned that in 1630 he issued a proclamation requiring the gentry to reside on their estates.

Herbert did not think it amiss in this as in other matters to descend to particulars for exactness lies in particulars (XXXII). The married gentleman has two objectives ... the improvement of his family, by bringing them up in the fear and *nurture of the Lord, and secondly, the improvement of his grounds by drowning* [the flooding of water meadows] *or draining or stocking or fencing and ordering his land to the best advantage* (XXXII). Herbert counsels that such a man might be a Justice of the Peace, an office of which he writes:

> *No Common-wealth in the world hath a braver institution than that of Justices of the Peace, for it is both a security to the King . . . and an honourable employment of a gentle or nobleman in the country.* (XXXII)

But he warns against *the abuse of it by taking petty country bribes . . . The heirs are to prepare . . . against the time of their practice* and Herbert advises them to watch their father's example and to *read books of law, and justice* (XXXII); to *frequent Sessions and Sizes*, to travel *cutting out the Kingdom into portions . . . When there is a Parliament he is to endeavour by all means to be . . . there*; in one way such advice is surprising, when compared with his own unsatisfactory experience of this office. He commends those who are elected, that they *must not only be a morning man but at committees also*. He continues:

> *when none of these occasions call him abroad, every morning that he is at home he must either ride the great horse or exercise some of his military gestures. For all gentlemen that are now weakened and disarmed with sedentary lives are to know the use of their arms . . . so must they fight for and defend them when occasion calls.* (XXXII)

Such advice prefigures events ten years after Herbert's death and again is surprising from one of known pacifist inclinations. But his concern for the growth of idleness and dissipation in its various forms is a constant theme in Herbert's writing. Like other contemporary commentators, he believed that it is the preference of the gentry for lives of idleness and leisure that lies at the root of many social problems; he condemns particularly those whom he finds *spending the day in dressing, complimenting, visiting and sporting*. To these he suggests foreign travel, particularly in Germany and France, as an opportunity to see how they manage their agriculture, industry and civic affairs.

In all these matters Herbert shows himself a shrewd observer and a wise commentator on contemporary affairs, as someone with an interest in and concern for his neighbours. Herbert, like country clergy in every generation, knew that the pastoral ministry depends upon a knowledge and a sympathy for those whom the clergyman has been called to serve. Whilst Ferrar was an ascetic who enriched the Anglican tradition with an experiment in community life based on his own household, Herbert always remained in close touch with the lives of those around him, and sought to draw them into the praying community that was his vision of the parish church. His advice is always realistic and direct; he treats the eternal temptations of youth with a vigorous common sense: *Wholly abstain, or wed; Drink not the third glass; Take not his name, who made thy mouth, in vain: It gets thee nothing, and hath no excuse; When thou dost purpose ought (within thy power) be sure to do it, though it be but small; Do all things like a man, not sneakingly.* (III; V; XXVI and from his poem *The Church & Porch*).

The country parson is exceeding exact in his life, being holy, just, prudent, temperate, bold, grave in all his ways (III). *The country parson's library is a holy life* (XXXIII). As with so many of the leading figures in the Anglican pastoral tradition, it was neither Herbert's sermons (of which no copies exist) nor the organization of his parish that impressed those who knew him; it was the quality of Herbert's life that caused him to be regarded as 'little less than sainted'. Herbert gently chides those who imagine that theological expertise and the possession of a good library are the main qualifications for the priesthood. Certainly, Herbert was well read, and he says of the country parson, *he often readeth lives of the primitive monks, hermits and virgins.* Herbert indicates not only that he knew some of the patristic sources but also the schoolmen and the classical authors. But for Herbert the source of his preaching was to be found not in a library but in the priest's own life.

*Some in a preparatory way, whose aim and labour must be
not only to get knowledge, but to subdue and mortifie all
lusts and affections; and not to think, that, when they have
read the Fathers or Schoolmen, a minister is made and the
thing done. The greatest and hardest preparation is within.*
(II)

It is ironic that Herbert is largely remembered today as a
man of letters rather than as a parish clergyman, as 'holy Mr.
Herbert', the exemplary country parson. Holiness, as Herbert
knew, is not the product of a resolute determination to lead a
devout life according to set rules; it is to do with the acceptance
of God's grace, of that changing of the heart through the
warming and nurturing of God's grace. Herbert, as a parish
clergyman in a small country parish, was beloved and revered
by all who knew him because they saw the unmistakeable
action of God's grace within him, his evident holiness and
goodness. Though Walton has been blamed for beatifying
him too easily and enthusiastically, nonetheless Ferrar, Oley
and his brother Edward are all early witnesses to this reputation
for sanctity; and the beauty of Herbert's own character is
discernible in his writing. He is a man of deep, hard-won,
unsentimental goodness; a man who in his early life had
sought fame and honour through the channels of conventional
ambition, but who found it in self-surrender to the love of
God and in the disciplined and consecrated life of a parish
clergyman.

Thus Herbert knew that the country parson's most powerful
sermon was not that which was preached from the pulpit, but
his own way of life; and to this end large sections of the book
are devoted to the life and character of the country clergyman.
His life should be characterized, as Herbert writes in Chapter
III, by a confluence of the theological and cardinal virtues. *The
country parson is exceeding exact in his life, being holy, just,
prudent, temperate, bold, grave in all his ways.* Above all, it is
important that he does nothing to *the dishonour of his person
and office*; the country parson is required to be in command of
himself, *that he may be an absolute master and commander of
himself* (III). Herbert realized that people will judge both the

Gospel and the Church, in large measure, by the clergyman's own life:

And first, because country people live hardly, and therefore as feeling their own sweat and consequently knowing the price of money, are offended much with any who by hard usage increase their travail, the country parson is very circumspect in avoiding all covetousness, neither being greedy to get, nor niggardly to keep, nor troubled to lose any worldly wealth ... Secondly, because luxury is a very visible sin, the parson is very careful to avoid all the kinds thereof, but especially that of drinking, because it is the most popular vice ... Neither is it for the servant of Christ to haunt inns or taverns or ale houses to the dishonour of his person and office ... Thirdly, because country people (as indeed all honest men) do much esteem their word, it being the life of buying and selling and dealing in the world, therefore the parson is very strict in keeping his word, though it be to his own hindrance, as knowing that if he be not so, he will quickly be discovered and disregarded; neither will they believe him in the pulpit whom they cannot trust in his conversation. As for oaths and apparel, the disorders thereof are also very manifest. The parson's yea is yea, and nay nay; and his apparel plain but reverend and clean, without spots, or dust, or smell; the purity of his mind breaking out and dilating itself even to his body, clothes, and habitation. (III)

In his house the country parson leads a disciplined and well ordered life.

The parson in his house observes fasting days, and particularly as Sunday in his day of joy, so Friday his day of humiliation, which he celebrates not only with abstinence of diet but also of company, recreation and all outward contentments, and besides with confession of sins and all acts of mortification. (X)

He acknowledges that there are some who cannot or should not fast (for injury to their health) and that there are varying degrees of fasting; eating less, eating plain food, and abstaining from meat. Herbert was a lover of the good things of life and he knew how easily these things in excess could damage and distort a person's life. The country parson is a disciplined man, and that discipline must start with himself. The lover of fashionable and courtly dress now realizes the importance of plain *but reverend and clean* clothes; this is not courtly fastidiousness but a desire to see everything as subservient to the single goal of commending the gospel.

Herbert's views about marriage are not readily discerned:

> *The country parson considering that virginity is a higher state than matrimony and that the ministry requires the best and highest things is rather unmarried.* (IX)

And yet he believed that there were personal and parochial reasons, as a consequence of which *he is rather married than unmarried* (IX). Herbert himself provides a welcome example of a married saint whose wife understood and shared his life to the full.

> *If he be married, the choice of his wife was made rather by his ear than by his eye; his judgement, not his affection found a fit wife for him, whose humble and liberal disposition he preferred before beauty, riches or honour.* (IX)

He speaks of the respect that a husband must give his wife, particularly before servants and other people, and says that she must have *half at least of the government of the house* (IX). He implies that marriage is a significant pastoral advantage to a clergyman:

> *as the temper of his parish may be where he may have occasion to converse with women and that among suspicious men . . . he is rather married than unmarried.* (IX)

Herbert acknowledges those problems and difficulties that have always existed for unmarried clergy:

> *If he be unmarried and keep house he hath not a woman in his house, but finds opportunities of having his meat dressed and other services done by men servants — at home, and his linen washed abroad. If he be unmarried and sojourne, he*

never talks with any woman alone but in the audience of
others and that seldom and then also in a serious manner. (IX)

In the case of married clergy, his children (in Herbert's case the
three orphaned wards), who are the principal concern of his
wife, are to be brought up to *truth and diligence and neatness*
or cleanliness; just as *in the house of a musician all are*
musicians, in the house of a preacher all are preachers. Even in
the management of his house everything is to be subservient
to the one aim of commending the gospel to the people; his
home is to be *a copy, a model for his parish.* (X)

As to the house itself:

the furniture of his house is very plain but clean, whole and
sweet . . . His fare is plain and common but wholesome,
what he hath is little but very good; it consisteth most of
mutton, beef and veal; if he adds anything for a great day, or
a stranger, his garden or orchard supplies it or his barn and
back side [kitchen garden]. (X) In his household *he admires*
and imitates the wonderful providence and thrift of the
great householder of the world. (X)

The country parson is not only a father to his flock, but also
professeth himself thoroughly of the opinion, carrying it
about with him so fully, as if he had begot his whole parish.
(XVI)

Herbert's concern for his parish stretches to all aspects of its
public and personal life. *The country parson at spare times*
from action standing on a hill, and considering his flock . . .
(XXVI) is on the watch against sin and self-righteousness: *a*
man may be both covetous and intemperate and yet hear
sermons against both. He knows that *country people are full*
of . . . petty injustices being cunning to make use of another
and spare themselves. He gives as an example a man who has
the money to buy a spade of his own but prefers to wear out
his neighbour's. (XXVI)

The country parson wherever he is keeps God's watch . . .
there is nothing spoken, or done, in the company where he is
but comes under his test and censure. (XVIII) He is especially

on the watch against the sins of country people, particularly
drunkenness and gluttony ... *if after dinner they are not fit
(or unwieldy) either to pray or work, they are gluttons* (XXVI).
He acknowledges that country people have a difficulty in
understanding the point at which something becomes an
abuse. He is a guardian against strange doctrines and their
damaging consequences, at a time when there was great public
interest in witchcraft and the occult (for example, John Aubrey
appears to have been particularly interested in witches,
supernatural occurrences and astrology).

> *The country parson, if there be any of his parish that hold
> strange doctrines, useth all possible diligence to reduce them
> to the common faith.* (XXIV)

The country parson is constantly among his people:

> *The country parson upon the afternoons in the weekdays,
> takes occasion to visit in person, now one quarter of his
> parish, now another. For there, he shall find his flock most
> naturally as they are, wallowing* [engrossed] *in the midst of
> their affairs.* (XIV)

He does not seek to escape from the responsibility of
questioning people closely about their own religious practice:

> *If the parson were ashamed of particularizing in these things,
> he were not fit to be a parson; but he holds the rule, that
> nothing is little in God's service ... The parson questions
> what order is kept in the house, as about prayers, morning
> and evening, on their knees, reading of Scripture,
> catechizing, singing of psalms at their work and on holy
> days; who can read, who not.* (XIV)

His pastoral visits will take him into every home without
distinction:

> *Wherefore neither disdaineth he to enter into the poorest
> cottage, though he even creep into it and though it smell
> never so loathsomely. For both God is there also and those
> for whom God died.* (XIV)

The country parson takes his civic duties responsibly:

*The country parson is sincere and upright in all his relations.
And first, he is just to his country; as when he is set at an
armour, or horse* . . . (XIX)

Periodically country gentry were required to finance the local
militia and this duty was frequently discharged in a
dishonourable way by hiring both men and horses that were
hardly fit for the task (XIX). At the same time the clergyman is
respectful to his diocesan bishop and observes the visitations
and *keeps good correspondence with all the neighbouring
pastors round about him, performing for them any ministerial
office* (XIX). He also encourages the churchwardens both to
attend the visitation and to read the canons of the church
(XXIX).

*The country parson is full of charity; it is his predominant
element* . . . *When he riseth in the morning he bethinketh
himself what good deeds he can do that day.* (XII)

In his own parish he makes sure there are no beggars or idle
persons, *but that all be in a competent way of getting their
living* . . . *by bounty, or persuasion or by authority, making
use of that excellent statute* (XII). This is a reference to the
Poor Law of 1601 which required overseers of the poor in each
parish to provide work for the able-bodied so that they could
earn a living.

. . . *at hard times and dearths giving some corn* and
employment for those who are destitute but this charity is
always subject to his principal purpose. He gives *most to
those who live best.* (XII)

Thus he rewards those who can say the creed and the ten
commandments. *This is to give like a priest.* (XII)

*The country parson owing a debt of charity to the poor and
of courtesy to his other parishioners, he so distinguisheth
that he keeps his money for the poor and his table for those
that are above alms.* (XI)

The country clergyman is hospitable and welcomes his parishioners to his house. In the course of a year he tries to invite all people to dinner. He makes sure not to miss anyone out *because country people are very observant of such things and will not be persuaded but being not invited they are hated.* (XI)

> *Now love is his business and aim, wherefore he likes well that his parish at good times invite one another to their houses and he urgeth them to it; and sometimes, where he knows there hath been or is a little difference, he takes one of the parties and goes with him to the other and all dine or sup together.* (XXXV)

In every way the parson tries to reconcile and to promote neighbourliness and friendship within his parish (XXXV). He also treats cases of conscience:

> *He greatly esteems also of cases of conscience, wherein he is much versed . . . the greatest ability of a parson to lead his people exactly in the ways of truth . . . Now if a shepherd know not which grass will bane [poison], or which not, how is he fit to be a shepherd? Wherefore the parson hath thoroughly canvassed all the particulars of human action, at least all those which he observeth are most incident to his parish* (V). *So the country parson who is a diligent observer and tracker of God's ways sets up as many encouragements to goodness as he can, both in honour and profit and fame, that he may, if not the best way, yet any way, make his parish good* (XI). *Thus both in rewarding virtue and in punishing vice, the parson endeavoureth to be in God's stead, knowing that country people are drawn or led by sense more than by faith, by present rewards or punishments, more than by future.* (XX)

> *The country parson desires to be all to his parish and not only a pastor but a lawyer also and a physician. Therefore he endures not that any of his flock should go to law; but in any controversy, that they should resort to him.* (XXIII)

Thus Herbert advised *reading some initiatory treatises in the law*, and he suggests William Dalton's *The Country Justice* (1618), a book which remained in print for a century and whose fourth edition was printed in the year Herbert went to Bemerton. Clearly Herbert was aware of the tension which might exist between the ministerial and the magisterial role (a problem which caused considerable concern for the nineteenth century parochial clergy). As so often, he illustrated this point with an example:

> *If the poorest man of the parish detain but a pin unjustly from the richest, he absolutely restores it as a judge; but when he hath so done, then, he assumes the parson and exhorts to charity.* (XXIII)

Above all, it is the country clergyman himself and his presence around the parish that is important:

> *The country parson, when any of his cure is sick or afflicted with loss of friend or estate, or in any ways distressed, fails not to afford his best comforts, and rather goes to them than sends for the afflicted, though they can and otherwise ought to come to him.* (XV)

At this time there were no doctors or medical practitioners of any sort available in country parishes, and therefore the large houses maintained herb gardens and some understanding of rudimentary medicine. Herbert seemed to be particularly interested in matters relating to health and diet as a consequence of his own prolonged ill-health. Walton records how he sought cures for his constitutional weakness but eventually he 'became his own physician and cured himself of his ague'. Towards the end of his life he translated the *Treatise of Temperance and Sobrietie* by Luigi Cornaro, a Venetian nobleman, himself an example of his own good advice, as he wrote the treatise at the age of 83 in 1558 (it seems that Herbert translated into English a Latin Version published in Antwerp in 1623, and it is suggested that he did this at the request of his friend Francis Bacon). In his parish, Herbert encouraged both the clergyman and his wife to develop their knowledge and to have *skill in healing a wound or helping the sick.* If they cannot do this themselves, they should maintain some young practitioner, but, as Herbert wrote, anyone who can read has only to buy the appropriate books, and he recommended Jean François Fernel's *Universa Medicina* (1586). Fernel was Physician to Henry II of France and his book was frequently reprinted during George Herbert's life. His brother Edward left three of Fernel's works to Jesus College, Oxford. In Chapter XXIII Herbert gives a list of the herbs which should be found in the country clergyman's gardens, which includes *rosemary, thyme, mint, fennel, hyssop, valerian, mercury, adder's tongue, yarrow, St John's wort, elder, camomile, mallow, and comfrey* (XXIII). Herbert shared with many of his contemporaries (particularly his step-father's elder brother, Lord Danvers, the founder of the Oxford Botanical Garden) an interest in gardening. His friend Francis Bacon wrote, 'God Almighty first planted a garden; and indeed it is the purest of human pleasures.'

The country parson is full of all knowledge (IV); this includes not only knowledge about farming and the management of his glebe but also carpentry and gardening (which he used both as example in his preaching and as a way of getting alongside his parishioners). Herbert, as Walton mentions in *The Compleat Angler* was a fisherman, and much concerned and interested in the countryside which surrounded him and the skill and understanding of those who worked in it. It was this feeling for people, their circumstances and their welfare, that must have played such a part in commending Herbert to his neighbours, *his parish being all his joy and thought* (XVII).

Barnabas Oley, the first editor of *The Country Parson*, commented in the introduction that he had heard men censure Herbert 'as a man that did not manage his brave parts to his best advantage but lost them in a humble way'. Having enjoyed a modestly successful academic and political career in his early life, it seems that Herbert was well aware that the country parson, in the eyes of the world, was a lowly occupation, held by many in contempt and ridicule. But Herbert believed that the service of God in a parish church and the spiritual leadership of the village community was the highest vocation, and he regarded himself as honoured to be called by God to this service. It seems that few contemporary Englishmen were as wise as Sir Thomas Fairfax, the father of one of Herbert's friends at Trinity College, Cambridge, who, when he heard that his son Henry wanted to become a country parson, gave his promising and well-educated son his complete approval and called it 'the happiest profession that can be. All other service be bondage, but this is pure freedom.' Herbert was aware of the 'general ignominy' which was cast upon the clerical profession by those who regarded it as unsuitable employment for a man of his ability and standing.

Walton recalls that when Herbert told one of his 'court friends' of his decision to seek ordination, his friend tried to persuade him to change his mind, as he regarded being a clergyman 'as too mean an employment and too much below his birth and excellent abilities and the endowment of his mind'. Walton records Herbert's reply:

> It hath been formerly judged that the domestic servants of the King of Heaven should be of the noblest families on earth; and though the iniquity of the late times have made clergymen meanly valued, and the sacred name of the priest contemptible; yet I will labour to make it honourable by consecrating all my learning and all my poor abilities, to advance the glory of that God that gave them; knowing, that I can never do too much for him, that hath done so much for me, as to make me a Christian. And I will labour to be like my Saviour, by making humility lovely in the eyes of all men, and by following the merciful and meek example of my dear Jesus.

Elsewhere he wrote:

> The country parson knows well, that both for the general ignominy which is cast upon the profession and much more for those rules which out of his choicest judgement he hath resolved to observe, and which are described in this book, he must be despised. (XXVIII)

This he recognized as the common fate of clergy and he expected to be despised, *because this hath been the portion of God his master and of God's saints, his brethren ... Nevertheless ... he endevours that none shall despise him ... in his own parish he suffers it not to his utmost power, for that where contempt is, there is no room for instruction. This he procures first by his holy and unblameable life ... secondly by a courteous carriage and winning behaviour ... thirdly by a bold and impartial reproof even of the best in the parish. (XXVIII)*

At another place, Herbert gave an example of what this meant in practical terms:

A godly man ... out of reverence to God's house resolves whenever he enters into a church to kneel down and pray ... but he spies some scoffing ruffian, who is likely to deride him for his pains; if he now, shall either for fear or shame, break his custom, he shall do passing ill; so much the rather ought he to proceed as that by this he may take into his prayer humiliation also. (XXXI)

In *The Country Parson* there is no word of the anxiety or the feelings of inadequacy which Herbert so often expressed in his poems. There he gave voice to his grief and bewilderment that ill-health and other troubles should thwart him when he had at last dedicated himself to God's service. But in *The Country Parson* the constant note is that of joy, *his parish being all his joy and thought* (XVII). Sunday is his day of joy and on Sunday evenings *he thinks it a very fit time, both suitable to the joy of the day ... to entertain some of his neighbours, or to be entertained by them* (VIII). *The pulpit is his joy and his throne* (VII). Although he writes of the general ignominy that was cast upon the clergy, it is clear that Herbert himself thought of the priesthood and of *the dignity wherewith God invested the priest* (XXXVI).

'Holy Mr. Herbert' was not the invention of Izaak Walton writing thirty-seven years after his death and without first-hand knowledge; it was the contemporary estimate of his character. His brother Edward wrote: 'His life was most holy and exemplary, in so much that about Salisbury, where he lived ... he was little less than sainted.' *The Country Parson,* which he described as *a mark to aim at*, bears witness to the high standards of devotion and pastoral practice which George Herbert set himself and to which he calls clergy in every generation.

5

The Changed Church

George Herbert was born four hundred years ago this year and wrote *The Country Parson* towards the end of his short three-year ministry in Bemerton. The book contained ideas and understandings about rural ministry which have remained relevant in every generation, but in order to assess their significance for the Church today it is necessary to understand something of the way in which the Church and the countryside have changed in the intervening period; it is with this that the next two chapters are concerned.

When George Herbert wrote *The Country Parson*, the Church of England had already achieved a measure of stability and confidence after the upheavals of the previous century. Elizabeth I, the daughter of Henry VIII and the zealously Protestant Anne Boleyn, grew up to appreciate the dangers of theological debate and kept her religious views to herself; but her preferences were displayed in the appointment of Matthew Parker as Archbishop of Canterbury, a man of moderate reforming views, who had taken advantage of the permission for clergy to marry, given in Edward's reign. Though monarchs changed, Parker remained his own man, capable of both compliance and opposition, as when he spoke out against further expropriation of church property. Much of the ethos and shape of the Church of England is owed to his energy, tact and moderation. The chronic problem of country parishes during Elizabeth's reign, a problem which had been building up since the middle of the fourteenth century, was that of the shortage of clergymen. In 1559, fewer than half of the parishes in the diocese of Canterbury had a resident clergyman. Although the situation had improved slightly at the time when George Herbert was writing, the shortage of clergy, particularly in the north and west, remained severe.

With the outbreak of the Civil War in August 1642, nine years after Herbert's death, there began a period in which there was much devastation of church buildings and church property. Many churches bear marks of axe or bullet, or record that Cromwell's cavalry was stabled within them. Certainly, the Cromwellian troops thought themselves to be fighting against the Church and made the churches and their ornaments a natural object of destruction. Many works of art which had escaped the attention of earlier generations, or had been placed in the churches during the Laudian period, were destroyed. Hammer-beam roofs were peppered with Cromwellian shot, the more accessible statues were mutilated and decapitated, stained glass was smashed, and vestments cut to pieces.

Archbishop Laud, who had tried to recreate the clergy once again as an estate of the realm, independent nationally of Parliament and locally of the squire, was executed in January 1645. The new Directory of Public Worship, compiled at the Westminster Assembly of 1643, was introduced in place of The Book of Common Prayer, which had formed the centre of Herbert's life. By this stage, many clergy were either Puritan at heart or at least willing to sign the Covenant and continue in their parishes as Presbyterian ministers. Of the 10,000 parochial clergy, only 2,425 were evicted and replaced by 'intruded' ministers. The number of clergy removed varied from diocese to diocese; in the diocese of Ely, of 121 parishes, 45 incumbents were deprived under the Commonwealth. Among the deprived clergy a few went overseas to exile, as their predecessors had done a century before, some were committed to prison, but others were given posts as tutors and chaplains in private houses.

The King's execution, on 30 January 1649, outraged the deepest feelings in the country and alienated many who had been, or might have continued to be, supporters of Cromwell. In the country parishes the distress of 1649 was great; a bad harvest, high taxation, and the general dislocation caused by the war bore heavily on the families of the village. The use of The Book of Common Prayer continued to be prohibited though there is evidence that Anglican services were held discreetly in many places, especially baptisms, weddings and funerals (even the Lord Protector's daughter was married at Waterperry in Oxfordshire according to the Prayer Book service). Some attempt was made to tackle the perennial problem of the poverty of the country clergy by supporting the lowest paid ministers with some of the land which had once belonged to the bishops and the cathedrals. But a more radical restructuring was not carried through; Cromwell had at first promised to restore the tithes but later changed his mind. However, it is easy to overestimate the degree of disruption that occurred during the period of the war; two-thirds of the English parishes had no change of minister under the Commonwealth.

Cromwell died in 1658; his son resigned as Protector in 1660 and Charles II arrived on 29 May amidst universal acclamation. The clergy exiled on the Continent had prepared the ground well and the Church of England was restored as the only legal and established Church in the land. The Book of Common Prayer was used in the King's Chapel; bishops were appointed and they set out, with the vigour of men long kept waiting, for the task of revitalizing the Church. On St Bartholomew's Day, 24 August 1662, the day the Act of Uniformity became law, 700 Puritan clergy were ejected from their livings.

In 1661 the elections to Parliament produced a House of Commons eager for revenge on the rebels, and this spirit was taken up at the Savoy Conference. At the second session in 1661, the 1552 Book of Common Prayer, with some alterations (especially the Baptism for those of Riper Years, for those not baptized during the Commonwealth) was included in the Act of Uniformity. The hasty revision of the Prayer Book had been carried out by a committee which included Izaak Walton's friend George Morley, who had now become Bishop of Winchester. However, The Book of Common Prayer was accepted in the House of Commons by a majority of only six, and they, believing reforms should be more radical, insisted on the right to debate further changes. The prohibition of Anglican practices in the fifteen years previously had a profound effect on the Settlement of 1662, and gave it a hint of intolerance which troubled Church and state for long after that date. There followed a series of Acts, known as the Clarendon Code, which among other things required all in public office to be communicant members of the Church of England and made non-Church of England religious services illegal. This was to have a profound effect upon the Church in the countryside.

The solidarity of the Restoration Settlement was tested by James II who was not only a Roman Catholic but made it clear that he wished to instal his co-religionists in positions of authority and influence, particularly in the army and the universities. The birth of a son to his wife precipitated the events that led to his flight from London, on 18 December 1688, and the arrival of the Anglican Mary and her Dutch Calvinist husband Prince William of Orange in the City on the same day. The revolution of 1688 achieved what the Civil War had failed to achieve, both in the name of religion and civil liberty. In the years after the restoration of the monarchy, the Church of England was not only firmly re-established but defended in law, and the clergy turned again to find in the writings of George Herbert, and his life, published by Izaak Walton in 1670, a model for their life and ministry in country parishes.

The patrician nature of the Church at this time was evident at many points, and the clergy were often heavily dependent upon the goodwill of the family that lived in the large house. When, in 1671, Viscount Scudamore built a rectory for the previously homeless vicar of Hempstead in Gloucestershire, the second incumbent caused this Te Deum to be carved:

> Who ere doth dwell within this door
> Thank God for Viscount Scudamore.

The Church of the eighteenth century is customarily seen through the eyes of Victorian writers, who have portrayed it as uniformly decadent and lethargic. Certainly, the Church was weakened by the loss of the Puritans; the sudden collapse of Calvinism as a factor in English religious life is one of the most significant changes in the English religious tradition. There is no doubt that in the late eighteenth and early nineteenth centuries the ministry of the Church was in considerable disarray. There was an acute shortage of suitably qualified candidates; clergy stipends were low; many vicarages and rectories had fallen into disrepair. Historians have portrayed the clergy of this period as of low social status on account of their humble social origins, their lack of education and the poverty of their benefices, the rusticity of their lifestyle, and particularly the socially degrading tasks they were forced to engage in to supplement their meagre stipends.

The country parson of the early eighteenth century is described in Henry Fielding's novel, *The Adventures of Joseph Andrews* (1742), as being 'a parson on Sundays, but all the other six might be more properly called a farmer. He occupied a small piece of land of his own, besides which he rented a considerable deal more. His wife milked his cows, managed his dairy, and followed the markets with butter and eggs. The hogs fell chiefly to his care.' Lord Macaulay wrote, of the same period, that the clergy were 'regarded, on the whole, as a plebeian class . . . his boys followed the plough; and his girls went out to service'. The Curate of Lastingham in the early eighteenth century had thirteen children to support on a stipend of £20. His wife kept a public house and he was able to convince the archdeacon that his indirect clerical management and his fiddle playing caused the parishioners to be 'imperceptibly led along the paths of piety and morality'.

In 1704, the establishment of Queen Anne's Bounty was a means by which some of the Church's revenues were used to create a fund for the relief of the ill-housed and poorly paid clergy. This followed a survey in which it was revealed that half the benefices were worth less than eighty pounds a year and that many of the curacies were worth less than twenty pounds a year. The plunder of the Church which resulted from the impropriation of livings had left many benefices below subsistence level, and the practice of impropriation had taken place in approximately 4,000 of the 9,284 livings by 1603. In practice, the lay rectors took the lion's share, as in Hornchurch in Essex, where, at this time, the benefice income amounted to £800 but the vicar's stipend was £55. At

Hogsthorpe in Lincolnshire the benefice income was £80 but the vicar received £10. Ruely, an early eighteenth-century vicar, remarked that the clergy got leavings not livings. Impropriation led directly to non-residence, absenteeism, pluralism, unqualified and other unsatisfactory clergy, and the general demoralization of the Church at the local level. In the county of Oxford in the 1780s, approximately one hundred of the one hundred and sixty-five incumbents were non-resident; at the same time, in the diocese of Exeter, one hundred and fifty-nine out of the two hundred and ninety were non-resident. The poverty of many clerical incomes demanded that clergy seek alternative means of support, many as school teachers, and the ideals which were set forward by George Herbert could not be followed. Tindal Hart quotes from a sermon preached at Danbury in 1787 which linked low incomes to an uneducated clergy. The clergy of that time were condemned on four counts: 'immoral conduct, professional ignorance, inattention to duty, and, lastly, attachment to the world'.

In areas where the clergy were largely non-resident, such clerical work as was done was performed by 'gallopers', curates who were known principally for their dexterity in speeding from one church to another, to serve as many churches as they could on a Sunday for a fee of half a guinea per service. The procession of curates leaving the city over Magdalen Bridge on a Saturday afternoon to serve the parishes of Oxfordshire was considered one of the sights of Oxford in the mid eighteenth century. On 9 December 1775, James Woodforde recorded that the snow stopped the curates leaving the city. The various effects of this system were that single duty became the rule; that curates were forced to hurry through the service, and that Sunday services were at no fixed time. Charlotte Yonge recorded that at Otterbourne, at the end of the eighteenth century, there was only one service and that the bells were rung when the curate could be seen riding towards the church. Numerous anecdotes point to the careless performance of the services and they bear witness to what must have been a common experience. George Horne (later Bishop of Norwich)

wrote in 1787 of his visit to a country church. Having described
the dilapidated state of the church and the churchyard, he
continued:

> The minister of this noble edifice was answerable to it in
> dress and manner. Having entered the church he made the
> best of his way to the chancel where he changed his wig, put
> on a filthy iron-moulded ragged surplice; and after a short
> angry dialogue with the clerk, entered his desk and began
> immediately without looking into the book. He read as if he
> had ten other churches to serve that day, at as many miles
> distant from each other. The clerk sang a melancholy solo —
> neither tune nor words of which I have ever heard before.

The neglect of church attendance had caused concern before
the last quarter of the eighteenth century, but there seems
little doubt that it had now reached much larger proportions.
John Butler, shortly after his translation from Oxford to
Hereford in 1788, sent out visitation queries and compared
the results with the diocesan survey last made in 1747. The
decline in church attendance was so distressing that he was
unwilling to divulge the results. The church attendance figures
had been by no means high in 1747 and, when the increase in
population was also considered, the results must have been
even more alarming. The report of a group of country
clergymen in Lincolnshire, published in 1800, revealed that in
seventy-nine parishes, with a population of 15,042, the average
number of members of the congregation was 4,933. Edward
Stanley (later Dean of Westminster) recorded that, when he
took over his family living in 1805, the established practice
was for the clerk on Sunday mornings to stand in the
churchyard and only call the vicar if someone came to church.
When the country clergy of the mid and late eighteenth
century are compared with the generality of parish clergy in
the Caroline period, it can be readily seen that as a group they
were more wealthy, lived in better houses and were in every
respect more significant figures in the rural community than
had been their seventeenth-century predecessors. A number
of diaries of mid-eighteenth-century parish clergy have been
edited, and they allow a composite picture of that century's

parish clergyman to be presented. The tendency to see the eighteenth century through the eyes of Victorian writers has partly obscured the fact that by their own rights many of the clergy were conscientious and endeavoured to fulfil the duty of their office according to the understanding of the times. However, the rising price of agricultural commodities, the enclosures and the consequent commutation of the tithe for a block of land, had the effect of making the clergy, both individually and corporately, significantly more wealthy. This fact was reflected in their houses, which, in the mid and late eighteenth century, more closely resembled the hall than the farm house, and in the adoption of new modes of recreation and dress suitable to their new status. (In 1752 William Halfpenny, 'architect and carpenter', published *Useful Architecture in Twenty-One New Designs for erecting Parsonage-houses*.) Benjamin Newton, rector of Wrath at this time, combined the duties of rector with the interests and occupations of a moderately well-to-do country gentleman. He hunted with all the neighbouring packs; he shot over the manor, for which he had the deputation of sporting rights; he fished; he kept greyhounds; and he attended the race meetings at Richmond and Catterick, as well as the local balls. He farmed, on a considerable scale, his own glebe and rented land; he bred horses; he sat on the county bench; and he visited and entertained his friends in a constant round of hospitality.

It is estimated that of the 3,128 Enclosure Acts between 1757 and 1835, in 2,220 instances the tithe was commuted, and, in the overwhelming number of cases, commuted for land. The conditions of commutation were remarkably generous to the clergy and the value of benefices increased accordingly. At Long Melford the income of the benefice rose from £450 in 1790 to £1,220 in 1819. Inevitably, as benefice incomes rose, at a time when respectability was gauged in acres and the owners of the soil derived from it not only wealth but high social status and the right to govern, the Church attracted men of higher social status, particularly the sons of the lesser squires, who were severely hit by the inflation of the eighteenth century and the development of the large estates. In 1756, Lord Chesterfield wrote to a father who asked his advice: 'I entirely agree with you in your resolution of bringing up all your sons to some profession or other.' He went on to suggest 'general rules by which I would point out to them that profession which I should wish them to apply to; I recommend the army or the navy to a boy of warm constitution, strong animal spirits and a cold genius; to one of quick, lively and distinguished parts, the law; to a good, dull decent boy, the church'. A glimpse of the clergy of this period is caught in the novels of Jane Austen, who was both the daughter and the sister of a clergyman. John Skinner wrote of the Reverend Mr Gunning of Farnborough, a recently arrived neighbour:

> He seems an open hearted man, but I do not think exactly calculated for a clergyman, as he keeps his hounds and having no other pursuit, thinks more of the hare than he does of hunting out what may benefit his parishioners.

However, it was the widespread practice in the late eighteenth century of appointing clergy as magistrates, that most clearly indicated their rising significance in the rural community. It has been shown that in the county of Oxford, of convictions recorded at Quarter Sessions in 1790, 86% bore the signature of a clergyman. The diary of Benjamin Newton reveals that he was an active magistrate, not only in his attendance at Petty Sessions and Quarter Sessions but also in the smaller matters of the magistrates' duty in the local community. Blomfield (later Bishop of London) when at Dunton, wrote in June 1813:

> My time will be somewhat more occupied than formerly as I am now a Commissioner of Turnpikes and a Justice of the Peace and the county business will never get on without me. I must study Burn with diligence before I can indifferently administer justice . . . I shall moreover probably be a Commissioner of Property Tax, all of which offices will a little interfere with Greek.

Thus it can be seen that the clergy came to conceive of their role in a significantly different way from that described and practised by George Herbert. These differences partly arose from changing understandings of the clergyman's role and his status in society, but also from the widespread mid and late eighteenth-century abuses of pluralism and non-residence. As a consequence of these, itinerant curates now performed much of the pastoral ministry which George Herbert had described. This meant that the amount of Sunday duty performed by the clergy as a whole continued to decline steadily. Single duty, as has been mentioned, now became common in as many as 40% of the churches, so common that in the early nineteenth century, in visitation enquiries by the Bishop of Exeter, he omitted the words 'twice every Lord's day'. James Woodforde, although he was constantly resident, had only single duty and even this had to be cancelled on occasions when the church was being cleaned or the weather was bad, or Woodforde, being ill or away, was unable to find a substitute.

However, in this period, there was a strong sense that the church belonged to the community, for the English Reformation above all else had established lay supremacy in many areas of church life. In the eighteenth century almost all patronage was in lay hands, and a clergyman was appointed not infrequently by the resident squire. Where church patronage was a valuable asset, it was reserved for a member of the family; where this was not the case, the clergyman was often appointed in the same way as the upper servants of the large houses, and could expect treatment not dissimilar. The church was not his church, in the way that it came to be regarded by clergy in the Victorian period, but belonged to the community in general and to the squire in particular. In many instances, as the lay rector, the squire had the responsibility of repairing the chancel, and would have exercised his right to occupy a pew in the chancel during services.

The services themselves were essentially an offering of the whole community in which many people played their part. The clergyman's duties were those of reading the service (or that part of it which the clerk did not read) and preaching the sermon, which came at the end of the service, unless it was a Sacrament Sunday. It was inevitable that the educated clergyman, who took pains to express himself as a scholar, in carefully composed literary exercises, spoke only to the educated members of his congregation. The clergyman who took the university disputation as his model, as Herbert had done on his first Sunday at Bemerton, or who composed, with the aid of references from Greek and Hebrew text, a sermon the preparation of which occupied him for a considerable part of the week and took more than an hour to read, or the clergyman who simply read his father's or grandfather's compositions, would have some difficulty in holding the attention, even of the educated members of the country congregation. For the rest, the sermon could often have had little meaning, particularly when a clergyman, such as the Reverend John Coleridge of Ottery St Mary, introduced lengthy Hebrew quotations into his parochial sermons; Coleridge regarded Hebrew as the 'immediate language of the Holy Ghost'. Clearly, Hogarth's cartoon of the sleeping congregation recorded an experience with which many could identify and a large part of the appeal of Nonconformity lay in the more energetic and colloquial preaching of its ministers, whose social and educational situation more closely approximated that of the congregation.

In the eighteenth century, preaching was dominated by the example of Archbishop Tillotson. His sermon, 'His commandments are not grievious', typified an age in which the doctrine of the divine wisdom and God's benevolence achieved pre-eminence. Tillotson established a school of preaching markedly different from that of Lancelot Andrewes, which Herbert had himself criticized. His preaching was centrally concerned with morality, and made its appeal to reason and common sense (natural wisdom) rather than to divine revelation. Many clergymen did not compose their own sermons but read those of eminent divines, or patronized the ingenious Dr Trusler, who, in the late 1770s, established a business in abridging the sermons of eminent divines and printing them in copperplate, so that if the pulpit was overlooked by the gallery the occupants would think that the clergyman was reading his own composition. Later attacks on the clergy constantly drew attention to their being content to read from the pulpit sermons which they had not written.

At the same time, the musicians and singers were responsible for the music, and in the eighteenth century they were usually accommodated in a west gallery. During the service the congregation stood and turned west during the musical parts of the service (hence the expression 'to turn and face the music'). The musicians had a considerable reputation for independent action and were liable to meet any interference by the clergyman with a demonstration of their disapproval, often during the service. A large number of country clergy had 'trouble with the musicians', as did Woodforde on several occasions. The standard of performance was often low, and Oxenden wrote of the Barnham musicians: 'the singing was almost ludicrous, provoking laughter rather than an expression of praise'. However, in other places high standards were aimed at; Arthur Gibbs, in Gloucestershire, wrote of the Chedworth band; 'These musicians are the descendants of the village musicians who, to quote from the Strand Musical Magazine of September 1897, "led the psalmody in the village church sixty years ago with strings and wind instruments". Mr Charles Smith of Chedworth remembers playing the clarinet in Handel's *Zadok the Priest* performed there in 1838 in honour of the Queen's accession.'

In addition, the parish clerk, whose liturgical functions customarily included leading the responses, reading the notices and briefs, and reading over the psalm before it was sung by the congregation, played a major role in the service. The office was freehold, and in some parishes hereditary. The Reverend George Woodward identified a fellow-traveller in a stage-coach as a parish clerk by the particular way in which he said 'Amen'; clerks were often known as 'Mr Amen'. It appeared that the clerk was often a source of considerable mirth and irreverence in the eighteenth-century church, being quite unequal to his duties. James Woodforde recorded in his diary on 14 April 1791: 'Poor old John Smith my clerk made a shocking hand of it singing this afternoon in church; much laughed at.' Whatever may be said about eighteenth-century Anglican worship, and there are many testimonies to its dullness, it was in a real sense the offering of the whole community in an act of worship, which included the village choir and band, with fiddles, bass, viol and serpent, the charity children in blue uniforms under the eye of the parish beadle, bell-ringers in the tower, and the parish clerk. In many churches, scenes such as that depicted in Thomas Webster's picture of the village choir must have taken place regularly every Sunday, as at Great Milton, in Oxfordshire, where both instruments and music from this period are preserved.

This period in the history of the rural church may rightly be described as the patrician period, if only because it was the time in which the church was most evidently under lay control. In many parishes the resident squire was both the lay rector and the patron of the living, and, through direct and indirect means, he controlled almost everything that happened in the village, including the church. The clergy may be seen in some ways as an occupational appendage of gentry status; though their role was, at every turn, an ambiguous one, for at times the clergyman could find himself treated as an equal, at other times as a servant. This inherent ambiguity in the clergyman's role, which is still experienced by the country parson today, has its origins in this period, as do many elements of the relationship between the clergy and the local community. However, this was to change significantly in the mid nineteenth century as the clergy increasingly saw their role in professional terms.

By the second and third decades of the nineteenth century, changes were taking place which were radically to alter the nature of the clergyman's role, for society was no longer disposed to accept the combination of rich rewards with minimal duties which had marked the eighteenth-century church. As William Cobbett observed after completing his tour of Hampshire, Berkshire, Surrey and Sussex in 1823:

> I cannot conclude my remarks on this Rural Ride without noticing the new sort of language which I hear everywhere made use of with regard to the parsons, but which language I do not care to repeat.

The mounting wave of agitation broke heavily on all ancient institutions and they were subject to every sort of attack, including physical violence. The unreformed Hanoverian Church found itself assaulted on every side, in an age which would no longer tolerate the abuses and privileges which it harboured. It was widely agreed that a sizeable proportion of the national wealth could no longer be set aside for the maintenance of the clergy. The Ecclesiastical Commission, established by Peel in 1835, was the means by which it was hoped by laymen and progressive churchmen alike that the obviously archaic structure of the Church of England could be remodelled, so it could more effectively discharge its pastoral duties. The Church, unlike Parliament and the universities, proved a difficult institution to reform, not least because of its dispersed and local nature, and the achievements of the Commission were principally to improve its administration and the use of its resources. A series of Acts were passed by Parliament in 1813, 1817, 1828 and 1836 which sought to compel clergy to reside in their parishes; to limit their extra-ecclesiastical activities; to encourage them to pay curates properly and to keep the parsonage house in good repair. When change came to the country church it came suddenly; in 1827, approximately half the benefices had non-resident incumbents; by 1850 this figure had dropped below ten per cent. In Cornwall in 1831 there were only 89 resident incumbents; by 1869, the year of Bishop Henry Philpotts' death, 219 out of the 232 incumbents were now resident in their parishes.

A mid-nineteenth-century clergyman wrote:

> You must remember that the tone of feeling that existed in the church, even twenty and five years ago, both with respect to duties and amusements, was very different from that which is to be found among us at present. At that time a person in holy orders might have been seen at Ascot or Newmarket without any very great scandal. But were a clergyman now to be seen on a racecourse he would, even by worldly people, be considered to have disgraced himself and his profession.

In a manner book of the period, *The Habits of Good Society*, published in 1855, the following advice is given: 'One must never smoke without consent in the presence of a clergyman, and one must never offer a cigar to any ecclesiastic over the rank of a curate.' Bishop Blomfield's biographer wrote: 'In character, habit, attainment, social position, and general reputation, the ordinary clergyman of 1860 is a very different being from a clergyman of 1810.' Speaking generally, the remark of Mr Thomas Grenville, who died in 1846 at the age of ninety-one, may be taken as true, that no change which had taken place in his lifetime was so great as the change in the clergy of the Church of England.

It was at this time, after a long period of neglect, that the country clergy rediscovered *The Country Parson*. Whether of Tractarian, Evangelical or Broad Church inclinations, the country clergy found in George Herbert's writing the seriousness of intent and the simplicity of life which enthused their highest aspirations. Many came to see, in the writing and life of John Keble, in its preoccupation with purity and sanctity, a poetic mind and a pastoral ministry that had strong similarities to that of George Herbert. Thus Herbert's pastoral was rediscovered in the mid nineteenth century; Hurrell Froude wrote, in March 1827, to Samuel Wilberforce (later Bishop of Oxford):

> I will advise you to go into some bookseller's shop to buy George Herbert; a new edition of his came out last year so that it must be easily procurable . . . among the ideas which it has instilled in me, it has made me determined to learn medicine, which in a parson is quite different from in a doctor; as you will not fail to perceive from a most delicious chapter in G.H.

At about the same time, John Keble himself wrote to one of his contemporaries: 'Do not forget George Herbert's *Country Parson*.'

In the mid nineteenth century the residence legislation meant that, in many country parishes, there arrived for the first time a resident clergyman, trained at one of the new theological colleges and determined to introduce higher standards into parish life. Many of these newly resident clergymen started on the church building itself, and attempted to improve the conduct of the services. They were unwilling to put up with the rustic standards, particularly of the clerk, whose activities were often fatal to the new sense of reverence and decorum at which they were aiming. One such clergyman wrote of his clerk: 'He can read but little, he can sing but one tune of the psalms, he can scarcely write his own name or read.' The dismissal of the clerk frequently caused less trouble than that of the musicians and singers. Many diaries record the struggle which the clergyman had to achieve this end. However, by the late 1850s and early 1860s, hymns, which had not been common in the 1840s, were widely introduced; and the old musicians were often incapable of meeting the new standards demanded of them. In many parishes the musicians made way for a new harmonium and a choir of children from the parish school, both placed in the chancel and under the clergyman's eye and immediate direction (or that of his wife). Implementing these reforms was not easy and they were often undertaken against a background of bitter opposition from the displaced musicians. T. T. Carter describes the removal of the gallery and the break-up of the choir at Clewer as 'a terrible grievance'. Thomas Hardy, in his novel *Under the Greenwood Tree*, described the last days of the gallery musicians and singers in a Dorset village and the introduction of an organ, played by the schoolmistress, into the chancel. He wrote in the preface to his story:

> Under the old plan, from half a dozen to ten full grown players, in addition to the numerous more or less grown up singers, were officially occupied with the Sunday routine, and concerned in trying their best to make it an artistic outcome of the combined musical taste of the parish. With the musical executive limited, as it mostly is limited now, to the parson's wife or daughter and the school children, or to the school teacher and children, an important union of interests has disappeared.

At the village of Stanground, near Peterborough, a newly erected barrel organ was installed in time to celebrate the Treaty of Paris, signed on 30 March 1858, at the end of the Crimean War. It played twenty-four hymn tunes and six chants. The case was handsome and the tone was reported to be rich and powerful; it was paid for by subscription, with the vicar himself subscribing more than half the cost. These changes had a profound effect upon the nature of worship, and were indicative of the new understanding of the role of the clergyman in the village. Reluctantly, one of the musicians (in Hardy's novel) was forced to concede that in changed times new ideas had replaced those of former generations: 'Parson Maybold, every tradesman'd like to have his own way in his workshop, and Melstock church is yours.' Few statements could describe so accurately the new professionalized view of the clergyman's role, which was increasingly seen as limited to those specific activities sanctioned by the Ordinal. Many clergy in the mid nineteenth century were anxious to remove the box pews which dated from the previous century and which they saw as symbols of a social division no longer compatible with a house of prayer. However, in some cases the wood salvaged from the box pews was used to erect a chancel screen, itself the symbol of another form of divisiveness.

Increasingly, worship in the parish church ceased to be the offering of the whole community, many of whom participated in different ways, and became something which was organized and performed almost totally by the clergyman himself. Worship tended to become a professional service offered to the village by a qualified practitioner, rather than the offering of the whole community. As Hardy noted, while the quality of church services was improved, this was achieved at the cost of an important 'union of interests' between the clergyman and his parishioners. This transformation of public worship in the mid nineteenth century may be regarded as indicative of a more fundamental change in the way in which the clergyman perceived his role, and, as a consequence, his relationship with his parishioners. In brief, while in the former period the parishioners were customarily participants in the worship and life within the church, in the late nineteenth century they tended merely to be 'consumers' of a service provided by professional personnel. Like the services provided by other professional men, there was a marked tendency, which has persisted strongly in rural areas, to regard the public aspects of religion as essentially something which is done to and for individuals or groups of individuals by professional personnel. Just as the clergy were called to meet new expectations of their pastoral and spiritual role, so other functionaries such as the Poor Law administrator, the political agent, the teacher, the registrar, the doctor, the policeman and the sanitary engineer took over functions which the clergyman had previously been content to perform in an essentially amateur and untrained capacity. In Warwickshire, in the early 1830s, Sir J. E. Eardley-Wilmot, Chairman of the County Quarter Sessions, declared himself in principle against the appointment of clergy as magistrates, but conceded that, in some areas, it was necessary in the absence of other suitably qualified men. His successor, the Earl of Warwick, was equally opposed to the appointment of clergymen and, by 1868, the clergy consisted of only seven per cent of the Warwickshire bench. In many country areas doctors were selected to replace the clergy on the magistrate's bench.

Country life, in the mid nineteenth century, was often portrayed as boorish and uncultured if not wild, savage and brutal. It must have appeared even more so to the newly ordained clergyman who had left the seclusion of Oxford to take up a college or family living, and found himself in the midst of a community at best indifferent and frequently hostile. In a letter of 1828, the incumbent of Checkendon in Oxfordshire advised Samuel Wilberforce, his successor, not to allow his man to sleep in the village. He said it was his practice to have his man on guard at night carrying a loaded gun and a sword-stick. The whole period was pervaded by the atmosphere of war, revolution and social instability, certainly until the 1840s. Even ten years later, the new rector of Ilmington in Warwickshire, the Reverend J. C. Young, wrote: 'The attractions of the rectory house and grounds are somewhat neutralized by the accounts which reach me from all quarters of the depraved condition of the parish.' By this he meant 'deplorable attendance at church, drunkenness, bastardy, poaching and even serious riot'. Apparently the previous incumbent, 'a man of amiable and retiring disposition', had even had his life threatened: 'his nerve was so shaken as to render residence elsewhere essential to his health and peace of mind'.

Along with all his fellow clergy, the Reverend J. C. Young sought to solve this problem by founding a range of parochial institutions, which included provident clubs, penny readings, magic lantern shows and, most important of all, a village school. Village schools are the enduring monument to the work of the parochial clergy in the mid nineteenth century, for neither their system of provident institutions nor their elaborate restorations of the church have survived subsequent changes in taste and local demand. However, the system of parochial primary education which was largely established through their efforts, and, in many cases, financed from their private resources, has remained unchanged in many of its essential features. The primary school, with its separate entrance for boys and girls, its prominent foundation stone (in all probability bearing a date between 1840 and 1870) and the schoolmaster's house attached to it, was considered an essential part of the parochial machinery in the mid nineteenth century, and many incumbents considered that their most important work was done within its walls. Between 1811 and 1833, 7,000 schools were built or assisted by the National Society (the Church's organization for financing schools), which educated 500,000 children. By 1842, the number had more than doubled to 17,000. (The legacy of their work may be seen in the fact that today 60% of all primary age children in Oxfordshire attend church schools.)

As the clergyman sought to concentrate on the work of the church and the school, so his involvements in many other aspects of village life contracted, and his role was marked by a new professional character which allows us to speak of the 'Victorian rural clergyman' as a recognizable figure. Within the church, the removal of the village musicians and band and parish clerk and the new emphasis on sacramental worship (full eucharistic vestments were used for the first time in 1849 in Wilmcote in Warwickshire) altered the way in which the clergyman and the church were regarded. At the same time, while, in the eighteenth century, pastoral work, as it later came to be understood, seemed to be neither practised nor looked for, in the nineteenth century, the active clergyman busied himself in a constant round of visiting the homes of his parishioners and organizing social and recreational activities (often aimed at drawing them away from the public houses).

However, as the clergyman went round his parish he often found himself separated from his parishioners by an unbridgeable gulf, for he was no longer indistinguishable from the yeoman-farmer clergyman of the early eighteenth century. He had become a professional man and a member of the professional upper middle class. Edward Monro, himself a country clergyman, found it necessary to write, in a handbook for clergy, advice aimed at helping them to 'get alongside' the working men in a country parish. Monro wrote in 1850: 'The visits of a clergyman to his poor must lose very much force unless he lays aside the magisterial air, so very commonly used. He has no right to cross the poor man's threshold with a covered head, nor in any degree to demean himself as a superior within the walls of the cottage.'

The last decades of the nineteenth century and the early years of the twentieth century, before the First World War, are often portrayed as the golden age of the country parson. Certainly, in many rectories, where the income allowed the employment of a number of servants, the clergy were able to sustain a style of life which, though less grand, approximated in many respects to that of the manor and the hall. They were able to send their sons to public schools, to professional careers in the army, the Church and the Empire, and to provide a comfortable and an appropriate lifestyle for their wives and daughters. However, the Whig reformers, who had wished to see a resident clergyman in every parish and whose legislation had done much to awaken the clergy to the nature of their duties, had had the effect of settling many country clergy in parishes that were too small or too poorly endowed. The decline in agricultural prices in the last two decades of the nineteenth century had resulted in a sharp decline in clerical incomes, particularly for those dependent on the letting of their glebe. In certain areas some clergy had to face a number of years where their fields remained untenanted. The Reverend E. B. Rutherfield recorded that the value of his benefice fell from £1,500 per annum in the high farming years of the 1860s, to £300 per annum in the depressed 1880s. At Ansley in North Warwickshire the value of the living fell from £236 in 1884 to £160 in 1904, by which stage the practice of making Easter offerings as a gift to the incumbent had become widespread throughout the Church. Less income led indirectly to the dismissal of the curate, more modest contributions to the village charities and organizations, and less support for the school.

However, poverty must have seemed easier to bear than the vague presentiment of a life passing by, which many rural clergymen were beginning to feel. Richard Jefferies provided a touching vignette of a country parson in the 1870s, as seen through the eyes of his wife:

> But the work, the parish, the people, all seem to have slipped out of my husband's hands . . . But surely his good intentions, his way of life, his gentle kindness would carry sway. Instead of which the parish seem to have quite left the church and the parson was outside the real modern life of the village.

In an age characterized by activity and achievement, success and boundless opportunity for the energetic and determined, there was increasing concern for the isolation, loneliness and stagnation of the country clergy, some of whom ministered to very small country parishes. Three country parishes in south Warwickshire, Atherstone on Stour, Preston on Stour and Whitchurch, which then had a total population of 500 people, were served by three separate incumbents during this period. Inevitably, many of the clergy found other interests to occupy their time and the Rector of Whitchurch at this period, the Reverend Harvey Bloom, became well-known as an anti-quarian and historian, who catalogued the libraries of Warwick Castle and Worcester Cathedral.

It is no coincidence that the first criticisms of the patronage and freehold system should date from this time, when H. Rider Haggard (well-known as an author but also a substantial East Anglian landowner and farmer) wrote:

> In future, although it may be distant, I believe that all will be changed; priests will not be pitchforked into livings by the arbitrary decision of the owner of the advowson, which in practice often means their own decision, but will be selected by proper authorities in consultation maybe with the

representatives of the parishes, for their quality and nothing else. Also, perhaps, the revenues of the church will be paid into a general fund and portioned out according to local need, to be supplemented, if need be, by the contributions of the laity . . . of one thing I am certain – if the church does not, or cannot, reform itself, 'ere long the laity will lose patience and take matters into their own hands.

Though written just before the end of the last century, this quotation prefigures many of the changes that have happened in rural parishes in recent years. It was at this time, when agriculture was depressed and when the life of the nation seemed to be centred on the urban and industrial areas, that the country clergy became increasingly aware of themselves as having been left in a backwater. Some asked for no more and pursued faithfully a lifelong ministry in a small village; but others could not accept this reality with equanimity. Dr A. Jessop, vicar of Scarning in Norfolk, wrote in 1890:

When the rector, on his induction, takes the key of the church, locks himself in and tolls the bell, it is his own passing bell he is ringing. He is shutting himself out from all hope of a future career on earth. He is a man transported for life, to whom there will be no reprieve . . . for the day he accepts a country benefice he is a shelved man . . . once a country parson always a country parson.

But of all their troubles, the poverty of the benefices was perhaps the most significant. As Rider Haggard wrote in 1899:

The poor parsons, how will they manage to live, I wonder? It is undoubtedly to the advantage of this parish that a clergyman should be able to keep up a modest position; that he should not at least be notoriously struggling with debts or visibly out at the elbows. Yet in eight cases out of ten, how is he to do so in these days . . . ? There are very many benefices in these counties [East Anglia] that do not return £300 clear per annum.

Seven years later the average income of a clergyman was revealed to be only £150 per annum.

The First World War was a critical time for the Church of

England in particular and for the countryside in general and it marked a period of abrupt change. It saw the erosion of many of the social conventions which had previously sustained church attendance (notably 'the English Sunday') and, in the village, the clergy became aware of the competition of other leisure activities. In 1899, Bishop Randall Davidson devoted part of his charge to his clergy in the Diocese of Winchester, to observing that the bicycle was having a particularly deleterious effect on Sunday church attendance. In the last quarter of the nineteenth century, the number of clergy continued to rise until it reached a peak of 25,235 in 1901. But from this peak their number began steadily to decline and almost every rural area which now comprises a rural deanery has lost approximately one clergyman every fifteen years during this century. By 1931, the total number of Anglican clergy had already fallen by over 6,000. Whilst for a short time, in the late nineteenth century, it appeared possible to provide one clergyman for almost every parish no matter how small, already by the 1920s it was acknowledged that this policy had to be abandoned, and neighbouring parishes were linked together under the charge of one clergyman.

At the same time, many clergy, particularly the 3,030 commissioned as Chaplains in the First World War, were determined to see changes in the Church's structure. In 1919, the Enabling Act was passed, followed by the Parochial Church Councils Measure in 1921. At the service of thanksgiving, Archbishop Cosmo Lang said: 'For the first time, the laity in every parish throughout the land are offered voice and vote in the management of the church.' It may reasonably be questioned whether this quotation is historically accurate, for as can be seen during the patrician period in the eighteenth century, the laity had a major role both as patrons and in the running of the local church in the countryside. It was the rise of Victorian clericalism, what Owen Chadwick has called 'the long period of clerical absolutism', that had denied the laity their rightful place in the running and management of the local church. But from now on the vicar could not run the church without reference to anyone else, for the measure declared: 'it shall be the primary duty of the Councils in every parish to co-operate with the incumbent in the administration, conduct and development of church work, both within the church and outside'.

However, two further problems particularly concerned the country clergy in this period, those of glebe and tithe, and those associated with the benefice house. In 1836, the Tithe Commutation Act was passed, and payment in kind was superseded by a cash payment called the tithe rent charge, assessed on the average price of corn for the previous seven years. Opposition to the payment of tithe always intensified during periods of agricultural depression, and, during the 1880s, there was widespread agitation. However, this died down as a result of the Tithe Act of 1891, which transferred liability for these charges from the tenant to the owner of the land. As the large estates were broken up in the period after the First World War there was a consequent increase in the number of owner-occupier farmers who were liable to pay the tithe, and once again agitation mounted. In 1930, a Tithe Payers Defence Association was formed in Kent and, in the following year, in Suffolk, Norfolk and Essex. Ultimately there were fifty such county organizations in England and Wales, and a National Tithepayers' Association was established, which fought against what its members regarded as the major injustice against the farming community, in that they were expected to pay a charge which other sections of the community did not meet. In one year alone, 16,000 applications were made to the courts, mostly by the ecclesiastical authorities, for the restraint of goods following default of payment. Effigies of the Archbishop of Canterbury and Queen Anne were burned on a bonfire at Beechbrook Farm, Westwell, near Ashford in Kent, on 5 April 1935, following an abortive auction sale of nine cattle seized for rent arrears.

In 1934 a Royal Commission was established to enquire into and report on the whole question of the tithe rent charge in England and Wales. The resulting Tithe Act of 1936 provided for the termination of the charge in 1996. Under the new arrangement the Government paid the Church and lay tithe owners (such as Oxford and Cambridge colleges) large amounts in compensation for the abolition of tithe, but sought to recover the money from farmers over a sixty year period. Tithe collection was now a much quieter matter and compulsory redemption was carried through when land came onto the market. In June 1976, Parliament decreed that from October of the following year the collection of this charge would cease; the cost of collecting it had become too great. Thus ended the historic system of supporting the Church and its ministry in rural areas; perhaps the most remarkable feature of this system is that it has not left behind a permanent legacy of bitterness.

The second problem which troubled the country parson and particularly his wife was that of the benefice house. Built in a period of limitless fuel and many servants, a large number of these houses were now increasingly inappropriate and many of them had not been maintained to a sufficient standard for several generations. One clergyman's wife told the Church Assembly, in 1933, that a brass band playing in the kitchen could not be heard in the drawing room of her twenty-one-roomed rural rectory. The Ecclesiastical Dilapidations Acts of 1871 and 1882 had led to the appointment of diocesan surveyors, who were required to produce a schedule of repairs and to issue certificates when these were completed. This ended the period in which the claims and counter-claims of outgoing and incoming incumbents had often to be settled in the courts. Almost the first Act of the new Church Assembly was to pass the Ecclesiastical Dilapidations Measure, which enforced a single, compulsory system, whereby incumbents were charged an annual rent and their houses were inspected on a five-year basis. This system worked well until after the Second World War when there was a considerable backlog of dilapidations and the annual assessments had become very much higher (though they were increasingly met by the Parochial Church Council). The Dilapidations Commission was established in 1958, and a new measure took effect in 1972, whereby the diocese took over from the incumbent all responsibility for the repair of the parsonage. By this time many dioceses were well advanced in the process of selling off the older and larger houses, and building rectories and vicarages in villages which were more appropriate to the circumstances of the clergy and their families in the second half of the twentieth century. Though many parishes have regretted the loss of what has become 'The Old Rectory', few clergy have sufficient income to live with even moderate comfort in these large houses, and the Church was unwilling to shoulder the cost of keeping them in repair.

Thus, in the nineteenth century, the clergy became in many ways similar to other professional men, providing services for people, who in some respects could be regarded as their clients. Though the historic idea of parish ministry remained, the notion that the church and its life were the exclusive responsibility of the clergyman became deeply embedded in English rural society at this time. It led to the development of attitudes of deference and dependence upon the clergyman which had not been present in the rural church of the eighteenth century and which have persisted. For the model of the clergyman as a professional man has remained influential, and, in some senses, the dominant model of the clergyman's role throughout the twentieth century. However, in the period after the Second World War, and particularly since the 1970s, at a time when the professions themselves were changing significantly, both the clergy and many lay people became increasingly dissatisfied with inherited models and assumptions about the nature of the clergyman's role. The growing awareness of the decline of the Church's resources both in money and ministerial manpower; a reluctance to accept the clergyman's domination of all aspects of church life and a new understanding of the theology of the Church resulted in a new emphasis on the role and importance of the laity, and, by implication, sought to redefine the clergyman's role and his relationship to the local church community.

Increasingly, at this time, the Church looked to business corporations and to the role of the manager to find an appropriate model. At a time of scarce resources in any institution, skilled management (particularly financial management) becomes an important priority, to which, in some respects, all other activities have to take second place. At the same time, many country clergy were now being asked to care for an increasing number of parishes, for which they required enhanced administrative and managerial skills. Thus, the 1970s and 1980s were characterized by a developing understanding of the clergyman as a church manager; books were written on 'Ministry as Management'; clergy attended courses on 'Church Management by Objectives'; dioceses developed strategic pastoral plans (based on the county structure plans) and it became acceptable to some to speak of the rural dean as the Church's middle management. John Tiller, in his report, accurately describes this new model:

> In secular terms the parish priest is regarded as the branch manager of a service industry. Some of the clergy, especially those who have been employed in managerial positions prior to their ordination, fit into this administrative and organisational role very easily.

Increasingly, the clergy were seen by others, and came to see themselves, as church managers, whose primary responsibility was for the organization of church life, for which they needed appropriate skills and understandings. Whilst the professional model remained important, this gradually gave place to new understandings derived from management studies. The conflict between the understanding of the priest as a professional man (the guardian of a socially useful and important area of knowledge), and as a church manager (carrying primary responsibility for its plant, finances and human resources), has become increasingly apparent in recent years and is referred to in Chapter 8.

In the face of declining financial resources and progressive loss of membership, it was plain to many, particularly members of the laity, that the Church needed to be organized in a more efficient and effective manner. This task came to be seen by many as the primary task of the clergyman, who found himself forced to accept this estimation of his role with varying degrees of reluctance. Country clergy, in particular, found that a significant proportion of their time was spent directly or indirectly on what others would call administrative tasks associated with the maintenance of the church building; the organization of services; the compiling of rotas and the deploying of volunteers, as well as on fund raising. Significantly, the room in which the clergyman worked increasingly came to resemble an office rather than a study and the tools of his trade were the word processor and the laser printer. The degree to which the clergy are involved in administration varies considerably. Most clergy imply that the amount of administration in which they are involved is a considerable burden and takes up a large amount of valuable time that could be deployed elsewhere. The Rural Church Project, interviewing clergy in 1989, found that 19% of a rural clergyman's week was spent directly on administration.

However, the gradual move from seeing the Church as a professional organization and its clergy as professional men, to seeing the Church as a management structure and its clergy as that structure's local managers, has accelerated in recent years. Gradually such expressions as 'market share', 'product image' and 'corporate identity' have entered the currency of some clerical debates; a recent discussion on the Church as an organization ended with this statement: 'What is urgently needed is a new radical style of leadership based on sound management principles.' Thus, the older view of the clergyman as a member of a learned profession has gradually given place to an altered understanding of his role; this has happened gradually, but its impact on rural parishes can be seen as dating from the report of Leslie Paul, *The Deployment and Payment of the Clergy* (1964).

Schemes for the amalgamation and rationalization of parishes, based on population and acreage, had been produced in the last quarter of the nineteenth century. In 1894 the Reverend W. Awdry of Amport near Andover produced a plan for the reorganization of parishes in the deanery into what would now be called a deanery team. Owen Chadwick records: 'He argued that the population was decreasing and that the bicycle allowed effective administration in more than one village.' But the report written by Dr Paul, a sociologist, was the first attempt to apply the principles of systematic planning and corporate management to the increasingly evident problems of the Church of England. In 1961, there were 15,488 full-time clergy; Leslie Paul predicted that there would be 18,940 in 1971; in fact there were only 15,223. In the next ten years there was a further significant reduction of 4,000 to 10,922. The decline, however, has been spread unevenly across the country and, as Leslie Paul indicated, a larger proportion of the clergy worked in rural areas; for, whereas there was one clergyman for every thousand of the population in rural areas, there was one clergyman for six thousand of the population in urban areas. He pointed out that half the benefices of the Church of England contained only 10% of the population (in the rural areas), whilst less than one tenth of the benefices contained one third of the population. As a consequence of these observations, in 1974, the Church looked for ways to rectify this imbalance between urban and rural areas, and the Sheffield Report of that year contained a formula for the deployment of the clergy which would result in a significant redistribution in favour of urban areas. The Sheffield Commission took four factors into account: the total population (8 points); the number of places of worship (3 points); the size of area (1 point); and number on the electoral roll (3 points). This formula was accepted by the dioceses in the General Synod, and, thereafter, annual target figures of stipendiary clergy were allocated to each diocese based on the agreed formula; this is one of the principal manifestations of the management approach to the organization of the Church. Despite minor modifications the system still controls clergy numbers across the country on a diocesan basis. The result has been a proportionate increase in the number of stipendiary clergy in urban and inner city areas. Furthermore, the formula has played a part in withstanding the drift of clergy to dioceses in the southern half of the country.

However, the decline in clergy numbers in rural areas has been dramatic. In the Hereford Diocese between 1956 and 1986, the total number of clergy fell by 43%, but this overall decline masks the fact that rural clergy declined in number by 57% whilst market town clergy (places with populations over 1,500) actually increased by 36% The present (1992) number of parochial clergy stands at 10,315. This figure represents the total number of diocesan parochial appointments for men according to the Sheffield deployment formula. In addition, there were 715 women ministering in Sheffield appointments; making a total of 11,030. Those serving their title (in the first three years of ministry) and those in non-parochial appointments are not included in the Sheffield formula. The total number for all stipendiary clergy (men and women) in 1992 is 12,359. In addition, there are 1,600 non-stipendiary ministers licensed to parochial ministry. There are also 4,393 men and 193 women who are listed as 'active retired' (source: Advisory Board of Ministry). However, the number of ordinations and the age structure of the present clergy suggests that there will be a 10% decline in the next fifteen years. There is evidence to suggest that if present policies continue this will be translated into a 20% decline in most rural areas.

Traditionally, the professional man worked alone, and a manifestation of the influence of managerial thinking felt by all professions during the post-war period has been the creation of collaborative task-oriented teams, in which different professional members contribute a variety of specializations and skills. Further proposals of a more developed and radical nature came in the Morley Report (1967) and in the Tiller Report, *A Strategy for the Church's Ministry* (1983). Although the Church Assembly (before the creation of General Synod in 1972) rejected the proposals of the Paul Report, many of his proposals shaped the Pastoral Measure (1968; revised in 1983). This Measure allowed various forms of pastoral reorganization to take place, principally by the union of two or more benefices to form a new benefice with the parishes either having united or continuing district church councils; the formation of group and team ministries; the alteration of parish, deanery and archdeaconry boundaries; the declaration of redundancy of a consecrated church no longer required for public worship, together with the provision for the future of the building and the use of 'closed' churchyards and burial grounds (and the buildings within them). The freedom given to the Church to restructure its ministry in rural areas resulting from this legislation has produced the present pattern of rural ministry. A further piece of legislation that had equally far-reaching effects, though in a different way, was the scheme of 1971 enabling clergy to retire at sixty-five, with compulsory retirement at seventy; and the legislation of the following year which transferred to the diocese the ownership and management of glebe, thus removing the last vestiges of the ancient link between the local agricultural economy and the income of its clergyman.

However, collaborative ministry in rural areas had its origins in the period immediately after the last war; for in 1947, the Bishop of Lincoln established the South Ormsby Group of parishes in the Lincolnshire Wolds. This came into full operation in 1952: twelve small parishes with a total population of 1,100 in approximately 75 square miles, previously served by six elderly clergy, were welded together to form a single group, served by a rector, two assistant clergy and a deaconess. In 1961, ten parishes in the northern part of the Breckland area of West Norfolk, then without pastoral care, were formed into the Hilborough Group. In many respects this was modelled closely on the lines that Archdeacon Smith had drawn at South Ormsby, with ten parishes, a rector, a senior curate and an assistant curate. In the next ten years, seventeen groups were established in Norfolk, and by the time of the retirement of Bishop Launcelot Fleming in 1970 approximately a third of the parishes and a third of the clergy in that diocese were involved in collaborative ministry. In operation, the groups varied considerably, as did the nomenclature; some referred to themselves as groups, others as teams, while others described themselves as a team of clergy ministering to a group of parishes. However, each group sought to provide, in an extensive area, a pastoral ministry which combined pastoral care with centralized planning of localized services and other activities such as youth and children's work, adult education and confirmation classes. Like the Methodist circuit system, the groups were seen as a means of allowing the strong to support the weak and permitting the clergy to work as a team to their own and the parishes' mutual advantage.

Gradually, through the 1970s, the number of groups increased, as did the number of dioceses in which they were established, despite the fact that collaborative ministry has always suffered from being regarded as a regrettable necessity rather than a hopeful and effective way of developing the ancient parochial system. By the late 1970s, the continuing decline in the number of clergy increased the number of dioceses which were prepared to regard collaborative ministry as part of their strategy for rural areas. By 1983, in the Church of England as a whole, 10% of the clergy worked in collaborative ministries, comprising in total 333 teams and 91 groups. Currently there are proposals for Bemerton to be included in a new Salisbury City Team Ministry. Such ministries, by pooling the resources of an area and by allowing the clergy to work together as colleagues, have brought new life and vigour to many rural areas and have encouraged younger clergy to work in the countryside. However, such ministries are not spread evenly across rural dioceses and a small number of dioceses, including Salisbury, Bath and Wells, Norwich and Exeter, together account for a significant number of rural collaborative ministries.

However, Leslie Paul recorded that statistically he received more cries of despair from incumbents in rural areas than from those in towns. The debilitating problems of raising consider-able sums of money from small communities to repair historic buildings, coupled with indifference, isolation, poverty, large parsonage houses and gardens, non-payment of clerical expenses, the feeling of being ignored or irrelevant, appeared to dull the faith and encouraged despair in the hearts of many caring and able priests. One such clergyman wrote: 'The amount contributed for all church purposes last year was £23. I have had five confirmation candidates in seventeen years. There is no parochial church council, no organ, no choir, no verger, no heating in the winter.' This seemed an extreme case, but the report cited others which were equally depressing and Paul finished this section of his report by recording: 'One conclusion presses itself: the inflexibility that exists in parochial systems is an impediment to the exercise of the church's pastoral ministry.'

The impact of the management model on the country clergy has been uneven, and its ideas were received with greater enthusiasm by those at the centre of the diocese and in the larger urban and suburban parishes. Whilst it was undeniably helpful for the country clergy, particularly in large multi-parish benefices, to improve their administrative skills and to attend such courses as those on time management, it remained the case that most country clergy, and their congregations, did not regard the Church as an organization directly comparable with a business corporation, or their role as one which was similar to that of a branch manager within such a corporation.

A distinctive feature of the management model is the awareness of the local outlet as being part of an integrated organization, with hierarchical tiers of management and statements of coherent policy and approved practice. Though the word 'hierarchy' has religious connotations, and, in some dioceses, management plans were produced, the dispersed nature of authority and power in the Church did not allow such simplistic analogies to be drawn. To speak of the country clergyman as being in a line management situation with the rural dean and the archdeacon bears little relationship to the operational and legal realities of the Church. At the same time, many of the pastoral strategies developed in the early 1970s could not be implemented because they foundered on the realities of patronage and the parson's freehold. These epitomize and encapsulate the dispersed authority of the Church of England, which is one of the principal marks of the reshaping of the Church in the sixteenth century.

In the 1970s and 1980s there was a marked increase in the growth of centralized bureaucracy both at the national and diocesan level. The growth of centralism is always perceived as disadvantaging those at the margins, and, during this period, there was a significant growth in the degree of criticism of the cost of such bureaucracy and the impact of distant decision making upon the life of the local church. Whilst the country clergyman himself may or may not have been influenced by management thinking, it was widely perceived that the Church as a whole was becoming an organization in which such understandings and models predominated. However, the laity, as reflected in responses to the Archbishops' Commission on Rural Areas, were not convinced that such an understanding of the Church was appropriate or that they wished to be managed by their local clergyman; partly because they looked to their priest for other things and partly because they themselves were often the possessors of greater management skills. In many places the country clergyman found himself having to mediate between a view of the local church embraced by the diocesan staff (as a unit within a management structure) and a view of the Church which more accurately reflected the local reality (as a voluntary associational organization). Any discussion of diocesan finances and that contribution which the parish annually makes to the diocese, is likely to bring these conflicting models of the Church as an organization into sharp focus.

Thus, a view of the Church increasingly gained ground, particularly in rural areas, which saw it as an organization in many ways similar to other local voluntary associational organizations in the countryside. Initially, country parishes were required, as a church community, to take responsibility for their own finance; in contrast to the earlier period in which the finances of the church had largely been controlled by and were dependent on the vicar and a small number of relatively wealthy laity. At the same time, many parishes developed varying degrees of lay ministry, once restricted to the reading of the lessons but now including the taking of services; running Bible study and confirmation classes and being responsible for certain aspects of the pastoral ministry. In this way, country churches invited comparison with other local voluntary organizations in which the leadership and the finance are both provided and controlled at the local level. The process of de-institutionalization, which has affected many organizations in English society in recent decades, has been accelerated in the Church by the financial difficulties encountered in recent years. As the local church community raised considerable sums of money for the maintenance of the church buildings and the church's ministry, so, inevitably, local congregations demanded more control over the way in which this money was spent.

Thus the local church increasingly saw itself in ways similar to that of other voluntary and community organizations in the village; as an essentially local organization, though loosely linked to a wider network and structure. In many ways the church became similar to such organizations as the Women's

Institute, at least in terms of its structure and operation. In recent years, with the rise of a non-participatory home-based culture, centred on the television, all such organizations have seen both a decline in activity and membership. For instance, the Women's Institute's membership has declined from a peak of 467,000 members in 1954 to 319,000 members in 1990. A significant number of Women's Institutes have been closed each year; 148 in 1989; 160 in 1990.

Voluntary associational organizations do not look for their leadership either to professional personnel or to managers. The professional – client relationship or the manager – managed relationship is essentially different from that which is found in voluntary associational organizations; indeed, de-professionalization is a part of the process of de-institutionalization noted above. The knowledge and skill once thought to reside only in the professional man or the trained manager is now seen as being widely available within the community; the professional man or the manager is seen as somebody imposed from outside, and therefore at variance with the essentially local nature of such organizations. Within such organizations, leadership is provided by the person who has the skill and personality to enthuse, motivate and lead others. Such a person (the term 'focal person' is frequently used and the significance of such a person in a voluntary associational organization is hard to overestimate) needs to possess particular abilities to motivate members of the group; to define the tasks and to enable a group of volunteers to achieve their objectives. A local community leader needs the skill to resolve the conflicts within the group; to optimize the contribution of group members; to identify and make available the appropriate resources and to recruit those who will enhance the operation of the group. In marked contrast to the professional or managerial leadership style, the nature of this form of leadership is heavily dependent upon the personality of the leader, and is more concerned with enabling and empowering a community group so that it can achieve its goals, than with the advising of clients or the directing of those to be managed. Far from inhibiting others and creating or perpetuating attitudes of deference and dependence, the principal object of this style of leadership is to encourage the group to function effectively as a corporate entity. Indeed, the long-term goal of the leader may be to develop the group to such a point that it can effectively take over the leadership function with only limited, though crucially important, support from outside. Increasingly, in the rural church, this style of leadership is sought in a clergyman who has the skill and the personality to act as the leader of a church, which is increasingly similar, in its local practice and operation, to other voluntary associational organizations.

Thus it can be seen that since the time of George Herbert the role of the country parson has passed through four identifiable stages as the Church has embraced different understandings of the role of a clergyman. Despite the fact that such significant changes have taken place within the Church, nonetheless, the principal understandings of ministry articulated by Herbert in *The Country Parson* have remained constant and steadfast, as will be shown in the final chapters.

6

The Changed Countryside

If, since the time of George Herbert, there have been far-reaching changes in the nature of the Church, so there have been equally significant changes in the village and the countryside which form the immediate context of the life and work of the contemporary country clergyman. In George Herbert's time, the benefice of Fugglestone with Bemerton was recorded as having approximately 400 inhabitants, who lived in the three settlements of Bemerton, Fugglestone and Quidhampton. Today, the parish of Bemerton has a population of 8,000. The village of Fugglestone and St Peter's church are now part of the Wilton benefice, and in Bemerton itself approximately 1,000 people live in the old village close to the river, the church of St Andrew's and Herbert's rectory. A further 7,000 live at Bemerton Heath, a large estate of post-war local authority and private housing. This settlement, in which the parish priest now lives, is only rural in the sense that it is situated in the countryside, but in its essential features it is a discontinuous suburb of Salisbury, and its problems and concerns are those reflected in the report *Faith in the City*. It is ironic that that part of outer Salisbury which most closely invites comparison with an urban priority area is that which is situated within Herbert's old parish. Nonetheless, this is a graphic illustration of the changes that have overtaken the countryside in recent years. The old village is still strongly aware of itself as a village community with its own school and St John's church, built in 1860 as a memorial to George Herbert. St Michael's church, built in the 1950s, serves Bemerton Heath, and at Quidhampton, which has never had a church building, there are Sunday evening services in the village hall. As has been mentioned in a previous chapter, plans have been drawn up to include Bemerton in the new Salisbury City Team Ministry.

As the Church increasingly takes on aspects which invite comparison with voluntary associational organizations, so it is inevitable that the local church will take a significant amount of its character, ethos and nature from the local community. There has been a growing awareness of the importance of the context in which the country clergyman ministers and the way in which this shapes and influences ministry in different areas. Whilst in George Herbert's time the overwhelming majority of parishes were rural, and almost all candidates for the ministry would have had a lifelong knowledge and acquaintance with the countryside, today few candidates for ministry come from rural areas. At the same time, society has become so varied that experience gained in one area may be of only limited relevance to a ministry in a different social context. By contrast, seventeenth-century society was, at least in this way, more homogeneous, and thus assumptions could be made (as they appear to be made in *The Country Parson*) about a priest's knowledge of the context in which he was to minister; assumptions which cannot be made so easily today.

It is clear that George Herbert had an intimate understanding of the countryside and village life, which he portrays at many points in *The Country Parson*. He did not have to learn how to relate to a country parish, because much of his previous life had been spent in rural areas, in a country which at that time was still very largely rural. In the mid seventeenth century, many features of rural society remained unchanged since the medieval period, though, as historians such as Alan McFarlane have shown, medieval rural society was, in many of its essential features, recognizably modern, and was based upon the rights and privileges of the individual against the wider group or the state. The traditional reading of English social history, the 'from peasant to industrial society' theory of social development, owes much to the ideology of nineteenth-century evolutionary social thinking and to the tendency for a former generation of historians, who had observed at first hand nineteenth- and early twentieth-century rural societies in

Poland, Italy and Ireland, to assume that traditional medieval England had been similar in its essential features. In Herbert's time the village comprised nuclear families of farmers and craftsmen who were mobile, both in the geographical and the social sense. Alongside them lived a number of small landowners and a significant number of waged labourers (not found in traditional peasant societies). The farms were individual economic enterprises owned by the farmer, whose activities were aimed at maximizing profit in order to have commodities or cash with which to pay rent, tithes and wages, and to purchase on the open market needs not supplied by the farm. There is much evidence to suggest that English rural society at this stage was a mobile, market-orientated form of rural society that differed in many of its essential points from traditional peasant society, in which there is no labour or land market, and in which the institution of servanthood hardly exists, and where the family, as a unit, forms the labour force.

The history of English villages, at this period, is dominated by the gradual breakdown of those factors that, in the early period, made villages isolated and in some respects self-contained. In the first period, physical and social containment broke down as a result of improved road and other means of transport. Eventually, the bicycle transformed many social patterns in the countryside and it is sometimes said that 'the Middle Ages ended in rural England with the invention of the bicycle'. As this process gathered pace, so kinship containment broke down, for in the early period villages had been kinship units, but, particularly in the late eighteenth and early nineteenth centuries, as can be seen in the parish registers, marriage partners were sought from a much wider geographical area. Throughout all this period, economic containment broke down as villages were integrated, first into a regional, and then into a national, economic system. In this the coming of the railways played a major role, both as a means of taking agricultural products to the large urban markets, and as a means of filling the shelves of the new village shops with factory-made produce. The communication of people, products and ideas broke down the old containment of rural England and it was against the penny newspapers and the railways that

such men as Thomas Hardy wrote, as they identified these as
the means by which the old isolation of the village and its local
culture were gradually changed.

George Herbert lived at a time when the population of rural
England was increasing considerably. By 1541, it was recover-
ing from the effects of the Black Death and had risen to 3
million; it increased to 4 million by 1600, and to 5.5 million by
1651. Farming in lowland England was dominated by arable
crops: wheat, barley and oats, with some beans and peas.
Wealthier smallholders and farmers kept cattle, and large
numbers of sheep were kept in the upland and depopulated
areas. In most areas fieldwork was done by oxen, which were
preferred to horses because they were less prone to illness,
and, being fed upon hay and straw, did not compete directly
with humans for scarce grain supplies. However, at this time
horses were taking over because of their greater speed and
strength, and their importance to the rural economy was
recognized in 1563, after which they could not be exported
other than under licence. Nonetheless, many villagers remained
loyal to oxen, not least because, in times of war, they were not
requisitioned. Herbert lived just before a major period of
change in farming and he did not see the new development of
seed drills and the introduction of root crops for winter feeding
that came in as a consequence of Sir Richard Weston's
Discourse on the Husbandrie used in Brabant and Flanders
(1645); methods popularized by such as Jethro Tull, and
particularly by 'Turnip' Townsend and Coke of Holkham, as
the 'Norfolk system'.

George Herbert's attitude to the countryside, in so far as it
can be interpreted from *The Country Parson*, was essentially
functional. As has been seen above, Herbert was concerned
with the countryside as a place of farming and employment for
the people in the village. As the life of the village centred
around the farming year, he learned as much as he could
about farming, so that he could enter into the hopes and fears
of the people in the parish. He shared their view of the
countryside as a place of work and agricultural production and
he clearly became knowledgeable about many aspects of
farming activity. In George Herbert's time, and up to the

industrial revolution, it was possible to speak of England as a society composed of thousands of small rural communities, which shared a common agrarian culture, to which there were few urban exceptions. In the late eighteenth century, when eighty per cent of the population lived in rural areas, such industrial enterprises as there were (such as the naval dockyards at Portsmouth) stopped work for a period of time at harvest, so closely were town and country interrelated. Commercial centres were also cattle markets and cities depended obviously and immediately upon their surrounding rural hinterland. Indeed, the notion of town and country, as separate environments and social systems, was not well developed in pre-industrial society.

It was the impact of the industrial revolution and the development of specialist manufacturing cities, such as Sheffield, that led to an accelerating division between urban and rural in English society. When 'the condition of England' came to be discussed in the mid nineteenth century, the Victorians were chiefly concerned to discover a new urban population which, in many of its essential features, was totally unlike the traditional rural society that, in many of its elements, had continued unbroken not only from Herbert's time, but throughout the previous thousand years. Though Disraeli's famous 'two nations' refers to rich and poor in Victorian England, it could easily have been applied to urban and rural society, so distinctive had they become in a relatively short time. Horace Mann's religious census of 1851 merely confirmed in statistical terms facts of which the mid-Victorian clergyman was becoming increasingly aware: namely that modern industrial society had created a new urban secular culture that was totally foreign to the environment in which George Herbert lived. In many respects this culture was wholly distinct from the older rural patterns and understandings, of which religion, and particularly the Church of England, had been so inextricable a part.

Most villages in England were already established on their present site by the time of the Norman conquest. Then, as now, the village was a group of dwellings clustered round the church and the green, which were both its architectural and social focus. The Saxon farmers, who developed these settlements, regarded the countryside as unfriendly and hostile. Unlike modern country dwellers, who site their houses so that they can enjoy the best view, the Saxons built their dwellings in a defensive ring facing inwards, with the backs of the houses to the hostile and threatening countryside. For them, the church was not just the centre of religious and social life of a community but also a strong point and place of defence from whose roof or tower a watch could be kept on the surrounding countryside. In pre-industrial society, the countryside was predominantly seen as hostile, primitive, violent and barbaric; the word 'pagan' literally means 'dweller in the countryside'. The walls of medieval cities were built not only to defend the inhabitants against attack but also against the encroachment of rural barbarism. In pre-industrial society, the countryside was the least desirable place in which to live, and men shared the 'Dick Whittington' myth that in the city alone refinement, wealth and culture could be found. The pre-industrial countryside was not the sunlit Arcadia of received opinion, but a place of poverty, disease, sickness in animals, fire and flood, and frequent starvation. Whenever the opportunity arose, people left the poverty, hardship, uncertainty and social and physical confines of rural life either for the developing industrial cities or to join the steady stream of settlers in the colonies. When Herbert became a country parson he was aware of the derision and sympathy of many of his friends; this in part was offered because he had become a clergyman, but in part because he had chosen to bury himself in the countryside away from the refinement and culture of the city.

If the Renaissance had its origins in the city (particularly the city-states of northern Italy) then the Age of Enlightenment had its roots in the countryside and in the formative influence of the concept of nature on religion, philosophy, ethics and law. Nature had been an important concept in Western thought since the classical period, but it was particularly in the eighteenth century that nature, as an alternative to all that was made by man, came to be seen as the dominant theme in European thought. One of the central motifs of eighteenth-century classicism was that of the pastoral idyll and the notion that life consisted of an eternal return to this primitive archetype. Philosophers and theologians, lawyers and economists, artists and scientists, all attempted to discover the natural (the divine and archetypal) laws which governed their disciplines: laws that were clear, authoritative and universal and that could be regarded as the outworking of the mind of God the Creator.

If theologians of the Renaissance and post-Reformation period had been preoccupied with the word of God, the eighteenth century saw a new concern for the works of God. As George Herbert's friend Francis Bacon had taught, science was the study of the works of God, and this should be almost, if not quite, as pious a pursuit as the study of his word. Thus, this interaction between theology and science played an important part in producing one of the dominant concepts of the eighteenth century, the divinization of nature. Such a materialistic perception did not dispense with the idea of God himself (at least in the eighteenth century) for the great machine presupposed the divine mechanic. This new emphasis in theology found an early expression in the writing of George Herbert's elder brother, Lord Edward Herbert of Cherbury, who aroused considerable interest by his *De Veritate*, published in Paris in 1624.

After the complexities and mysteries of medieval thought and the theological controversies that raged in the seventeenth century, men everywhere turned to nature as a source of authority and inspiration. The divinization of nature, which began in the Renaissance, proceeded during the eighteenth century and culminated in the works of William Wordsworth. The painter Turner, by all accounts a man almost without religious belief, proclaimed on his deathbed: 'The sun is God'. Scientific, philosophical and social writers all saw in nature the divine hand and the place where a true understanding of the world, in both a physical and a moral sense, could be found. European thought was profoundly influenced by the experience of Rousseau on his island refuge on the lake of Bienne. In his total absorption in the natural world he became aware not only of the beauty and innocence of nature but also of its moral order. Philosophers and missionaries praised the virtues of the unspoilt, natural man whose physique and morals, it seemed to them, put Europeans to shame. A number of black men appeared in the capitals of Europe as examples of prelapsarian innocence.

Partly because of the influence of these ideas, and partly because the wealthy in the early eighteenth century, at the end of the European wars, were able to travel more extensively in Europe, there emerged a changed attitude towards the countryside, an attitude which significantly affected the contemporary view of rural matters, as distinct from that of George Herbert. Such travellers brought home to the shire counties of England not only the paintings of Claude Lorraine, Poussin and Salvator Rosa but also new ideas about landscape, scenery and the countryside. If, in the medieval period, the countryside in a painting was seen through a window or over a garden wall and separated from the foreground, and invariably portrayed as a place of work, in the eighteenth century the countryside as scenery was recognized as a proper subject for painting in its own right. For now it was seen as a place of beauty and innocence, eloquent of the divine wisdom. Pastoral literature (which goes back to Theocritus, who, in his *Idylls*, adapted the popular songs and ballads of Sicilian peasant culture) enjoyed wide popularity. By the early eighteenth century Virgil's *Georgics* appeared in a flood of translations for a public eager to reclaim the pastoral tradition.

The medieval farmer had seen the countryside in simple terms: good land was easy to cultivate and yielded well; bad land did neither. While his attitude to the land was pragmatic and functional, the new concepts of landscape and scenery seemed to imply separation, observation, and a lack of that close involvement with the actual work of the land that characterized George Herbert's attitude. Humphry Repton (who remodelled two hundred estates) wrote his *Observations on the Theory and Practice of Landscape Gardening* in 1803, and claimed that 'a ploughed field was no fit sight for a gentleman's elegant mansion' and that 'the beauty of pleasure grounds and the profit of farming are incompatible'. Influenced by such ideas, the returning travellers commissioned the Palladian country houses of Burlington and his protégé

Flutecroft in styles of approved good taste and decorous elegance, and created, with Repton and Capability Brown's help, many fine examples of neo-classical pastoral landscape. The eighteenth-century gentleman, standing in his library with a book of poetry in his hand and gazing over his park and estate, came to be regarded as the embodiment of the age of enlightenment. Possibly the most celebrated example of landscaping is that at Stourhead, with its temples and grottos grouped around a lake in the centre of the garden. It was principally the work of Henry Hoare the younger (1705–85), who had inherited the estate in 1741. He sought to create a real landscape that would imitate the idealist Virgilian scenes painted in Rome in the previous century by Lorraine and Poussin.

However, for his poorer neighbours, these new under-standings of the countryside, which manifest themselves in enclosures and parks, served only to increase their distress further. For them the countryside was a far cry from the sunlit Arcadia filled with shepherds and shepherdesses wearing garlands and playing recorders and hautbois, as portrayed in Watteau's paintings. The new concept of landscape and scenery brought great changes to the mid-eighteenth-century country-side and their impact is graphically recorded in Oliver Goldsmith's poem *The Deserted Village* (1770). The title page was illustrated in the first edition by a drawing of an old villager, shown recounting the destruction of her village and pointing to the crumbling cottages which can be seen in the background. Goldsmith is thought to have been inspired by the case of Nuneham in Oxfordshire which was rebuilt as Nuneham Courtenay after the imparkment of the original village.

However, it was in the writings of William Wordsworth that this process of the divinization of nature reached its zenith. In some senses England was the first European society in which the widespread adherence to the Christian faith ceased, and it is no coincidence that the belief in the divinity of nature took a strong hold in this country. That ease of heart and soul, which George Herbert found as a country parson in Bemerton, Wordsworth found in contemplating the fields, mountains and the natural world. He came to see that only total absorption in nature could heal and restore his spirits, which were distracted by the realization of man's inhumanity as revealed in the French revolution. But neither Wordsworth nor his followers would have lifted up their eyes to the hills for such help if the eighteenth century had not unfalteringly directed them towards the visible universe as the clearest evidence of God. This new religion was a religion of feeling and response to the natural world, rather than one of learning and intellectual quest. Some aspects of this new attitude are prefigured and anticipated in the writing of Edward Herbert, sometimes called 'the father of English deism'. In one of his poems, his brother George speaks of man as being the priest of the created order, standing before the Creator on behalf of all creation, representing God to the world and the world to God and declaring the good intentions of the Creator for his creation. This poem, *Providence*, is quoted in the Archbishops' Commission on Rural Areas report, *Faith in the Countryside* (1990); it saw this idea of the human being as creation's 'representative' as lying at the centre of the understanding of man's relationship with the created environment.

In a relatively short period, both in poetry and art, there was a change from the grand and heroic to a concern for images drawn from the familiar, the homespun and the ordinary. Artistic and cultural life, which had been associated from the beginning with urban lifestyles and values, came to be dominated by images of the countryside. Constable's much admired painting, *Willows by a Stream*, portrayed an undistinguished section of muddy Suffolk river bank, with a distant view of a village, but it spoke eloquently then, as it does now, of the beauty and the melancholy of the natural world. If plain thinking and high living were the characteristics of this new religion, then country walks were its liturgy, for generations of English people have recognized the Wordsworthian insight that a country walk is a spiritual experience as well as physical exercise. As Lord Clark has commented, the countryside where Wordsworth himself walked in solitude is now almost as crowded with pilgrims as are Lourdes and Benares. John Burroughs wrote in 1912: 'Every walk in the wood is a religious rite . . . if we do not go to church as much as did our fathers, we go to the woods much more, and . . . we now use the word nature very much as our fathers used the word religion.'

In the late eighteenth century, stimulated by John West's guidebook of 1778 and cut off from Italy by the European wars, many people made their way to the Lake District, where a number of classical villas were built. *Morning among the Coniston Fells*, Turner's painting of 1798, showed a man and a woman with some sheep alone in a vast lakeland landscape; a quotation from *Paradise Lost* identifies them as Adam and Eve calling on the elements of the natural world to praise their Creator. It is no exaggeration to say that Wordsworth's book, *Description of the Scenery of the Lakes in the North of England* (1822), changed the way in which people looked at landscape and scenery. Without doubt his influence had a lasting effect on the English view of the countryside, but his name should be linked with that of Ruskin, whose successor in part he was (in 1844 they co-operated in a campaign which attempted to prevent the construction of a railway link between Oxenholme and Kendal). Ruskin saw the natural world as the direct revelation of God's glory, designed for the edification of man and to be read like a holy book, which it was his privilege to interpret as nature's priest. While he rejected the implicit pantheism of Wordsworth, nevertheless he saw the natural world in a similar light, as evidenced by his enthusiasm for the paintings of Turner, who, he believed, was alone among modern painters in his capacity to see the revelation of the divine in the natural world. Ruskin and Wordsworth shared the widely held belief that the spread of urban and industrial areas, in the late eighteenth and early nineteenth centuries, was to be regarded as the social equivalent of 'the fall of man'. When William Cowper wrote 'God made the countryside and man made the town', he was articulating the widespread belief that the countryside was a place of virtue, morality and religion, and that the town was characterized by lawlessness, greed, violence and atheism. Anti-urbanism became a predominant feature of mid-Victorian society and Ruskin denounced the 'great foul city, pouring out poison at every pore'. This polarisation between town and countryside, and its association with moral values, remains a vein in the English understanding of the countryside and is discernible in some modern writers, who tend to regard industrialization and the loss of the pre-industrial countryside as the cause and origin of contemporary social disorders.

The rural romanticism, which owed so much to Ruskin and was so strong a feature of nineteenth-century literature and art, appears to have arisen as the compensating shadow to the overcrowded offices and noisy factories of an increasingly urban and industrial society. The popular Victorian landscape painters suggested in their work a timelessness which was in its own way an implicit protest against the rapid transformation of both urban and rural areas in the late nineteenth century. Like Thomas Hardy, Myles Birket Foster (1825–99) portrayed a landscape which was being speedily transformed by factory-made products and by new means of communication, particularly the railways. Such men were the voice of the old rural culture with all its picturesqueness and poverty, its touching gentleness and its brutal violence. Helen Allingham's cottage scenes portrayed, in drowsy, warm, unnaturally still weather (which some people still call 'Tennyson weather'), the English virtues of rural domesticity, continuity and repose. However, at the same time, they are an accurate reflection of the living conditions of the rural poor in the late nineteenth century, and the poverty, the mud and the effects of poor diet and hard labour are clearly visible. It is part of the paradox of the Victorian treatment of the countryside that the idealization of the happy cottager and tenantry, supported by honest toil, appear side by side with an awareness of the poverty and squalor of their homes, and the melancholy and violent nature of much village life. Thomas Hardy, who was born near Tolpuddle only a few years after the deportation of 'the martyrs', portrayed the countryside as changeless and timeless but also as a struggling and developing community. He particularly identified new means of communication, the railways and cheap newspapers, as the destroyers of the old rural culture.

From the mid eighteenth century to the late nineteenth

century England was slowly changing from being a wholly
rural to a predominantly urban society. Increasingly, the
countryside came to be seen no longer as intimidating and
hostile, and village life as brutal and boorish, but both were
viewed with a wistful sense of loss by those now living in
urban and industrial areas. On the walls of their new houses
such pictures as Millais's *The Angelus*, with its aura of pious
humility and honest toil in the dreamy calm of an evening
landscape, spoke eloquently of community, continuity and
contact with nature, to those constrained by the pressures of
industrial and urban life. Rural romanticism and nostalgia
were one of the dominant themes of Victorian society, and
artists and craftsmen sought to bring indoors, by means of
carving, wrought iron, stained glass and paintings, the trees,
foliage, flowers and fruits of the countryside. The Gothic
Revival was in part an attempt to create the lost world of pre-
industrial society and to emphasize the social harmony,
continuity and simple piety which, it was thought, had been
eroded and destroyed by urbanization and industrialization.

It seems that whenever English society experiences a period
of disturbance and turbulence it seeks to reaffirm its rural
origins and roots (what Americans call 'the Jeffersonian
values'). It is as if there was a turning for spiritual nourishment
to the heartland of English society, whose lanes, as H. J.
Massingham wrote, 'lead to what the world calls nowhere,
namely, the hamlets, villages and farms which are the
cornerstone of England'. In the years before the First World
War, particularly on account of an subconscious sense of
impending change, the seemingly eternal changelessness of
the English countryside was widely celebrated in poetry and a
genre of writing known as the 'Norfolk jacket' school of writing.
Poets such as Thomas Hardy, Edmund Blunden and Edward
Thomas wrote what were, in a sense, elegies for the passing of
an immemorial rural order. Their work was edited and
published by Edward Marsh between 1911 and 1922 in five
anthologies of *Georgian Poetry*. About the same time, Edward
Thomas, who did much to popularize the works of Richard
Jefferies, and was a friend of Arthur Ransome, wrote a series
of topographical books: *The Heart of England, The South*

Country, The Icknield Way and *The Pursuit of Spring.* Perhaps no writer since Wordsworth can have walked so many miles through England and Wales, and, like Wordsworth, Thomas saw himself as a recorder of the slow destruction of a rural society and culture that stretched back to the time of George Herbert. It is interesting to note that these books by Thomas and the works of the Georgian poets, which had long been out of print, have recently reappeared in popular editions. At the same time, the emergence of similar themes and sources of inspiration can be seen among musicians, for after the German influence of Handel and Mendelssohn, there emerged around the turn of the century a new era of English music. Elgar and Vaughan Williams, Holst, Delius, Walton and Britten, all drew on the countryside as a major source of inspiration.

Although there were such landmarks as *The Shell Guide to the Flowers of the Countryside* by Rowland Hilder (first published in 1955); Nikolaus Pevsner's first volume of *The Buildings of England* (1951); and *The Shell Guide to Oxfordshire*, edited by John Piper and John Betjeman in 1938, nevertheless the thrust of this period was essentially urban. The 1960s may be regarded as the zenith of confidence in the urban future of man, marked in theology by the publication of Harvey Cox's *The Secular City*. However, the 1970s saw a dramatic resurgence in concern for and interest in the countryside. Just as in mid-Victorian England interest in the countryside and the village appeared to arise as a response to the threat of social and cultural change, so in the 1970s and 1980s a similar awareness appeared to prompt a similar reaction. Gradually the excitement and confidence which had been widely felt in the urban future of man gave way to an uneasy weariness and growing pessimism. The awareness of increasing levels of violence, privation and alienation drove people back to the countryside in the search for certainties and values, away from the corruption and violence of the cities. In a sense the countryside has become the dominant symbol for genuineness, integrity, authority, meaning and value in a society dominated by the instant, the expendable and the superficial. As people revolted against the technical standardization and commercialization of life in the

1970s and 1980s, so they developed a taste for dairymaid and peasant dresses (with their suggestion of rural values and pleasures, without any hint of rural toil), cottage-style scrubbed furniture and coffee-table books about the countryside. Advertizers used the countryside as a symbol of homespun goodness and simple virtues to market their products. In a world of change and profound insecurity there is a deep desire for the predictable, slow-moving world of the pre-industrial countryside.

As Peter Berger has commented, modern man suffers from a sense of homelessness, of futility, insecurity and moral confusion and loneliness. In one lifetime man has progressed from horse-drawn transport to space travel, and it is not surprising that he feels that he is left with a sense of rootlessness and insecurity. Such rootlessness makes people both hanker for the past and see the countryside in terms of pre-industrial patterns and lifestyles; by contrast, despite the turmoil of the previous hundred years there is no hint of nostalgia in *The Country Parson*. Rural nostalgia is the medicine that modern man takes for the side-effects of living in an age of the computer and the silicon chip. The coffee-table book about the countryside, of which there are so many, and the guidebooks to English villages, all portray the countryside not as a dynamic modern community but as a static and fixed way of life, as if it were something which was not the product of human labour but had dropped at our feet from a distant past as a remembrance from a simple and uncorrupt time. What such books lack is the realism with which George Herbert viewed the village and its inhabitants, and an understanding of the countryside as a place of work.

Thus it can be seen that since the time of George Herbert there has been a radical transformation of attitudes towards the countryside. The functional attitude of medieval man, of which Herbert himself was the heir (in this as in other things), and which treated the countryside as a place of work and valued it accordingly, was replaced by the picturesque attitude that can be said to have become the dominant view of the English countryside. In current debates about the future of the rural areas of Europe, it is noticeable that the British contribution places most emphasis upon landscape, while other countries (particularly France) place greater emphasis on the rural community as a social entity; thus England tends to criticize the agricultural policies of the EC (the Common Agricultural Policy) as being essentially social policies. In this as in much else, current attitudes are the heirs to a process of transformation which has radically altered attitudes to the village and countryside since the time of George Herbert.

The two processes of change that have transformed the village and the countryside since his time are the attitudinal changes noted above and the changes to the social profile of the contemporary village. Today, the village can be seen not as a single community centred around farming but as a community of communities made up of five identifiable groups: the farming community, the old village community, the commuters, the retired and occasional residents.

The recent history of farming indicates that it has always fluctuated between boom and depression. The period 1860 to 1873, known as the 'high farming' period, was one in which high inputs led to high profits in order to satisfy the increasing demand of the urban population for food. In 1873, a number of factors, of which the large imports of American grain was by far the most important, led to a sudden and dramatic fall in the fortunes of British agriculture, as has been noted in the previous chapter. Between 1871 and 1898, wheat prices fell by half; many farms were abandoned, and much of the countryside returned to rough pasture. It is ironic that this period of great depression and hardship for many farm families is remembered in much rural literature as the idyllic country-side of grassland and wild flowers in the period immediately before the First World War.

The United Kingdom entered the First World War only 17% self-sufficient in food and it was not until the Food Production Campaign of 1916 that serious attention was given to the contribution of farming. By the end of the war only a quarter of the food consumed in Britain and by its armies overseas was produced in this country. In the years after the war a period of depression again settled on the agricultural industry, following the repeal of the Corn Production Acts in 1921 (known at the time as 'the great betrayal'). In 1923, the price of wheat, which at one stage stood at 80s 10d, had fallen to 42s 2d. Throughout the 1920s and 1930s, farming was in the grip of a deep depression which lasted until the eve of the Second World War. No account of contemporary farming is complete without an assessment of the lasting effect which those years had on the attitudes and folk memory of the farming community. By the 1930s, sour, soggy and degenerating land, full of speargrass, bracken and brambles, together with dilapidated and out-of-date buildings, were common in many areas. On the lighter, less fertile soils, particularly in areas such as north Norfolk, farmhouse windows gazed emptily over derelict fields which were rapidly disappearing under a covering of gorse, thistles, docks and ragwort. In some areas, ditches and drains slowly filled, hedges began to thicken into copses and copses became woods. Landowners were forced to forgo the rent in order to ensure that their tenants remained on the farm. In north Oxfordshire the farming community can remember that a number of the most productive farms today were untenanted, covered with dense thorn-bushes during the worst of the farming depression. Game, rabbits and wild flowers all flourished in this neglected landscape, giving a pleasant aspect to what was in reality a deep agricultural depression and the ruin of many farmers. At its worst, almost any land could be purchased for £10 an acre and poorer land, such as the flinty chalkland of the South Downs or the Salisbury Plain, could be purchased for £2 an acre unfenced, or £5 fenced.

By contrast, the Second World War, during which England was isolated from the supply of overseas food, led to an immense national campaign to increase home food production. For a period, the increase in domestic food production was literally a matter of national survival, and the government established County War Agricultural Executive Committees with the widest powers to invigorate agriculture and, in particular, to plough up land which had not been used to the limits of its potential. In 1939, Britain produced 30% of its own food; by 1945 the figure had risen to 80%. During this period the percentage of farmland under cultivation almost doubled and again approached the levels of the 1860s and 1870s. The term 'mechanical agriculture' was first used in 1931, when the first farms were being run entirely without horses. Combine harvesters appeared in this country in 1928 and the introduction of the three-point linkage system in the early thirties revolutionized the design of tractors. In 1939, the combine harvester was still a rarity in the English countryside, but fifteen years later half the arable crops were harvested in this way.

The Second World War contributed to the radical restructuring of British farming and established a permanent relationship between the state and the farming community, formalized by the Agricultural Act of 1947. As wheat imports started in the immediate post-war period, so the farmers were determined that the depression which had followed the First World War should not occur again. The Act established a system of securing guaranteed prices (subject to the annual February price review) and a system of subsidies and grants for capital projects. At the same time it increased the security of tenant farmers; but above all it was the guaranteed prices that gave individual farmers the confidence and assurance to develop their farm enterprises and to expand in the following decades. Between 1947 and 1951, net agricultural production grew by 20%; between 1948 and 1978, the average yield of wheat in England and Wales approximately doubled.

However, the success of British farming within a European context has led to the problems of overproduction in many commodity areas. On 3 March 1984 milk quotas were imposed across the Common Market to limit the overproduction of dairy products, and this can now be seen as the beginning of a series of measures designed to limit production. These have included the fallowing of arable land, known as set-aside, and it is expected that British farmers will take one and a half million acres of arable land out of production, an area slightly larger than Devon. From a period of great prosperity in the decades after the Second World War there is evidence on all sides that farming has now entered another period of marked depression, reflected in the decline in the price of agricultural land, in the number of farmers now leaving the industry, in the decline in farm income and the poor prospects for the industry as a whole. At present, 1,200 full-time jobs are being lost in farming every month and farm incomes are in comparative terms at their lowest since the Second World War. It is said that three farmers per week commit suicide as a consequence of these pressures.

To add to the commercial pressure, farming has been subject to extensive criticism for its impact on the landscape and for ecological and environmental reasons. It is widely believed that Victorian farming in general, and the four-course rotation in particular, were an environmentally friendly method of farming, and that this has been replaced by a system which makes extensive use of inorganic fertilizers, pesticides and herbicides. In reality, levels of fertility were declining markedly during the period of the Norfolk four-course rotation and had not superphosphate become available in 1842, Victorian farmers would not have been able to feed the growing urban population. Much criticism of farming practices relates to attitudes towards the countryside described in the earlier part of this chapter. Calls for a less intensive method of farming, or for a fully organic system, have to be seen in the context of the fact that a 30% reduction in nitrogen fertilizers would reduce the yields of wheat by 20%, and consequently make the crop unprofitable for the average farmer. If nitrogen fertilizers were banned, it would need an additional nine million hectares (an area that exceeds the current lowland farmed area) to make good the deficit. If pesticides were banned, production would fall by 36% in the first year and by approximately 50% in the third year. Fully organic systems are heavily dependent upon livestock to replace soil fertility; however, for dietary reasons, livestock products, particularly meat and dairy products, form a less significant part of the diet of advanced Western society. In recent years, considerable work has been done to repair some of the aesthetic and ecological damage done to the farmed countryside in the 1970s and 1980s by new initiatives on hedgerow and tree planting and by a wide range of conservation initiatives.

Perhaps the most significant pressure on farmers today, which has led to the high level of suicides and the creation of farming support groups in many areas, results from the uncertainty with which farmers view the future and the wide range of advice that is offered. Some farmers believe that British farming can prosper in an international market if the best and most scientific methods are used on the best land, and that this country has climatic and other advantages which will make its products saleable on a world market. However, such an option may only be open to those farming the best land under highly favourable economic and agricultural conditions, and many speak of the emergence of two-tier farming, which has in effect already existed for many years; currently 80% of UK home production is produced by 20% of the farms. For the vast majority of farms, there is a need to diversify, both into other crops and into non-farming enterprises. In effect, farmers are becoming land resource managers and they may combine traditional agricultural usages of the land with recreational and other uses. If, in the future, it becomes necessary to produce fuel from bio-mass, the situation of farming, in a short time, might be radically altered. What is clear is that the farming community, whilst their attitude to the countryside remains similar to that of generations ago, is now a small part of the rural population; in many villages there may be only one or two farm families; certainly, in most areas, the farming community will no longer have the numerical dominance which it had in previous generations.

Second, in any village there is still a local resident population, which in some cases may be small, but in other villages may comprise more than half the population. In the popular imagination, villages are seen as being inhabited by those whose forebears lived there, and it is supposed that successive generations of the same family have crossed the same threshold to attend the baptisms, marriages and funerals that have marked the progress of the family's history. In reality, while it is possible to find some families with a long attachment to a particular village, or cluster of villages, their number is not great even in the most remote areas. For the old villagers, the centre of their life is their home and the local community to which they are linked by extensive family relationships. Often the old villagers have about them a sense of the past, a sense of loss and wistful regret that the cohesive, family-based community of their grandparents' generation has been dissolved into a modern village. But such regrets are often tinged with a realistic and grateful appreciation of the benefits which modern living have brought to village homes and the great improvement in their working lives, which were once lived exclusively on the farms. It was not until the 1950s and 1960s that piped water, mains sewerage and electricity arrived in many rural areas, along with television and a range of kitchen gadgets.

In English society there is a significant divide between middle and lower income earners in their attitude towards occupation and residence. In brief, middle income earners, once they have found a career line, pursue that career line and change houses (and areas) as their career proceeds. These are the 'colour supplement gypsies' of contemporary culture. Lower income earners, by contrast, remain in the same house, whether local authority, rented or privately owned, often for their whole lives, but change jobs according to the local employment opportunities of that area.

By nature, the ethos and character of the old village community is elusive and difficult to describe, not least because of the great variety among different areas of the countryside. Nevertheless, the members of the old village community, to a greater or lesser extent, are the heirs of the old working class solidarity, so characteristic of primary industries, by which the village was welded together by its common history of poverty, hard work, danger, insecurity, disease and suffering. Whilst the causes of much of this deprivation, as it was experienced in previous generations, have been eradicated, nevertheless the hidden memory of the old village is perpetuated, and attitudes formed generations ago are handed down. In a way, the old village community is dominated by a sense of displacement and loss; they feel that the village is no longer theirs, that they have been taken over by newly arrived people who have no knowledge of their tradition, history, and the value of the old village. This feeling of displacement can often mean that the old village community appears aloof and restrained, for they know themselves to be the real villagers and their new neighbours are but temporary residents in a place whose history they cannot inherit. Inevitably, history becomes a matter of great importance and not infrequently 'the sanctuary' of the old village community, which will often be focused upon the church building.

This group has particularly suffered as a consequence of the decline of village services and facilities (59% of villages have no shop; 40% of villages have no Post Office; and 51% have no school). In recent years they have been particularly affected by the rising price of houses in rural areas as these houses have been bought by wealthier people from urban areas. Recent reports have indicated significant levels of rural deprivation in certain areas, particularly in the more remote villages where there is a lack of transport and local facilities, and in some of the 'urban shadow villages', where the in-migration of people from urban areas has changed the social profile in such a way that villages can no longer support the type of facilities and services that used to exist. For a generation, people in the village have increasingly got used to the fact that their children will not be able to live in the village. That was a possibility when local authority housing was available, and has become a possibility in recent years for a limited number through the efforts of rural housing associations to provide affordable houses in villages. However, in the main, this group is now significantly diminishing in size in many villages in all but the more remote areas.

This change in the character of a village, which is clearly reflected in what a village looks like, is one of the most noticeable features of many rural areas. In recent years, many country villages have been transformed by what the planners call 'gentrification' or 'geriatrification', with a consequent change in the character of the village, the nature of the pub and the type of services and entertainments that the village supports. The new affluence of many villages has made them seem like discontinuous suburbs; one villager ruefully commented to the Archbishops' Commission, 'Neighbourhood Watch has taken over from neighbourliness.'

Third, in the nineteenth century, some people were disposed to regard the village as in some ways similar to an open prison from which those who could made their escape to the city. By contrast, in the twentieth century, an increasing number of people wish to make the journey in the opposite direction. The work of rural sociologists in the immediate post-war period, such as the study of north Oxfordshire villages by C. S. Orwin and his team, was principally concerned to bring home to a wider public the degree of social disintegration that had affected the majority of villages. Such studies make pessimistic reading, and their authors cannot be blamed for failing to anticipate the wave of migration into the countryside, as depopulation gave way to repopulation in the second half of the twentieth century. As car ownership became a possibility for middle income earners, so it was no longer necessary to live within easy walking distance of the public transport network. At the same time, the improvement to the rural infrastructure encouraged many to move into rural areas, and contributed to the transforming of the demographic structure of villages in this country, as in most European countries and in the United States.

In the mid nineteenth century, Surrey was a county of remote heathland and woodlands, less valued for agriculture than many areas, and, in consequence, one of the least populated of the Home Counties. The advent of the suburban railways, particularly in the Thames Valley and to the south of London, allowed the relatively wealthy to choose the option of living in the country and commuting to the town. The term 'commuting' is derived from the commuted rate at which railway tickets for regular journeys were issued at this time. It was around the major conurbations that commuting developed in the late nineteenth century and early twentieth century as an increasing number of people forsook the city and sought the peace and quiet of the countryside. As a consequence, the population of rural counties, particularly those accessible to the conurbations, has risen significantly in recent years, whereas the major conurbations themselves have lost population (inner London lost 18% of its population in the 1970s).

Those who move into the countryside often fall into one of two groups; the first is composed of those with a young family (often with the oldest child about to reach the age of five). Many new families, who arrive in the villages in the more

accessible countryside, are those with young children whose
father has a managerial or professional job, and who move
into a new house on a private development on the edge of the
village or purchase and restore one of the cottages in the
centre of the village. They look forward to living in an
identifiable community and sending their children to the
village school. The second group, who typically form a larger
proportion of new households in the village, are those who
have either reached retirement age or are anticipating retirement within the foreseeable future. It is well known that the
period of bringing up young children and that of retirement
are both times in the life-cycle when people have to adapt to
new circumstances, stresses and constraints. Indeed, there is a
complementariness between the two groups, for under the
dispositions of traditional society it was the grandparents who
played a major role in the lives of the young children. It is
possible to suggest that among the many and varied reasons
for making these moves, people in these two groups are,
consciously or unconsciously, influenced by a view of the
village as a warm, accepting community which will act in some
ways as a surrogate extended family. In an age when the
psychological need for the extended family is still evident, but
such families are often scattered across the country, the village
may be seen as a community which provides some of these
functions.

Dr Johnson may not have been thinking of commuters
when he expressed the opinion that heaven would contain the
joys of the countryside and the amenities of the town.
Certainly, those who move into the countryside often wish it
to conform to their own understandings both of what constitute
appropriate amenities (street lights, pavements, etc.) and
appropriate entertainment. Those who move into the countryside often place a high value on self-reliance, independence
and privacy which they believe to be more congruent with the
rural rather than an urban life. The garden is a symbol of all
these values and more British people have gardens than any
other European nation. Certainly, the home-centred culture is
a marked feature of the commuter's life-style. However, behind
this lies the predominant desire of modern man to separate

out the various elements of his life and particularly to distance his work life from his family life. Commuting is a desired life-style for many because work and family are separate to the point where there is almost no contact. Such a life-style, which characterizes modern society, is markedly different from that of the old village community, for whom work and family existed within the same social context and almost all aspects of life were regarded as 'public' rather than 'private'.

The new villagers tend to have strong views, not only about farming and farmers but also about what they like and dislike in the village. Characteristically, new villagers are active and articulate in preserving the village against changes which they regard as being at variance with their understanding of what the village should be like, and they know how to influence the public decision-making processes. A village which could boast only three graduates in the post-war period may now have a significant number of company directors, barristers and chartered accountants as well as retired diplomats and senior military personnel. Their wives' life-style is dominated by the car and by the journey out of the village, to school, to work or to the local station to collect their husbands from the train, to shop, or to go to other centres for recreational pursuits. Some new villagers live very private lives with little contact with the wider community, but others wish to become involved in village organizations, and their presence has done much to stimulate and revive village life in general, particularly that of the parish church.

The fourth group sees the countryside as a place of retirement, and retirement migration is the most significant factor in the changing demographic patterns of rural England. While the desire to retire to the countryside has existed for many years, it is only in the middle decades of this century that retirement migration has become a major demographic phenomenon, not least because the number of pensioners has risen so significantly. In 1900, only one person in twenty was over the retirement age; shortly the ratio will have reached one in five. Better pensions and larger sums saved during their working career have allowed people to move into the countryside, and the motorway and more widely available private transport have played an important part in opening up certain parts of rural England for retirement migration. The old person portrayed in a Victorian novel or painting was likely to be someone in his or her sixties or early seventies. Today, such a person is more likely to be the provider of voluntary services than a recipient. Retired people place a premium on the availability of services and facilities and so tend to retire into those areas where these are readily available. The problems of remoteness, isolation and high costs may be seen in their most acute form on islands. Alderney, for example, publishes a *Guide for those considering settling in Alderney*, in which it states: 'Persons in poor health, or with small means, or of advanced years would not find it a suitable place in which to retire.' It is clear that, to a degree, the same may be said for much of the remoter English countryside, but the problems of living in rural areas do not occur to those who have long dreamt of a retirement cottage far away from the disagreeable aspects of urban life.

Many retired people, with little previous experience of living in the countryside, are alarmed when they first observe contemporary farming at close quarters. The intensive nature of modern agriculture with large machines working day and night at certain times of the year bears little relation to their preconceptions. Recent research by farming organizations has indicated that retired people who have recently moved to the countryside are particularly prominent in those groups which are most critical of modern farming practice.

Many retired people, particularly the active early-retired, come to the village to be restored after an arduous working life. Many such people have held positions of responsibility and seniority and soon play a leading role in village activities, social, sporting or recreational. In some villages there is a degree of tension between the old village community and those who have arrived relatively recently. Whilst the old villagers appreciate the enthusiasm and resources that are brought to village activities, they often feel threatened by the ready assumption of leadership roles by the active retired. The old villagers find it difficult to relate to the newcomers, for fear that the village and its life are being taken over by their new, more affluent and articulate neighbours. The old villagers can appear to retreat into a hidden village life which is hardly visible to newcomers and from which the latter feel excluded. Whilst the newcomers may take over certain specialist activities such as the cricket club and the drama club and may form a keep-fit club in the village hall, or seek to convert a nearby barn into a squash court, the old villagers tend to retain a hold on such organizations as the parish council, the Women's Institute and the British Legion.

The old villagers are the possessors of the village history and frequently can make subtle use of it to mystify, and, at times, even to outmanoeuvre those who have arrived in the village more recently. There is a tendency for the old villagers to blame the newcomers and to make them the scapegoats for the disagreeable aspects of change in village life. Those who come in from outside are made to feel representatives of the hostile outside world and responsible for remote public decisions which have adversely affected aspects of village life. In many villages, new and old villagers relate well and benefit from the pooling of different insights and experiences, and, particularly in smaller villages, the interaction between the two communities can be beneficial and helpful to both; each respecting and acknowledging the contribution that the other makes to the village. However, in other villages, particularly those where the commuters are in a position of considerable numerical dominance, the old village community can easily feel that they have become strangers in their own village.

Finally, the occasional residents are those with second or holiday homes in the countryside, who spend either the weekends or holidays in the village. Although second-home ownership and occasional residents have a long history, it was the availability of private cars and the development of the motorways that precipitated 'the country cottage boom'. The effect of second-home ownership is largely determined by its scale. Occasional residents tend to be located in particularly favoured areas and their presence is most noticeable in the more remote areas. In the main, second-home owners do not make a major contribution to the local economy, for they tend to bring many of their needs with them and their presence is increasingly resented in those areas where they compete with local families for scarce housing or where their impact on a local rural culture is seen as detrimental. This process can be seen in Wales and in parts of rural France, such as the Dordogne, where over 30,000 houses were purchased by English families by 1989. Throughout rural France it is now thought that one in thirteen rural dwellings are owned as second homes, largely by English and German families. If present trends continue, French politicians speak of a time when 80% of houses in parts of the Dordogne will be owned by foreigners, and in some areas (such as Harfleur) consideration is being given to the imposition of a ban on further purchases by foreigners. In English villages, occasional residents have always caused some resentment, as a result of competition for the housing stock in a situation where those from outside, with greater financial resources, are able to buy up the available housing. In part this has led to the movement to provide affordable housing for local families in rural areas. Frequently, second-home owners come to the village to relax and to be restored and as a result play little part in the life of the community, and this too can form the subject of resentment.

Thus it can be seen that the countryside has been totally changed since the days of George Herbert's ministry, when the village was a coherent occupational community centred around the farming year. In many ways this understanding of the village remained until the early decades of this century, but since the First World War the processes of change have accelerated, particularly in recent years. Whilst the village used to be made up of a coherent community of those directly involved in farming, either as landlords, farmers, farm workers or those who provided the services and allied crafts, today, the village is made up of a number of identifiable different groups with different attitudes towards the village and the countryside. It is the interaction of these different groups in the village, based on different understandings of the village and the countryside, that can lead to a measure of conflict in contemporary village life. Ministering in such a situation requires a clergyman to understand the different attitudes and presuppositions which are held. In effect, a clergyman has to be multilingual in order that he can both understand and speak to the different communities that exist within a single village, which is more accurately described today not as a single community but as a community of communities. It is this, together with the fact that the church has now taken on many of the features of a voluntary organization (as noted in the previous chapter), that comprise the two major differences that have transformed the church and the village since George Herbert wrote *The Country Parson*. However, despite these far-reaching changes, many of George Herbert's insights and understandings remain of continuing importance for those who seek to minister in the much changed contemporary village.

7

The Tasks of the
Country Clergyman Today

The previous two chapters have described the changes that
have transformed the Church and the countryside since the
time of George Herbert's ministry and the writing of *The
Country Parson*. Since that time the life of the village has been
radically altered, but no less far-reaching have been the
changes to the Church, although these are less easy to assess,
as so much that dates from the earlier period continues in the
life of the contemporary Church. It might be thought that the
ministry of a priest in a rural parish today would be radically
different from that of George Herbert as recorded in *The
Country Parson*. However, there is much continuity between
Herbert's time and today, particularly in those areas that might
be thought to belong to the essential nature of ministry as
recorded in the Ordinal. The modern country clergyman finds
in the heart of his ministry much that would have been familiar
to George Herbert and, as is clear from *The Country Parson*,
formed part of his own ministry.

In every generation, the pastoral strategy of the rural church
has been founded on the consecrated building and the
ordained clergyman; on the holy place and the sacred person.
The term 'parish' was unknown in pre-Conquest England and
does not occur in the Domesday Book, where the word 'manor'
was commonly used. By the mid seventh century the kingdom
of Kent had been parcelled out into parishes by Archbishop
Honorius (627–53), but it was Archbishop Theodore (668–90)
who is usually credited with the creation of the parochial
system in its modern form. He encouraged the Saxon
landowners to erect churches (the majority of them wooden)
on their estates, and he granted them the right of perpetual

patronage (the origins of the present system). In other areas, away from the more populated south-east, minsters were established (as at Stourminster, Wimborne Minster, Kidderminster, Minsterly and Minster Lovell).

From the Domesday Survey it is not possible to estimate with any accuracy the number of parish churches in the countryside as a whole. The number of churches actually mentioned in the survey is less than 2,000, of which half are in the counties of Norfolk, Suffolk and Lincolnshire. In some areas the only churches named are those liable to pay dues to the Crown and in two counties (Cornwall and Middlesex) no churches are mentioned at all. However, the record is sufficient to allow it to be seen that in some areas, particularly in Suffolk, where over half the villages had their own church, the tradition of a parish church and a resident priest (*ibi ecclesia et presbyter*) was already becoming part of the fabric of the English countryside.

Fourteenth-century rural England was increasingly polarized between the landless poor and vagrants, and the newly-wealthy farmers, landowners, wool merchants and staplers, whose wealth resulted from the rapid development of sheep farming (those 'eaters of men', as Sir Thomas More was later to call sheep, for the extension of highly profitable sheep farming was regarded as being responsible for much rural depopulation). It seems that much of this new money was used to build, not only country houses, but also magnificent parish churches in the perpendicular Gothic style of the period, that essentially English style that originated at Westminster and was perfected, after 1331, at Gloucester. The expression, 'as sure as God is in Gloucestershire', testified to the great number of churches in that county dating from this period. The new wealth and the piety of individual parishioners led to the rebuilding of a large number of churches at this time. In the county of Norfolk there are six hundred and fifty medieval parish churches; in Suffolk, five hundred and fifty. The largest churches are to be found in Norfolk, the richest county in England in the fourteenth and fifteenth centuries, and in those areas such as the Cotswolds which benefited most directly from the wool trade.

More than eight thousand parishes had been registered in the survey of 1291 and further evidence suggests that there were possibly as many as one thousand five hundred more. Although some parishes, particularly in the north, were extensive, it is estimated that on average parishes contained approximately three hundred people. It is possible that there were as many as twenty-three thousand priests, serving parishes which were predominantly rural at this time; today there are fewer than half this number.

As has been shown in Chapter 5, throughout much of the history of the Church of England there has been concern about the number of clergy, and a belief that numbers are not being maintained at a sufficient level to meet the pastoral needs of the country. Even in the late nineteenth century, when numbers again approached the levels of the thirteenth century, there was much contemporary concern that more clergy were needed, particularly in rural areas. Today, the number has been reduced by nearly half and there are currently 10,315 stipendiary clergy in parochial appointments serving in the Church of England. (For the detailed figures, see above, pp. 124–5.) As a consequence, just as George Herbert served two parishes, so today most country parishes are linked to their neighbours in clusters served by a single clergyman. In Oxfordshire approximately half the clergy serve three or more parishes and one cluster, in Lincolnshire, includes seventeen. In some such clusters, parishes have developed close relations with their neighbours, whilst in others they remain essentially separate communities who share little except the same priest. There is a sense in which the multi-parish benefice (the technical description by which these clusters have become known) has become the common experience of rural ministry today, and it may be regarded as an extension of the pastoral situation which faced George Herbert in his two small parishes. Herbert's answer to the problem of serving a parish in which he did not reside was to appoint a curate at Fugglestone, and eventually, when he became seriously ill, he also appointed a curate at Bemerton. Reduced clergy numbers mean that this option is not available to the Church today.

It has been seen in Chapter 6 that the rural church today

operates in a totally changed social context. In some parishes the vestiges of the old agriculturally-based rural community remain, but, in almost every area, the countryside has been transformed. The old pastoral strategy of the Church based upon a building and a resident priest, working in a knowable and coherent community, can no longer be maintained. The multi-parish benefice, which has become increasingly common in the decades since the last war, is becoming the predominant form of ministry in most rural areas.

In considering the tasks of the country clergyman today within such a context, it must be recognized that the clergyman is the inheritor of expectations and understandings about ministry that were formed in the earlier periods. Over the generations in the English countryside, there has grown up an understanding that the life of the Church and its ministry rests entirely in the hands of the clergyman. This view had its origins in the theology and practice of the medieval Church, particularly in the twelfth century, but was powerfully reinforced in the post-Reformation era, when the clergyman was seen as the father and teacher of his parish, a view reflected in Herbert's own writing. Clericalism reached its zenith in the Victorian Church and there are many testimonies in diaries and journals to the strength of Victorian clericalism, particularly in country areas.

This resurgence of clerical domination in the Church followed a period in which that domination had been considerably weakened. The desire of the clergy to see themselves, and to be seen by others, as a profession, served to reinforce such attitudes, and there developed a pattern of church life in the countryside which was characterized by attitudes of deference and dependence. In effect, the clergyman ran the local church in much the same way as the schoolmaster ran the school or the grocer ran his shop. Although church-wardens had a distinctive role both in fact and in law, in the Victorian village, the clergyman ran the church (and much else that went on in the village), and frequently paid for it out of his own pocket.

Thus the village church became largely dependent upon the energy and direction of its clergyman, and his removal or retirement exposed what has been described as 'the parson-shaped hole' at the centre of local church life. Increasingly, after the Second World War, it was impossible to find replacements for those who retired, and the process by which a number of parishes were placed in the hands of a single clergyman, and multi-parish benefices were created, began to accelerate. A consequence of this was the sale of a number of parsonage houses, and contraction in the number of services and the programme of church events which had once been the centre of much village life. As a result, there exists in the rural Church today the widespread though rarely expressed feeling that the Church is living in reduced circumstances which bear little comparison to a golden age that existed at the end of the nineteenth century. However, such comparisons tend to focus on the well-remembered major occasions, and there are many testimonies to the dullness of some services, the dirtiness of some churches and the eccentric and inappropriate behaviour of some of its clergy. By contrast, today, it is almost certainly true that rural churches have never been so well maintained nor so frequently visited; and an increasing number of clergy (especially younger clergy) seek appointments in the country-side, because they regard rural ministry as a demanding and important part of the Church's total ministry.

It might be thought that the circumstances of the Church today are entirely different from those of the first half of the seventeenth century in which George Herbert ministered. However, in many of its essential features, the tasks of the clergyman remain those that were identified by George Herbert. He saw the life and work of the country parson as a single entity: praying, preaching, visiting his parishioners, providing spiritual leadership within the community; these were merely four aspects of the one reality. However, the arrangement of *The Country Parson* implies that it is possible (at least analytically) to divide the work of the country parson into a number of parts. As has been seen in Chapter 4, these may be summarized under the following headings: priest, pastor, teacher and shepherd.

Priest

The Church exists to offer worship, and its primary task is to share in the unceasing prayer of Christ, to bring before God the prayers of his people present within his Church, which is his Body. The Church above all else is a community of prayer. Communities differ according to what nourishes them; some are nourished on conflict; others are nourished on nostalgia, others on grievance; but the Church is nourished by its life of prayer, and in prayer and worship the Church is most truly itself.

As a consequence, the primary duty of the country clergyman is to pray; to make the Church a community of prayer; to draw people into a loving and ever deeper relationship with God in prayer, and to pray for them. He must be a man of prayerfulness himself but also one who can teach others to pray. At a time when a parish is vacant the bishop meets members of the congregation and they will invariably ask for a prayerful man, who not only says his prayers, but can lead others and can share a knowledge and awareness of God. People find it hard to express what they want but in different ways they express their desire for a priest who has a visible regularity in prayer and who acknowledges that it is one of the priest's chief duties to pray with his people, for his people, and to teach them to pray.

George Herbert was in no doubt that the offering of worship was the principal task of the clergyman and in some senses the country parson's defining activity. The regular offering of the offices in church are his primary obligation and the central act of the Christian community around which everything else pivots and finds its meaning. Its value has nothing to do with the number of people who come to the services and in many cases the clergyman may find himself alone. But in saying 'O Lord open thou our lips' the priest is acknowledging that these prayers are offered on behalf of the whole Christian community. Such prayer is to be public, corporate and on behalf of the people whom the priest is called to serve, and these points are made more clearly when the offices are said in church. But the local parish church is not an isolated community; it is joined in a fellowship of Christian congregations as it enters into the cycle of prayer with the whole Church.

It is clear from Herbert's writing that his best energies and efforts were devoted to the life of prayer in his parish, and it is this for which contemporaries particularly remembered him. Today, 10 o'clock (the canonical hour for Matins) may not be the most convenient time, but it makes the point that the principal work of the clergyman is prayer and that Morning Prayer is not something to be hurried through before the major concerns of the day are addressed.

The life of prayer, and particularly the offices, should be the regular and visible centre of the life of the parish. Parishes are praying communities, and whenever possible the priest should say the daily office in church, just as Herbert did, and invite his parishioners to join him in this act of worship.* The centre of the life of the parish should revolve around the rhythm of daily worship, which is common prayer, rather than simply the private act of the clergyman by himself. The importance of this being public and in church (even if at times the clergyman is alone) cannot be overestimated. The members of the Archbishops' Commission, as they travelled around the country, were particularly impressed by the significant number of rural parishes in which a serious attempt is being made to maintain a daily pattern of public prayer. By tradition, Anglicans are the people of the office, though this has been obscured in recent years, partly because of the parish communion movement, partly because of the folk memory of the dullness of Matins in previous generations, and partly because the office has come to be seen as the private act of the clergyman. The recovery of common prayer depends upon it being made clear that this pattern of Morning and Evening Prayer is the essential rhythm in the life of the church. People increasingly look for a deeper seriousness and profundity in worship than may be found in many parish communions or

* This is not to imply that the 1662 form of Morning and Evening Prayer will invariably be used today. Many will prefer post-Cranmerian versions, which retain an ordered pattern of scripture, psalmody, canticle and prayer, but do so in a simpler form, as in *Celebrating Common Prayer* (Society of St Francis 1992).

family services, and there is good reason for thinking that the number of people who attend the offices said quietly in country churches has risen significantly in recent years.

A priest in a modern multi-parish benefice faces the problem of deciding whether to make one church the centre or to divide his time equally between the many. It seems that in many multi-parish benefices a rota is followed by which Morning and Evening Prayer is said in one of the churches of the benefice every morning and every evening. In the nature of things, on occasions, the priest may be prevented from being present and on such occasions others take responsibility for the service. The offices belong to the whole Church and are not simply the private possession of the priest, and the establishing of a rota of this type does much to make it clear that the Church is above all a praying community. Thus the rhythm of daily worship becomes the central action of the Church.

The way in which Sunday worship is organized in modern multi-parish benefices varies considerably. All such benefices have to make a compromise between the desire of some for a full range of services in every small village and others who favour a centralized pattern of 'benefice services'. In practice, most multi-parish benefices achieve a compromise between the two, having benefice services either on the first or the fifth Sundays and local services on other Sundays. The organizing of a programme of Sunday worship in a number of different villages can be extremely complex. Most churches today prefer a service which starts either at 10 o'clock or half an hour before or afterwards. Achieving a suitable pattern can be a lengthy and difficult matter and it is important that there is some body such as a 'benefice council' or a meeting of the churchwardens which can be regarded as the forum in which final decisions are taken. A priest who tries to do this himself will often find himself under continuing pressure from those parishes who believe that the new arrangements do not ideally suit their requirements.

As in George Herbert's day, the small size of rural congregations is an important consideration, particularly with regard to worship. In some country churches, when a certain group of people have arrived, the start of the service need no longer be delayed, for no one else is expected. The empty rows of pews and the weakly sung hymns serve only to reinforce the private rather than the public nature of such an act of worship. In the post-war period, and in some rural areas until relatively recently, it was still customary to find country churches where there was an expectation that Sunday services would take place at 8 a.m., 11 a.m. and 6.30 p.m., possibly with a Sunday school either during the 11 a.m. service or in the mid afternoon. Each service tended to have its own following and to be marked by a different character. For example, the particular atmosphere of the early service was, for generations, almost the defining characteristic of rural Anglicanism; for others, choral Matins, which was solemn, unemotional and majestic, and had about it something of the atmosphere of the public school chapel in the era of the Empire, was what characterized the country church. In the evening, the service tended to be sung with the choir again present, but the sermon was shorter and more colloquial in style and the service less formal than in the morning.

However, this pattern of worship was already breaking down even in the inter-war years, and, certainly in the post-war period, a number of churches dramatically altered this traditional pattern. First, the decline in the number of clergy and the linking together of parishes, inevitably led to an overall decline in the number of services. Only the larger villages and market towns were able to maintain a three-service Sunday pattern and increasingly the smaller country churches had only single services on Sunday. The loss of Evensong, according to contemporary sources, was particularly regretted, and had the unintended consequence of tending to unchurch many people who had previously been attenders only at evening worship and had never been confirmed.

Second, in the 1960s, the parish communion movement, which had taken firm root in suburban parishes, gradually began to make an impact in rural areas. In a different age, and when one service per Sunday was becoming the norm in many country churches, it seemed to many that Matins was no longer suitable or appropriate as the only morning service on a Sunday. Many country clergy sought to change the pattern of services so that a service of parish communion became the regular Sunday morning worship, partly for reasons of theological preference, partly for more practical reasons. Such a service aimed at a different atmosphere, for among other things the service had to be 'child-worthy'; in many places it was both brighter and more obviously a congregational service. At the same time, as liturgical revision progressed, so the various new orders of service were adopted in village churches. These services, which led to the publication of the Alternative Service Book in 1980, contained a subtly different theology of the Church from that found in The Book of Common Prayer. The theology of the Church in the new service books, which was that of the Lord's people gathered round the Lord's table, tended to supplant older understandings of the nature of the Church as the offering of the whole community to God in prayer; an understanding of the Church which more clearly articulates the situation of a church in a country parish.

Some critics have seen in these changes the impact of suburbanization on the rural church in this period. Certainly, while a century before, many Church of England clergy were born and bred in the countryside, the number of such clergy has rapidly diminished. In previous generations, many clergy brought to their ministry an instinctive understanding of the nature of country villages and their churches; today, the picture is totally different, for the overwhelming majority of ordinands come from urban and suburban parishes and naturally bring to rural ministry urban assumptions about the nature of community and of the Church, that are reinforced in their theological colleges and early ministerial experience. Thus, some have suggested that the parish communion movement has had an unintended consequence of distancing the church from the mainstream of village life, and as a result of this and other changes, the rural church in many areas has come to assume the character of a eucharistic sect as opposed to that of a community church. Certainly, as Canon Charles Smyth once observed, the spirituality of country people 'has never been naturally sacramental, but was, in the early period, mystical and more latterly moral'. However, it is undeniable that the adoption of the parish communion as the single and only service in many country churches has altered the nature of the rural church in a much more profound way than merely altering the service-book or the form of worship.

If it is possible to speak in such terms, an average multi-parish benefice has a combination of parish communion services, family services and evening services (though the latter are not found everywhere). Family services (sometimes now called 'all-age worship', and not to be regarded as 'children's services') recognize the reality of church life, that in many villages it is families rather than individuals who attend church and worship needs to be structured in such a way that there is something to engage the interest and commitment of all age groups. The family services range from those which have a fixed order and, in a sense, are modern versions of Morning Prayer, to those that are unstructured and in which there is much congregational participation; indeed, an increasing number are conducted entirely by members of the congregation, following a pattern worked out at the weekly meeting of the 'worship committee'. Such services allow the less committed access to the worshipping life of the Church where a greater commitment can develop. Evening services have been severely hit by competition from television and other entertainments and the general decline of 'the English Sunday'. It is customarily said that the television serialization of *The Forsyte Saga*, which was shown in 1967 on Sunday evenings, had an effect on Evensong attendance from which many churches have never recovered.

One consequence of recent changes in patterns of worship in rural churches, and particularly the emphasis on parish communion, has been that the provision of services is now even more closely tied to the availability of the clergy. The coincidence of the decline in the number of clergy, and the emergence of a pattern of worship increasingly dependent on the presence of a priest, has led to a situation in which the availability of the clergy increasingly shapes this and other aspects of church life. The need for rural clergy to be present in the largest number of churches on a particular Sunday has led to the situation in which it is now normal for the clergyman to arrive from a previous service at the last minute and sometimes to disappear during the last hymn (the singing of which is partly drowned by the roar of his departing car). Whilst it has been widely appreciated that this is an unsatisfactory situation, attempts to remedy it have only been partially successful. In some areas non-stipendiary and local clergy have been ordained; other areas have adopted 'extended communion' (by which consecrated elements are taken from one church to another and administered in the second church by a deacon or a lay person), and, in many churches, the pattern of services includes the family services led by members of the congregation. However, the fact remains that many churches regard a communion service with their parish priest present to be the only acceptable form of worship. The report, *Faith in the Countryside*, recommended that a clergyman should take no more than three celebrations of Holy Communion on a Sunday, but it is clear that in many areas this is significantly exceeded.

Another feature of modern rural ministry is the complicated pattern of services produced in a multi-parish benefice. The need to satisfy the demands of a number of different country churches often produces a complex pattern of services which differ for each Sunday in the month. This has provoked its own reaction and recently there have been calls for churches to hold their services at the same time every Sunday. The implication of this would be that the majority of services would have to be taken by readers or members of the congregation, as the priest would be able to visit a particular church possibly as infrequently as only once a month, as almost all parishes would choose to have their service at a similar time.

A further aspect of worship in country churches is that of finding an acceptable compromise between the different preferences of various groups that can be found in the contemporary village. One group may prefer the 1662 Prayer Book and a formal approach to worship; whilst others may prefer the Alternative Service Book and a more relaxed and informal style of worship, that can absorb noisy children in moderate numbers. Differences of preference can be extreme, as between those who prefer a Christmas Carol Service led by a village choir accompanied by an American organ much damaged by mice, to those who would rather listen in silence to taped music from King's College Chapel, Cambridge. Such contrasts between local involvement and supreme excellence are only one dimension of these differences. Much attention has been focused in recent years on the relative merits of adherence to The Book of Common Prayer or the use of the Alternative Service Book. What seems to be clear, above all else, is that it is the way in which the service is conducted, the care, concentration and thought that go into the planning and conduct of the service, that is the most important factor. Services that bear the unmistakeable mark of hasty preparation, partly covered up by being conducted with jovial informality, in a manner which owes much to the television compère, fail to meet the spiritual needs of many, and contrast markedly with worship conducted by a priest who spends an hour preparing the prayers for Evensong.

Finally, baptisms, marriages and burials are simply extreme manifestations of the general proposition that the people in the village still expect the church to be the means by which they find significance and meaning in life, and they expect their parish clergyman to preside at these important family events. Many families, who do not attend church regularly, still expect to bring their babies to baptism and their children to marriage in the church and will be puzzled and mystified if they are met with anything other than a welcome or by attitudes which tend to exclude all but the most dedicated. For the village church is not a gathered church, in the sense that that term is used of suburban churches, but is the symbol of the presence of Christ at the centre of a community. Such a church needs to be inclusive rather than exclusive; it needs to be welcoming and to have thresholds which are easily crossed by the less committed on their journey in faith.

One of the prominent features of George Herbert's ministry was his concern for the church building itself, as can be seen from *The Country Parson* and from his restoration of Leighton Bromswold church. The church is a holy place, set aside, consecrated for the primary task of the Christian community, of which it is itself a symbolic presence. Where a clergyman prays, alone or with a few people, the building itself is a symbol of the representative nature of that act. A church that has itself been regularly prayed in, whose walls have been hallowed by prayer over many generations, and, where, on the priest's desk his books lie open, has a different, but difficult to define, atmosphere. A building imbued with the worship of centuries, well preserved, lovingly used, bearing the marks of an active religious life is, to the casual visitor, one of the most effective instruments of mission that the Church has to hand. For, if the church building is a place of prayer, it is also a place of proclamation. The church by its very presence says things about the nature of the gospel and the Kingdom. It is an icon of God's glory, a window into eternity, and the paintings on the walls, the glass in the windows and the doom above the chancel arch, for many centuries held the central doctrines of the Christian faith before all who saw them. At a more subtle level, today, the church building speaks of values and understandings at variance with those found in the wider society. For here is a building, large and costly to maintain, only used for a relatively short period each day. Everything it stands for seems to contradict the quantifiable judgements made about most things in contemporary society. It is a standing witness to the truth that beauty, peace, space, stillness, order and tranquillity are of importance in human life; and that man does not live by bread alone, but by values and understandings which are enshrined in such a building, which itself declares eloquently the truth that God's Kingdom is not of this world.

The church, the sacred building of special use, is found in the earliest Christian period with its emphasis not on sacred space but on the holy people among whom God's presence can be found. The theology of the church building as a sacred space developed in parallel to the ideas and the practice of the royal court, and English churches and their design are rooted in this tradition. However, in the 1960s and 1970s there was a marked return to the 'theology of the tent' rather than that of the temple; and many clergy came to express, either directly or by implication, criticism of church buildings which they saw as having developed into cultic objects in their own right. In addition to this, many clergy felt that much of their and their congregations' time, money and energy was absorbed by the maintenance of the building. If only, it was said, such resources could be deployed elsewhere where the real work of the Church was to be done. Certainly, the care of four or five ancient country churches can impose considerable administrative, financial and other burdens upon the incumbent and churchwardens, who, in the last resort, bear legal responsibility. However, attitudes have changed in recent years and many have come to see and value country churches in a new light (in many places encouraged by the activities of the county Historic Churches Trusts). In reality, few country churches have been made redundant and almost all churches are cared for to a high standard. The building itself has come to be seen as a major agent of mission in the contemporary countryside. George Herbert himself clearly saw the importance of the church as a building and as a presence at the centre of the community, and that understanding has been recaptured in many country parishes.

Pastor

While other Churches are known for their mystical and spiritual writers, the Church of England has a quieter genius and its saints are men like George Herbert, John Keble and Edward King; men who served God as the pastors of country parishes. For the Anglican clergyman, pastoral work, in its many dimensions, has come to be seen as the central and almost defining aspect of his role, and generations of clergy have heard the Gospel from St John, with the image of the shepherd, read at their ordination service. Parishes value a clergyman who has what is sometimes called 'a pastoral heart': a man who places a high priority on visiting, and identifies himself closely with the joys and sorrows of all the people who live within the parish. It is clear from *The Country Parson* that Herbert placed a high priority on pastoral work. Every afternoon he was around the parish, *now in one area, now in another*, and he seemed to miss no opportunity of meeting his parishioners on their own ground, in cottages and gardens, in fields and farmyards. He took trouble to understand about farming and about the customs and work of the countryside so that he could talk easily and naturally to his parishioners.

Since Herbert's time there have been two principal changes. First, Herbert acted within his parish in a number of roles that now have been taken over by other professionals or are no longer areas of life in which parishioners look to their priest for guidance. In the nineteenth century the country doctor and the country solicitor took over roles which Herbert had performed for his parishioners in Bemerton. It seems there is hardly any aspect of life on which Herbert was not prepared to offer guidance and advice. Second, it is not possible for the modern country clergyman, who may be the vicar of a number of parishes, to maintain the close pastoral contact which Herbert maintained with his parishioners.

When a new incumbent is instituted into a parish, he kneels before the bishop to receive the Deed of Institution and the bishop uses the same form of words which George Herbert himself heard: 'Receive this cure of souls which is both thine and mine.' He is instituted and inducted into the benefice which comprises not a church but a parish (or, today, parishes). He is not being asked to take on responsibility for a church (though that is part of his task) but to accept the role of pastor and spiritual leader for the whole parish. As Richard Hooker wrote: 'With us, one society is both Church and common-wealth.' It is clear that Herbert stood firmly within this tradition and against Puritan ideas of a gathered church of God's faithful people. George Herbert saw himself as the pastor and the shepherd of everyone in the parish.

The modern country clergyman needs to have an understanding of the way in which the church relates to the whole of the village and of 'community ministry'. He needs to understand the close and symbiotic relationship between the church and the community and to know that much of his work is effectively that of being present at all types of occasions within the village. He will know that, particularly where a clergyman serves many villages, it is important that he should be visible and accessible, and that he should attend functions and occasions where people gather and be visible and known to be about during the day. He will know the importance of occasionally being outside the school when the mothers gather to collect their children; or on the village green where the school bus brings them from another school; the importance of calling at the old people's lunch club in the village hall and of attending and showing interest in a wide range of village activities. Community ministry means associating himself with the many and varied aspects of village life including the pub, the British Legion hall, the horticultural society, the drama society, the youth club, the young farmers and the range of sporting and social activities that take place in many villages. By doing this he demonstrates that God cares and is concerned for people in the ordinary activities of day-to-day life. At the same time, when crisis or difficulty strikes a family, he will be in a much better position to help if he is already a familiar and trusted figure in the village, whom people have met on various occasions in different contexts.

Clearly, to do this in a number of villages can impose an enormous strain upon a clergyman. Whilst George Herbert could have done this in a single village, it cannot so easily be done in a modern multi-parish benefice. It is important that the priest and leading members of the congregation talk freely about how his time should be best used and make plans accordingly. What is certain is that he cannot do all this himself and one of his principal roles will be to draw together a team of people who together share certain parts of the pastoral ministry. Thus, in many parishes, young people's and children's work will be looked after by a group of people, whose responsibilities will include visiting the families as well as organizing services and activities. Another group of people may be involved in welcoming new arrivals; others may provide a lunch club and other activities for elderly residents. The modern parish priest may find much of his time involved in the training and support of these people, and that he is less able to involve himself in the primary pastoral encounters as they increasingly become the work of others. Pastoral work increasingly is the work of a ministerial team, and the clergyman's role is that of drawing together and supporting that team. Most parishes will decide that visiting the sick and those in particular crisis and difficulty should be the work of the priest, but they will also determine that other parts of the pastoral ministry should be done by other people.

There is a necessary relationship between quantity and quality. If the modern country clergyman is required to do the whole pastoral ministry unaided, it is inevitable that the quality of his work will suffer. Many of the handbooks written for clergy in the late nineteenth century, and, certainly, those in the early decades of this century, recognize that a clergyman must limit the range of his work and not spread himself too thinly over too wide an area. 'Many a parish', wrote Arthur Robinson in 1902, 'would be greatly the gainer if its clergy were less ready, and indeed eager, to do everything themselves.' Today, when pastoral circumstances have radically changed in many country parishes, this is an absolute requirement.

However, it is of the first importance that the modern country clergyman conveys to his parishioners the feeling that he cares for and cherishes the parishes that he serves. Pastoral visiting is of the greatest importance and the old-fashioned advice of the handbooks of former generations, about 'walking the parish' and the use of a bicycle, still has its significance. The visiting undertaken by a clergyman within the community can be divided into two parts: on the one hand there is the specific visiting of those in need, the bereaved, the sick, the housebound, the elderly, and those whose children are about to be baptized; and there are the general visits which a clergyman pays as a sign of the Church's presence within the community as a whole. He will seek to be a known and trusted and recognized figure because he knows that in distress people will seek out those they know or at least those they recognize. His visiting must encompass the whole village, and not just the congregation, for Christ came to save the world and it is to the world that the clergyman is sent; for the Church, in the sense of a visible ordered community, is the sacrament of Christ's continuing presence and ministry in the world, which the clergy epitomize and represent. The Church itself is a part of the gospel that we proclaim and is an instrument used by the Spirit to accomplish the purposes of God. The clergyman must not give the impression that he is concerned only with the few who attend church, but that he is equally concerned with the many who lie beyond. There is still enormous goodwill towards the Church of England and its clergy in rural areas, and there are country clergymen who, after a lifetime of service, can remember few occasions on which a visit was rejected. As his pastoral ministry in the community develops, so he will gain a position as a trusted and known person in that community; he will be appealed to to give a lead in many circumstances, to be a focus of the life of that community, and be better able to help people in individual distress and difficulty. However, the country clergyman will be aware of many allies who work in his villages in both the statutory and voluntary sectors. He will get to know the doctors, social workers, policemen, district nurses and the many volunteers involved in a number of caring agencies who are together concerned for those who live in the rural community and are active in providing for their needs.

In Anglican rural ministry, evangelism has always been seen in pastoral terms. Today, evangelism is sometimes spoken of as if it were a separate activity within the life of the Church, but in the country parish, the gospel is commended to people most effectively by the care and concern of the pastoral ministry. In the countryside, the principal agent of evangelism is the church itself, and a village can be seen as a series of concentric circles, with the worshipping community at the centre, graduating outwards to those with only the loosest connection with the life of the church (though in a country village almost everyone will regard the church as in some sense theirs). Rural evangelism aims at drawing people from the outer circles towards the centre and this is done by the quality of its worship and of its pastoral care. In any parish it is necessary for there to be a strategy, whereby stepping stones are created so that people can move from the outside closer to the centre. It is through the care with which the church and the modern country clergyman prepares people for marriage, confirmation and baptism; the way in which funerals are taken and the pastoral care which is associated with all these events in village life, that people are drawn further into the worshipping community of the village church.

Teacher

This function of the country parson's role is more distinct than the other functions, for preaching and catechetical teaching are clearly defined roles. However, there is a sense in which, like the other functions, teaching permeates all clerical activities, as the country clergyman seeks to guide, lead and inform his congregation. It is clear from the Ordinal that the teaching function of the clergyman's role is regarded as of particular importance in the Anglican tradition. Whilst, in the pre-Reformation Church, the priest was seen principally as the celebrant of the sacraments, in the post-Reformation Church, his duty is seen predominantly as that of teaching, expounding and familiarizing his congregation with the Scriptures. In this respect, the Church of England is the heir to the Protestant Reformation, for when the Prayer Book Ordinal was written it was only a few years after the Bible had first become available in English. It is clear that George Herbert attached considerable significance to this aspect of the clergyman's role. He saw preaching and catechizing as being central duties and, in later generations, clergy became the principal instruments by which a system of rural primary education was established. The clergy's contribution to primary education in rural areas has been considerable and continues today. In Oxfordshire, over 60% of primary age children attend church schools; and the parish clergyman will be a member of the governing body, if not its chairman. However, this chapter is not concerned with the country clergyman's contribution to the life of the school, significant though this is in many cases.

In its Anglican understanding, ministry has always been seen as having an interpretive function (in some literature this is referred to as the prophetic role of the minister). It is the role of the clergyman to relate Scripture and the Christian tradition to the personal and social events and issues of everyday life by preaching and in many other ways. The Church and its clergy provide meaning and understanding amidst the complexities and vagaries of personal and social life. Thus, the clergyman is provided with a stipend and other forms of security in order that he can spend time in study and lay the fruits of that study at the disposal of the parish through preaching and through other means. The modern country clergyman will set aside some time in his week for study, and will try to keep up to date in his theological reading. Much of his reading will be done as he prepares sermons, Bible studies and confirmation classes for his parish, but he will seek to keep a book of theology by him, from which he reads from time to time. It is almost inevitable that this is the part of the modern country clergyman's life which can easily be lost in the face of other more urgent demands of the parish. However, it is particularly important that the country clergyman continues to read, for part of what he offers to the community is a Christian interpretation of life on which he must continue to reflect.

However, in recent years parish clergy have not tended to see theologians as immediate allies in their work. This has arisen partly as a consequence of the growth in English religious life in recent years of an anti-intellectualism, which is itself, in part, a reaction to the emotionally constrained and over-academic approach of previous generations (one writer recalls a priest, formerly a classics master and retired to a country parish, who, on a winter's evening, with a small congregation in a remote country parish huddled around the coke stove, mounted the pulpit and began his sermon: 'Those of you who have been at Thermopylae will remember . . .'). It is also related to the erosion of the middle ground in religious debate, once occupied by a significant number of critical but committed Christians. Today such debate can seem to be polarised between the radical relativism of post-modernism and the reactionary irrationalism of religious fundamentalism. Many now look for expressions of religion which appeal principally to the heart, rather than the mind, and which are characterized by a warm, emotional and sentimental understanding. In many parishes, clergy with higher degrees learn that, whilst in other walks of life this would be an advantage, in the Church it may be seen as a disadvantage. At the same time, the negativity of much recent theological writing, and its perceived hostility to traditional and widely held understandings, has done much to create a situation in which theologians are seen as essentially hostile to the work of the parish clergyman. From all points of view this is a regrettable situation, for the development of a clergyman's understanding of the faith should be part of his life and ministry. Study should nourish his praying and his praying should enliven and infuse his study. However, the consequence of this situation is that many members of rural congregations know little about the faith or the Bible. This alarming level of theological undernourishment is discernible in the banality and shallowness of some family and 'all-age' worship, and in sermons which bear little comparison with the carefully composed expositions and exhortations of previous generations. As a consequence, members of country congregations have been left ill-equipped to take their place in a Church in which there are different theological and liturgical traditions, some of them markedly at variance with traditional understandings and patterns.

Today the modern country parson's teaching role is principally that of being the man who provides the resources to support the ministerial team and the wider congregation. His distinctive contribution to the work of the ministerial team will often be that of providing the intellectual and spiritual background and resources which that group will need to function. His knowledge of Scripture and the Christian tradition will guide and assist that group as together it seeks to exercise the community ministry in the parishes. Today his teaching ministry will be conducted in Bible study groups, in leading study groups and guiding the studies of those who are training for some ministerial office within the congregation. His principal role in the team will be that of the person who provides the needed resources, not of money, but the spiritual and teaching resources that will allow the team to develop and grow in its Christian understanding. As the community ministry grows in strength and confidence, so it will take over more of the pastoral and administrative tasks within the parishes and thus the clergyman will find that he has more time to devote to this, one of the central and principal aspects of his work.

Shepherd

It is the clergyman's duty to take responsibility for the life of the parish and this is the burden placed upon him by the bishop at his institution. ('Shepherd' is used in this section in the sense of 'leader'.) A clergyman is inducted into the parish, for the spiritual welfare of which he is responsible; all the people in that parish may look to him for the offices of the church, for pastoral care, for teaching and for spiritual leadership. Every settlement in England is within a parish and it is the ancient wisdom of the Anglican Church that at least somebody should sleep uncomfortably if the gospel is not preached in that place and the worship of God is not offered and the sick and needy are not visited.

Duns Scotus taught that baptism made people citizens, confirmation made them soldiers and ordination made them officers within the Christian community. Until quite recently this was regarded as an appropriate way of describing the Christian community. In the 1960s much emphasis was put upon the clergyman as the enabler of the Christian community, with the implication that older styles of leadership were now inappropriate. The churches in many country villages contain in their vestry pictures of their previous incumbents. These men ruled the parish and the church by the strength of their chin and the breadth of their forehead. Certainly, leadership cannot be understood in these terms today, but, at the same time, some of the language used in recent years has seemed to imply that the clergyman does not have a leadership role.

Today, leadership in the Church is very different, and requires a man who understands that he must lead from within a group of people, who are the Church in that place. One of his principal tasks as the shepherd of that Christian community is to give it direction or vision. Where a ship goes depends on the currents and the winds, upon the crew and the helmsman; the helmsman himself does not work alone, though his contribution is of the greatest importance. He is the man who has the knowledge (of the stars and the tides) that can keep the ship pointing in the right direction. By another analogy, he is the shepherd, who walks before his sheep, not driving them but encouraging them to follow him. It is the particular temptation of a community organization such as a rural church to become a comfortable local organization run for the personal and social satisfaction of its members. That might be appropriate for a sports club or a social club but it is the priest's task to keep the church pointing to the cross and the gospel. He is there to symbolize and remind people of the imperative of the gospel, which is not done by argument or aggressive proselytizing, but by being a practical example of loving holiness, characterized by a generosity of nature and spirit. At the centre of this lies the ability to give direction; to inspire; to allow others to share in a vision which will animate and enthuse the life of the local church.

He must accept the discipline and the responsibility of leadership. In secular life such a term is associated with the power to give commands, to impose sanctions, to invoke the traditions and the *esprit de corps* of the group and, perhaps most important, the ability to distribute rewards. For the modern country clergyman, leadership is a matter of being the servant of the Christian community, with no commands, no sanctions and no rewards. His task is to animate, invigorate, direct and motivate a group of people who will together form the community ministry in that place. In many country parishes there is still a strong desire for the old style of leadership, and it may be suspected that such congregations feel content and comfortable to leave matters entirely in the hands of the clergyman. Such a style, though it may be regarded as a success by some, will not lead in the long term to the deepening and the growth of the Church. Jesus' style of ministry was not to recruit followers but to train other leaders. It is said that strong leaders make for weak teams; Jesus' self-effacing style of leadership, characterized by meekness and humility, and an unwillingness to draw attention to himself, brought into being the leadership of the early Christian community. Such a style of leadership, which is not authoritarian leadership but the leadership of the servant, is always open to the criticism that it lacks strength and conviction; but the desire for strong leadership, in the authoritarian sense, may well be the sign either of an immature congregation or, worse, a sign of irresponsibility or laziness. Jesus himself drew a distinction between the authoritarian style of leadership practised by the Gentiles and his own style (Mark 10.42–45).

In 1915 Father Herbert Kelly wrote:

In our practice today the church is almost entirely dependent upon the clergy. The church in a parish consists of all those people whom the clergy can persuade to take an interest in religion. If the clergy possess the rare gift of influence — without which holiness and self-sacrifice effect little — things go well. If a vicar without gifts follows a vicar with gifts everything comes to a standstill. We are so accustomed to this way of thinking and working that it never occurs to us that there is or should be any other, although in fact our way is peculiarly Anglican. We do not observe that for the old creed 'I believe in the Holy Catholic Church' we have mentally substituted a new clause 'I believe in a holy and energetic clergy'.

Today, in a modern multi-parish benefice, it is clear that this style of ministry in which the clergyman did everything (what Kelly called 'the handcart style of ministry' — someone is needed from outside to push the cart) is no longer possible or appropriate. In a cluster of several country parishes, in which each parish has a church and parochial church council, each church will have its own pattern of services, church activities and church fund-raising events; each community will wish for the presence of the vicar at its principal community function and each parish will make a range of other demands upon the clergyman's time and energy. The mathematics of rural multiplication become acute at the major festivals, when a country clergyman can find himself celebrating Christmas, Easter, Harvest and Remembrance Day six times in different communities. Increasingly, it is recognized that ministry is the function of the whole Church, and, within that total function, a clergyman has a particular task of which his role as the servant-leader, the shepherd, is of particular importance. Today, the laity are being called to repossess their own priestliness, and it is the clergyman's task to assist them in doing this. At the centre of every benefice there should be a community ministry of committed people, who share together in the work of ministry throughout the parishes. The leadership of this community ministry forms one of the principal functions of the rural clergyman today.

Increasingly, the Church, as has been seen, takes the form and shape of a voluntary organization, and it is the role of the clergyman to act as a community leader, identifying and channelling the talents of those within the community ministry. It is his role to identify and train suitable people; to maximize their contributions; to minimize conflict. In practice, community ministry teams operate best where there is a clear understanding of who does what, and where there are known boundaries between different areas of responsibility. The setting of these boundaries, the holding together of a team of volunteers, is a highly demanding and exacting role. As the life of the community ministry develops, some members will leave and others will join, and new tasks will have to be addressed, and the clergyman's role as leader is particularly important in this.

There is a tendency in parish life for every disagreement to become a personal affront, and holding together a team of people can be a difficult and a costly task. Those who wish for a quiet life tend to do the jobs themselves because, at first glance, that appears to be an easier option. But that limits the size of the church to the energy of the local clergyman and limits its composition to those who are happy merely to be passive receivers of his ministerial activities. The training of a ministerial team, before which the clergyman must put a clear vision of his own understanding, is one of his most important tasks. That team will become the leadership of the local church and one of the common features of almost all growing churches is that they tend to have strong lay leadership. A leader must know accurately how things are, have some vision of how they might be and have some idea about moving people from one situation to another.

The difficulties of this should not be underestimated, and many clergy find that the level of conflict within congregations can be much higher and much sharper than they had anticipated. The clergyman is needed as 'the man from outside' who can enable a group to stay together or, as one person put it, 'We need the minister to keep us apart so that we stay together.' All this will involve the clergyman in many meetings, for which some clergy do not have a natural appetite, but what could be more important than equipping the community ministry within a parish? As the team grows in confidence it will become less directly dependent upon the energy and leadership of a clergyman, and its own role will be subtly redefined by these new circumstances.

The building up of the community ministry requires the clergyman to have different skills and understandings from those of previous generations. He needs to be the sort of person who can identify members of the community ministry, reconcile their conflicts and maximize the effective contribution of each member. Theologically, the priesthood exists for the building up of the priestliness of the whole Church, and this is a practical, day-to-day way in which this is achieved. But it requires different understandings from those of previous generations, when the clergyman led from the front and the only activity open to the laity was that of 'helping the vicar'. Today, clergy and lay people work together as colleagues within the community ministry. This requires, on the part of the clergy, an ability to share their task with others, which at times may be difficult. Arthur Robinson writes: 'Who does not know of cases where the weak health of the vicar has actually proved to be a blessing in disguise?' The modern country clergyman must be willing to share responsibility and tasks with others in order that the pastoral ministry of the whole Church may prosper; and the ability to work in a collaborative way in which the gifts of others are valued and optimized is one of the principal qualifications for ministry in the contemporary rural church.

Exercising such leadership in a small face-to-face community can be extremely difficult, yet such leadership is deeply important, and, where it is exercised quietly and effectively, it allows other people to fulfil their potential and to achieve things they would not have found possible under other circumstances. It is a style of leadership that liberates and frees the contribution of others in order that the whole Church may grow. In many places in the past, clerical leadership has been a personality cult which, when the personality is moved, leaves little behind except the photograph on the vestry wall. The fruits of true leadership may be seen in the growth within the congregation of a prayerful holiness and a new confidence and an ability to exercise the community ministry of the whole Church.

Thus it can be seen that the principal tasks to which the modern country clergyman is called — priest; pastor; teacher; shepherd — though very different in practice, are still recognizably those of *The Country Parson* and would have been understood and familiar to George Herbert. Nearly fifty years ago, those who wrote the influential report *Towards the Conversion of England* (1945), commented: 'George Herbert's *The Country Parson* still holds good as one of the best expositions of what a village ministry demands'. But putting this into practice, living the life of a country clergyman, has never been easy either in the time of George Herbert or today, and this is the subject of the next chapter.

8

The Life of the
Country Clergyman Today

As has been seen above, the tasks of the modern country
clergyman are similar in their essentials to those outlined by
George Herbert, but significantly different in detail and in
application. When an incumbent is inducted into a living
today, the monuments around the chancel walls and the
photographs in the vestry will remind him that he is but one
more name in a long list of those who have held that
appointment. Over the generations much historical continuity
has remained, although the issues with which a clergyman will
have to deal and the scope and extent of his work have
changed considerably in recent years. Nonetheless, the ministry
of the country clergyman today is still recognizably within the
tradition in which Chaucer's 'poor clerk' stood, of whom he
wrote:

> This noble ensample to his flock he gef,
> That first he wroughte and afterwards he taught . . .
> To drawen folk to hevene by fairnesse
> By good ensample this was his bysynesse.

Such a ministry was essentially local, static and stable; one in
which the personal example of the clergyman was of crucial
significance. As Jeremy Taylor wrote in a Charge to the clergy
of his Ulster Diocese in 1660: 'Men will strive to be like you if
you be like to God.' George Crabbe wrote in 1810 of his local
minister:

> Sober, chaste, devout and just
> One whom his neighbours could believe and trust.

Within the tradition of Anglican pastoral ministry, George

Herbert's book *The Country Parson* may be regarded as the archetypal description of this type of 'cure of souls'. At its best it was the drawing of a community to God through the personal example, leadership and care of its clergyman. Above all, it was the personal ministry of a known person in a knowable community, and, as an inevitable consequence, Anglican rural church life has centred round the person and the personality of its priest. In a real sense the priest became the Church, and people found it difficult to conceive of church life without a resident clergyman, whose job it was to represent the Church and to be responsible for the Church at every point. He was the *persona ecclesiae* and the nature and quality of his own personal life were of the highest importance. For, as has been seen, the clergyman's identity is defined not by what he does, but what he is. The way he lives his life, his personal attitudes and dispositions, the way he encounters and relates to other people in the community, will be more decisive for the effectiveness or otherwise of his ministry than any number of projects or schemes which he sets on foot within the parish. Who he is, as a person, matters above all else. His personal openness to people, his willingness to laugh and cry with them, his ability to serve them, at times at considerable personal cost to himself, will all speak much louder than any number of sermons. For he must demonstrate the self-giving, sacrificial love of God in his own person.

It is sometimes said that 'when two or three are gathered together' in the Church of England their purpose is to criticize the vicar. Certainly, it is hard to live up to the high standards of the priestly calling, but if parishioners may be demanding in their requirement of high standards and judgemental in their assessments, it is unlikely that they will be more so than the clergyman himself. For every priest knows the difficulty and impossibility of living such a life and the constant failures and shortcomings which must inevitably result. Being a priest will always be deeply sacrificial and costly, because it involves an entering into the priesthood of Christ, becoming oneself a part of that total self-giving in love which is the hallmark of all Christ's servants and saints. In the life of the modern country parson, however, the clergyman must face not just the ancient problems and ambiguities which attach to his role, but a range of specific difficulties of more modern origin.

In George Herbert's time the role of the country parson in the local community was widely understood and acknowledged. Although it is clear that practices varied considerably, the responsibilities and duties of his office would have been valued, acknowledged, and respected and affirmed by the local community. Today, the number of people who share these understandings has markedly declined, and, as a consequence, it is possible to speak of the clergyman's role as having lost social support. At one level this is part of a wider process of change involving the desacralization of culture, in which traditional authority figures, particularly where their authority is based upon these understandings, are no longer held in respect by the wider society. The Church, and the clergyman who represents it, is increasingly described as 'irrelevant', for it has lost its traditional position as the authorized interpreter of an accepted and universal tradition of revelation and natural law, and is no longer seen as relevant to the problems and issues of modern society. For some, the Church is seen as an institutional antiquity and the clergyman's role as one that belongs more properly to the life and times of previous generations. Even those who do not necessarily accept this are not unaffected by the widespread view that religion is something which people have outgrown and which modern enlightened man has discarded as unreasonable and irrational. People often feel obliged to begin a conversation with a clergyman by saying: 'I am not really religious . . .'. This is part of the decline in modern society of commitment to any definite point of view, and, in part, an assertion of the autonomy of individual conscience and private judgement. The consequence of both these understandings is that the clerical role is often seen both symbolically and actually as an attempt to impose views and understandings upon other people. These are all part of the problem of being a public representative of the faith and the Church, in a society where these matters have moved from the centre to the periphery; from the social to the private.

But the problems which the clergyman faces within the

church community itself are those which touch him most closely and which cause him most anguish and difficulty. As has been described in Chapter 5, changes in the Church as an organization have in recent years resulted in a movement away from assumptions based on the Church as a professional organization to the present situation where the Church increasingly operates, at the local level, on the modes and assumptions of a voluntary associational organization. The problem is that this movement of change has been uneven in church life; whilst certain areas still articulate values that relate to the Church and the clergy as a professional body (particularly central selection of the clergy, which encourages a sense of the clergy as a professional body with a well-developed centralized organization and career structure), at the local level, it is clear that the way in which the Church operates, in many country parishes, is closely akin to that of other voluntary organizations. Thus, one of the basic problems facing the contemporary clergy is the discontinuity between these two understandings of the Church and their role: that of the clergy as a professional body and that of a voluntary organization. There are times when the clergy find themselves having to interpret one view of the Church to those who hold another, and vice versa. This is particularly the case in financial matters which are highly centralized; for the payment of increasingly large sums of money by the parishes to the centre (which in turn pays the clergy) is now seen by many as incompatible with the growing localism and voluntaryism of the parish church which wishes to control its own finances.

However, there are many points at which difficulties and misunderstandings can be seen as a consequence of this changing understanding. For the clergyman, this dual system becomes particularly apparent at the time when he moves to a new appointment. Under the old professional assumption, a clergyman moved from one parish to another either because his bishop made the suggestion or as a result of his approach to his bishop or to another ecclesiastical patron, resulting in an offer of a new appointment. Today (since the Patronage [Benefices] Measure 1986), a clergyman can be appointed to a parish only with the consent, in writing, of representatives of the parochial church council. This is not simply a further manifestation of consumer choice but represents a fundamental shift in the way the Church sees itself as an organization. The problem for the clergy is that some of the assumptions remain those of a professional body, whilst other assumptions are increasingly those which reflect the Church as a voluntary organization.

The characteristic of a profession is that it has access to a body of knowledge which it places at the disposal of its clients, as was noted in Chapter 2. A professional man is valued primarily because of the degree to which he has mastered the knowledge of his profession and the degree to which he is able to make this knowledge available and accessible to his clients. Thus lawyers, doctors and clergy were once commonly referred to as learned professions. A priest was valued, among many other things, because he was a learned man, and there is a long tradition (within which George Herbert stands) of cultivated and scholarly country clergymen, whose sermons may not always have been understood by their parishioners, but whose learning was recognized and valued as important. As has been seen in Chapter 5, in the early decades of this century, there began a process of change that has accelerated rapidly in recent years. The clergyman is no longer seen as having a body of understanding and knowledge which is valued by his parishioners, but is seen as the person who runs the church. Increasingly, in the post-war period, theological colleges came to see themselves as training their students to 'run a parish' and the clergyman's role was increasingly seen as that of a management task rather than that of a professional person.

One of the particular uncertainties which George Herbert did not face, but which causes problems in many parishes today, concerns the nature of the relationship between parishioners and clergymen. The gradual supplanting of the professional understanding of the clergyman's role, and its replacement by an understanding of the clergyman's role as a church manager, have taken place at an uneven pace. In some parishes there is an expectation among certain parishioners that the clergyman will act as a professional person; whilst other parishioners will expect him to operate in a manner not dissimilar to that of a full time organizer of a voluntary associational organization. The older view is still found well represented in many country parishes, where a significant number of parishioners may regard shared decision-making as a sign of weakness and yearn for a confident, remote, professional figure on whom they can depend and to whom they can defer. On the other hand, there is an increasingly significant body of opinion that regards the clergyman's role as that of a church manager. There are many testimonies to the fact that the organization of volunteers is intrinsically one of the most difficult management tasks, because, by their nature, volunteers are always able to withdraw the moment any demand becomes disagreeable or inconvenient. A recent survey of voluntary organizations points to the high level of friction between volunteers and employed staff. Volunteers need to be inspired, led and encouraged, but they cannot be directed, driven or badgered. At the same time, the Church is increasingly aware of the rising significance of charities and charitable fund-raising in modern society, and finds itself in competition with other charitable organizations both for its personnel and resources at the local level.

The clergyman will occasionally find himself musing on the fact that he is asking people to do in a voluntary and unpaid capacity, in time that they have to sacrifice from leisure and family activities, those things which they and others may regard as his paid employment. Leading a group of volunteers requires personal skills of a high order and many clergy find this increasingly difficult. In matters of religion people are often at their most subjective, irrational and dogmatic, and the level of conflict can be considerable. Furthermore, the clergyman can find himself as the repository of a great deal of private and community anger. The Church and its clergy are often convenient scapegoats for the decline in moral values in society, the erosion of community and a whole range of personal losses, grievances and regrets. It has probably always been the case, but this is accentuated at times when such values are seen to be declining, and people still look to the Church and to its clergy as a repository of unchanging principles and practice. There is a sense in which people today expect the clergyman

to believe on behalf of an unbelieving society. As a consequence, any form of theological exploration, any deviation
from the strictest interpretations of credal orthodoxy by a
clergyman will be denounced loudly, often by those who may
have little understanding of the issues involved.

At the same time, for many people – the semi-believer, the
occasional attender or the non-attender who still believes the
Church to be a valued institution – the totality of the priest's
commitment can be a silent reproach to their weakness of
belief and the presence of the priest is a constant unspoken
invitation to an involvement they do not wish to pursue. Many
people feel uneasy in the presence of a clergyman because
they perceive that what he represents is a challenge to their
weak faith and lack of involvement in the life of the Church.
This manifests itself in the desire of many to fend off what is
perceived to be a threat, either by humour and caricature, by
exaggerated attitudes of respect and deference, or by criticism.
Initially a clergyman may find such attitudes irritating and
difficult to understand, but he will soon learn that the hands
of some people search constantly for the convenient stick with
which to beat the Church or to harass its clergy. On the night
of an institution, after the new clergyman has received the
Deed of Institution, the bishop asks the archdeacon to induct
him 'into the real and actual possession of this church and
benefice and to defend him in it'. The significance of the last
phrase has grown in recent years. New liturgical developments
of a relatively minor nature or small changes to the interior of
the church building can expose conflicts of a serious nature
that quickly become personalized. Not only is it uncomfortable
to live at close quarters to such conflict, but its very existence
undermines the message which the Church seeks to preach in
a rural community. As a consequence of this, the avoidance of
conflict can easily become, either consciously or unconsciously,
a high priority in some rural ministries.

As has been mentioned in Chapter 5, the tendency to see
the Church as a management organization has significantly
affected the way many people assess the clergyman's role.
Increasingly, there is a tendency for some to judge the clergy in
a way not dissimilar to football managers; if they do not

produce an increased attendance they are invited to consider their future. This is congruent with a culture which places a premium on visible success; in the case of the clergy reflected in numbers attending the church and an ability to raise money and create a 'successful' church community. This view tends to see churches as retail religious outlets which exist to satisfy the needs of their clientele. The effect of this management view of the clergy is to encourage them to perform in such a way that satisfies these criteria. By its nature much of a clergyman's work is not easily quantifiable, but, in recent years, there has been a notable tendency to place emphasis on those parts that can be readily quantified: buildings, budgets and attendance at church. Traditionally, rural clergy did not count the number of people attending Morning and Evening Prayer, and the numbers were recorded only for Holy Communion. This goes back to the period when not only numbers but also names were recorded, as many offices in civil and academic life were open only to those who were communicant members of the Church of England. Today, by contrast, considerable attention is attached to the counting of numbers of those who attend worship and a 'successful' clergyman is commonly defined simply as one who increases the number of those attending a particular church.

The pressure that the clergy feel to justify themselves leads to many clergy surrounding themselves with an atmosphere of intense busyness. They are always rushing from place to place, from meeting to meeting; diaries are full months ahead. A number of dioceses have introduced performance assessment programmes, and parishes have become noticeably more vocal in the condemnation of those clergy whom they perceive as under-performing by their standards. Though it is undeniable that many clergy can learn with advantage better administrative and other skills, many of these attitudes contain some mis-understanding about the essential nature of a clergyman's role, exemplified by a complaint made of a priest, who always said Matins and Evensong in church and had a period of intercession for the parish at midday, that he 'wasted far too much time in church'.

One of the principal distinctive features of ministry in rural areas is the high profile of the clergyman's role, for inevitably the country clergyman is more visible to the wider community than his urban counterpart. Everyone in the village will know where the rectory or the vicarage is, and a thick hedge or a high wall cannot insulate the clergyman and his family from the interest and comments of the village. People who live in a village find it difficult to be indifferent about their clergyman, and almost all writers on rural ministry have stressed the significance of a clergyman's personal example in a small community. Villages are very exposed places in which to live; it is difficult to hide there, and people naturally tend to know much more about their neighbours than they do in an urban area. Many who move to rural ministry find the high visibility of their role a particularly daunting factor (as do the members of their family); anyone who wishes to lead a very private life should not consider rural ministry. The countryside is no place for an anonymous and inconspicuous ministry, and a clergyman will find that the village will regard every aspect of his, and his family's, life as a legitimate subject for speculation and comment. Living in the public eye over a long period is in itself very demanding, and can make the clergy weary and cautious of social contact. The village is a place where, as the Prayer Book says, 'no secrets are hid'. A recent report of the House of Bishops explicitly states that the Church demands both different and higher standards from its clergy. It is paradoxical that as the majority of people become more casual in the observance of the codes and mores of society, so they become more demanding that their public figures should scrupulously observe these codes on their behalf, and less tolerant of those who fail. It would seem that the more society disregards certain rules, the more it demands that its role models adhere to them. Thus the clergy (and other public figures) will attract adverse criticism over matters that would pass without comment among the more anonymous members of the general public. This is part of the lack of privacy which many clergy find hard to bear over a number of years, together with the fact that what is most essential to them is something that they have to be prepared to talk about constantly in public.

There is in English society a powerful stereotype of the

country clergyman as a man who is a gentlemanly amateur, friendly, genial but naive and guileless, frequently muddled and usually ineffectual. George Herbert in his time was aware of the low esteem in which the clergy were held, and no doubt he, like clergy today, found it difficult to be regarded as a stereotype rather than as a person; for being a representative or public figure in a small community can place considerable demands upon the individual clergyman. These can be exacerbated by the tendency of communities to project their difficulties upon the Church and its clergy. Both at the national level, and locally, the Church and its clergy often act as lightning conductors for the confusion, anger, bitterness and disillusion that a community may feel. Communities at such times find it necessary to find a scapegoat for their own inadequacies, and very often the Church in general, and the clergyman in particular, are singled out. In the more serious cases, martyrdom, in its modern form, comes to the clergyman by courtesy of the local press.

The totality of the clergyman's life, and the fact that the understanding of his vocation and priesthood embraces his whole life, leads to a situation in which there are few acknowledged boundaries in a clergyman's life and work. It can be seen in George Herbert's book that he regarded his family life and his parish ministry as closely interrelated, to the point where his parish ministry was an extension of his family life (and his choice of a wife was in part determined by such considerations). There is a sense in which to ask a clergyman how many hours he works is not a relevant or easily answered question because he sees no division between work and leisure, family and parish. Many of the understandings that dominate the priestly role predate the concept of leisure (which in its modern form dates from the mid nineteenth century), and refer to a time when the ascriptive nature of roles (see Chapter 2) was dominant. It is probably the parts of Herbert's book that concern his family life that are the most difficult reading today, as clergy are encouraged to insulate their family life from what can be seen as the all-demanding nature of parish ministry. The clergyman is sometimes described as being in a 'bigamous relationship', that is to say, he has an absolute loyalty to his wife and family and also to his priestly vocation. This total understanding of ministry is reflected in the 1662 Ordinal in which the priest is instructed that he and his family should be 'wholesome examples and patterns to the flock of Christ'. The lack of boundaries, the fact that his work life can seem to have a domestic nature, or that his domestic life suffers from the constant intrusion of his work, is a prominent feature of traditional roles, and is another point at which the clergyman's role is similar to that of the farmer.

The fact that priesthood is fundamentally an ecclesiastical status rather than a functional role provides a further set of difficulties, which become apparent when a clergyman is asked to explain what he does. The fact that there is no simple answer to that question, and the fact that in an advanced society most people's identity is defined by their single coherent answer, poses significant problems, and many clergy feel the pressure of not being able to define their role in a way readily understood by others. This has been reinforced by the fact that some country clergy have been better known for their leisure activities than for their pastoral ministrations. Until relatively recently advertisements for country livings could be found in the columns of *Horse and Hound*; and the *Church Times* (30 June 1967) contained the following advertisement:

> Old-fashioned Vicar (Tractarian) seeks colleague. Left-hand fast bowler preferred. Good golf handicap an asset but not essential. Fine Church with good musical tradition. Parish residential and farming. Box H.V. 521.

In advanced society many traditional roles have effectively been defined as non-work, and this is particularly so in the case of the clergyman's role. This is reinforced by the advent of non-stipendiary ministry, as has been noted in Chapter 5, which carries with it the implication that the clergyman's role can be fulfilled as a part-time leisure-occupation. Whilst many clergy can live with the ambiguities which result from this, others find it necessary to seek refuge either in conspicuous busyness or in a substitute ministry. Many of the major voluntary organizations concerned with housing, social welfare, counselling, as well as part-time teaching, will find parish clergy well represented in their numbers. Whilst there is a long tradition of Anglican country clergy who have diverse interests and wide sympathies, care has to be exercised to make sure that these do not become a substitute for the main task of ministry in the parish, and move into the centre of a clergyman's life and concern. For instance, George Herbert, when he came to Bemerton, still retained some of his literary and musical interests, but there can be little doubt that his life was focused on the worship and ministry of his parish. Conspicuous busyness can be a response to both ambiguities about the clergyman's role and a desire to escape from the impress of the constant demands of the parish. Because open availability to the needs of parishioners can be mistaken by some for a leisurely and undemanding ministry, it is common for clergy to surround themselves with an atmosphere of bustle and relentless activity.

For Herbert, as for almost all parish clergymen, accepting a rural ministry meant the voluntary embracing of a life lived within narrow confines. In Herbert's time, when very few people lived other than a local life, such would have been expected and anticipated (though of course Herbert himself was an exception to this, having lived in Cambridge and London and been involved in the life of the university and the court). Today, when many people's lives are lived with a wide horizon and involve much travelling, to spend one whole working life in a small confine is part of the distinctiveness of rural ministry. In a world of fast-moving international events and concerns, the challenge of the ordinary, the prosaic and the everyday 'bringing the light of the gospel to those in your care' can seem a compressed and small-scale activity and consequently can appear to lack importance. In a world where many work with instant access to international means of communication, the priest on his bicycle seems an irrelevant and outmoded figure. Clergy work contains none of those things that appear to give importance to so many other people; no filled diary or attendant secretary; neither the urgency of the fax machine nor the importance of the chauffeur-driven car to the breakfast meeting; all those things which can make other jobs seem urgent and important. Many clergy find it difficult to reconcile the words of the Ordinal with the sameness and pettiness of much village life, the relentlessness and trivia of some aspects of clerical duty, and the everyday smallness of a country parish. But being a priest is a craft work and can only be done on a small scale, touching at any depth only the lives of a relatively few people. It is personal work, as George Herbert makes clear, dealing with the joys and the sorrows, the anger and the grief of people and communities; a life in which the needs and demands of others set the agenda and the timetable.

By contrast with the busyness and activity of the life of a country clergyman today, Bishop Hensley Henson wrote, in 1945:

> The majority of country clergy are no doubt underpaid, but they are also generally inadequately employed. They loiter through life in discomfort and discontent, steadily degenerating as age strengthens their prejudices, diminishes their powers and destroys the effect of such efforts as they make.

But at about the same time Canon Charles Forder wrote in his book, *The Parish Priest* (1949), of the daily timetable of a clergyman:

> Prayer will occupy the time from early rising until 9 or 9.30 a.m., with a short interval for breakfast. After day school, an hour or more for administration, leaving two hours or more for study before lunch. A short rest, with or without a book, is wise after lunch, and parochial activity occupies the afternoon. Tea and evensong will follow, and another short spell of administration. The evening is devoted to parochial organisations, but sometimes there are opportunities for study and visiting.

In examples such as this lie the roots of the ceaseless activity of many clergy today and the rise of the 'all day, every day' priest, a prey to workaholism. The ancient division of the clerical day into various parts, along the lines of monastic communities, in which adequate time was allowed for rest and relaxation, has much to commend it. A recent visit to a parish to assess the needs of that parish, before a new clergyman was appointed, led to an exercise in which the expectations of that clergyman were set down. In the end, it was found that if he was to satisfy all expectations, he would be working one hundred and forty hours per week.

'Will you strive to fashion your life . . . to be an example of Christ to your flock?'. The centre of George Herbert's message and the inescapable truth about the priesthood is that what matters above all else is the quality of the clergyman's own life. Parishioners, when they are consulted about a new clergyman, almost invariably lay the greatest stress upon his personal qualities rather than any skills that he may have acquired, and clergy know in their hearts the uncomfortable truth that it is who we are as people that matters most in priestly ministry. The priest who truly radiates the love of God in his parish will be forgiven almost everything else. He may preach incomprehensible sermons of great length, be a hopeless organizer, and be quite unable to remember anyone's name, but all this, and much else, will be forgiven him if he communicates in his own person something of the love and presence of Christ. This is why ministry is such an exposed and therefore costly, uncomfortable and sacrificial way of life.

The complaints that are made about clergymen, and those that are made by clergymen themselves, throw an interesting light on the changes which have transformed the country clergyman's role in the last hundred years. In the mid nineteenth century, the new standards required of the clergy, both by Parliamentary reform and by the desire of the more energetic clergy, that all should embrace improved and more spiritual standards, meant that it was the secularity of the clergy that was widely criticized at that time. There are few more perceptive assessments of this change than in Anthony Trollope's picture of the Reverend Mark Robarts in *Framley Parsonage* (1861). As he recorded in this novel, to the vast majority it was no longer acceptable for a clergyman to move easily and familiarly in secular society and to be a participant in its recreations. 'The young lady', wrote one clergyman, 'will scarcely care to recognise as her proper spiritual guide and friend, her partner at last week's Ball; and the dancing priest may well find it difficult to assume at once his ministerial character towards those with whom he has shared the small talk and trivial things of a cricket or archery club ball.'

Bishop Blomfield's biographer wrote: 'In character, habits, attainment, social position, and general reputation, the ordinary clergyman of 1860 is a very different being from the clergyman in 1810.' Speaking generally, the remark of Mr Thomas Grenville, who died in 1846 at the age of 91, may be taken as true, that no change which had taken place in his lifetime was so great as the change in the clergy of the Church of England. Thus, by the second half of the nineteenth century, certainly among those clergy influenced by the Tractarian and Evangelical movements, new standards were required which emphasized the distinctiveness and the sacramental and spiritual character of the clergyman's role. Whilst, in the previous century, many clergy, such as those whom Jane Austen knew, were indistinguishable in lay society, by the second half of the nineteenth century the clergyman was called upon to be distinct, recognizable and increasingly to conform to a pattern of behaviour and style of life to which the name 'the rectory culture' was eventually given. As a consequence, the clergy increasingly found themselves distanced from the mainstream of rural society and its activities, and it is from this time that concerns are first expressed about the loneliness and isolation of the country clergy. For many, the acceptance of loneliness was simply part of the costliness of the priestly vocation. However, this was often exacerbated by the fact that many country clergy served for long periods in a single parish. Whilst such ministries were often highly valued, nonetheless there was an ever-present danger that as the years progressed, a clergyman would lose his enthusiasm and dedication. This is well described by Canon Wilfrid Browning:

> Parishes notice a creeping staleness and loss of previous enthusiasm; punctuality is no longer a strong point; he is less diligent about visiting the bereaved: does not bother to see that the linen is spotlessly clean; is eager to assert any authority in the remaining areas where a clergyman has authority by being difficult with 'fringers'; impatient of

criticism, he is himself very critical of 'the diocese', much
given to days off and long holidays abroad; not too
scrupulous about what is charged to the parish expenses . . .
perhaps the most sinister temptation of all is for the priest to
suppose that he has a God-given right to be exempt from
any kind of suffering.

However, by the end of the century it was not their secularity
which caused comment, both among the clergy and the laity,
but the circumstances and conditions under which many of
the clergy now worked. The rising numbers of parochial clergy
during the second half of the nineteenth century inevitably
led to circumstances in which clergy were inducted to livings
that comprised a single small parish with an equally small
income. The poverty of the clergy was exacerbated by the fact
that much clerical income was derived either from the rent of
glebe land or from tithes. At a time of agricultural depression,
when wealthy landowners could afford to mitigate and in
some cases set aside rents, the clergyman, dependent on the
rent of a small farm, found himself in a difficult position in
which he had to negotiate with neighbouring farmers, who
were themselves parishioners, and in some cases, churchwardens. Discerning laity, such as Rider Haggard in Suffolk,
saw that the poverty of the clergy was now a serious problem
for the rural church. He wrote in 1899:

> The poor parsons, how will they manage to survive, I
> wonder? It is undoubtedly to the advantage of this parish
> that a clergyman should be able to keep up a modest
> position; that he should not be notoriously struggling with
> debts or out at the elbows. Yet in eight cases out of ten, how
> is he to do so in these days?

For many clergy, the benefice house provided a further
problem. Rectories and vicarages varied enormously in their
size and standard, but many were now too large or too
dilapidated to be maintained on such slender clerical incomes.
In the eighteenth century, clergy had been able to borrow
money (from Queen Anne's Bounty) against the value of the
benefice, to build houses which were larger than might have

been built in other circumstances and which mirrored the tastes and style of the manor rather than the farmhouse. In the nineteenth century, the prosperity of the clergy, particularly in the high farming years, allowed for the extension or rebuilding of many of these houses. Thus, by the last quarter of the nineteenth century, many benefices had houses which were over-large, and slender clerical incomes meant that such houses had not been adequately maintained for a number of years. The system of 'dilapidations', whereby the outgoing clergyman (or not infrequently the deceased clergyman's estate or his widow) paid a sum of money to the incoming clergyman in respect of such deterioration as had taken place in the building during the period of his occupancy, was a system guaranteed to cause disputes frequently ending in legal action. However, in many cases the outgoing clergyman or his widow did not possess the means to pay these dilapidations.

The widespread augmentation of rural livings in the period after the First World War, the slow reduction of the number of clergy working in the countryside in the inter-war years, the widespread recognition that clergy should be paid working expenses, the improvement in clergy pensions and retirement regulations, all had the effect of making concern for the clergyman's financial welfare a diminishing problem in the twentieth century. Though in relative terms clergy stipends are still low, the gradual removal of the disparities between what were previously regarded as 'rich livings' and 'poor livings' has been a considerable achievement. Today, all beneficed clergy are paid the same amount, with the consequence that those with young families and wives who remain at home to look after their children find themselves in very straitened financial circumstances, whereas those towards the end of their career, whose children have left home and whose wives have a job, find themselves enjoying a standard of living which many country clergy have not known for over a century.

Today, the complaints of the clergy tend to be not about secularity or about the terms and conditions of their employment, but centre upon the perception of the clergy as being an occupational group under stress. A number of books, conferences and seminars have focused attention on the problems of clerical stress, clerical 'burn-out' and 'priestly fatigue'. Such discussions concentrate on two aspects of the problem, first that many clergy find themselves over-busy in a job which has no easily defined boundaries. The demands made upon the modern rural clergyman, who may be looking after three or more country parishes, are extensive. If generations ago a clergyman's life was seen to be one of quiet, calm reflection, today the average clergyman spends his week responding to a wide range of demands made upon him and his time. Second, the clergyman's role is seen as lacking in support, and there is much demand for increasing contact with bishops and archdeacons, who are required to provide counsel and support (often in contexts described as 'assessment and evaluation') of a type which was unknown to the clergy in previous generations. Clearly, clergy stress arises from a wide range of factors but it may be suggested that one of the principal causes lies in the lack of clarity which many have about their role. In an earlier chapter (see page 4) it was noted that an experienced country priest has written 'time and again we met clergy who are bewildered, frustrated, unclear about what they should be doing'. It may be suggested that this uncertainty about the content of the clergyman's role today is the principal source of frustration and stress for many clergy.

The effect of stress on clergy, particularly in mid-career, takes a number of recognizable forms. For some it manifests itself in the adoption of an alternative ministry but for others it can be recognized in such responses as a retreat into invalidism or domesticity or the advocacy of extreme opinions and constant criticism of 'the diocese' and its representatives. For others it can take the form of adopting a confrontational attitude towards the parish and thus being constantly 'at odds' with the PCC or 'being difficult' with individual parishioners. As can be seen from the above, many pressures have been brought to bear upon the clergyman's role in recent years, and he now contends with difficulties and circumstances which George Herbert could have neither known nor anticipated. Nonetheless, what he describes remains the essential core of the country clergyman's role, and the four principal tasks outlined in the previous chapter remain the centre of rural ministry wherever it is practised.

But what sort of man is the modern country clergyman today? Being a priest is not a job in any conventional sense, but is more accurately described as a way of life; a life based on prayerfulness and formed by the disciplined simplicity of Anglican worship. People rightly desire to see in their clergy, both in their faces and in their behaviour, a sincere desire to serve God with a disciplined heart and mind, so that they can receive from them a sense of the holiness, trust and faithfulness, which comes from the knowledge and love of God. The modern country clergyman needs to communicate in his own person a thoughtful holiness that makes God both real and accessible to the people around him. The awareness of God, and the sense of his working in the world, together with a deep experience of prayer, a strength of conviction and an inner calm, are all qualities that are looked for in the modern country clergyman. These will only be achieved in a life that is centred and focused in prayer, in which prayer and worship are important, and through which others can recover a sense of reverence and holiness.

His life is one of unproclaimed self-discipline and pervasive prayerfulness. For any clergyman, what ultimately matters is not what is written or spoken but what a person actually is. Any long-serving church member in a rural area can recount the way in which the life of a particular parish has gone up and down, and a principal factor that determined these movements is the personality of the clergyman. He should radiate not frustration or anger (though these he may feel from time to time) but a quiet happiness and a strength that comes, not from toughness, but from dignity, integrity, stability, and friendliness, abundant good nature and quiet enthusiasm. He must be the master of himself, modest, self-contained, abstemious, reflective, self-effacing, calm and unhurried, gentle and courteous. He must readily accept his own strengths and weaknesses. He must have the ability to handle criticism, rejection and conflict, which will at times call for deep reserves of moral courage to resist what others might regard as the consensus of right-thinking opinion. In this, he must not

develop a hard outer shell, which can lead to a form of
spiritual and emotional enamelling, whereby things may be
said and done which might seem appropriate, though it is
clear to all that the heart is not in it. He will need to avoid that
smugness and self-satisfaction which has been the bane of
religious people in all generations. He will need to develop
ways of moving through the local community that do not draw
overmuch attention to himself, in a low profile but recognizable manner. A gentle but vigorous spirituality, and a
patient, unobtrusive yet painstaking pastoral care are his
hallmark.

Inevitably, following the way of Christ will bring suffering.
Archbishop Michael Ramsey said to a conference in Bristol in
1963: 'In your service of others you will feel, you will care, you
will be hurt, you will have your heart broken. And it is
doubtful if any of us can do anything at all until we have been
very much hurt, and until our hearts have been very much
broken.' It is a truth of the gospel that Christ calls into his
service wounded men and women, and sometimes those
wounds are both obvious and painful. Not least of the wounds
are those of being misunderstood and having one's motives
questioned, for forbearance can often seem like weakness;
thoughtfulness and reflection can seem like indecisiveness.
God asks impossible things of improbable people, but it is he
who gives them, as he gave George Herbert, the strength to
understand and fulfil their task.

9

The Future of the Rural Church

The English country clergyman has a long history, but now questions are being urgently asked about whether he will have a future. In much that has been written about the future of the rural church clergy have sought to lift the curtain and anticipate what lies ahead. Almost all such writing makes depressing reading, and portrays a Church in which the number of clergy in rural areas will continue to decline, a growing number of parishes will be unable to raise sufficient money to maintain the present pattern of church life, and it will be necessary to make an increasing number of rural churches redundant. At the same time it portrays a Church which is becoming increasingly distanced from its historic understandings and roots in the local community, and is taking on many of the principal features of an urban sect.

Whilst there are many lively and vigorous churches in rural areas, it is certainly true that there are some which are dismal and depressing, which communicate little of the presence of God and the joy of Christian living, and to whose worship people only go under a deep sense of duty. Such writing varies from the elegiac to the angry; from the plaintive to the outright protest. In the main, it offers few insights into the future of the rural church; clergy are portrayed as having to cope as best they can with an increasing number of parishes and being more firmly chained to a treadmill of fund-raising activities. But the fact remains that the parish has proved a remarkably durable social institution; and despite the impact of much writing in the 1970s and 1980s which prophesied, and in some cases demanded, its demise, the parish and parochial ministry remains at the centre of the Church's life. It is noticeable that most of this writing comes from the pens of clergy who tend to underestimate the durability of the parish and the loyalty of country people to their church. There is about the faithfulness of rural Christians to their church a doggedness, an unsinkability, which clergy often underestimate, or rather, mistake for unthinking conservatism. Whilst they may be inclined to criticize certain aspects of country parishes and the prominence which the maintenance of the church building assumes, nonetheless it is these characteristics which have maintained the church in the countryside not just from natural decay but from those who have planned a very different future for the rural church.

Twenty-five years ago it was confidently predicted that church life in rural Norfolk could not be sustained and that there would have to be a widespread closure of churches and a rationalization of the ecclesiastical network. Twenty-five years later not one of the ten churches in the Hilborough Group of parishes, which serves approximately 1,600 people in West Norfolk, has been closed. Those who made such prophecies have been proved mistaken, partly by the determination of country people that this should be so, partly by the faithfulness of the clergy who have served in these areas, but also by the new levels of support available for church buildings (particularly through English Heritage), and through the widespread development of multi-parish benefices, which are the heirs to the understandings of ministry developed in the East Anglian rural group and team ministries of the 1960s and 1970s. The multi-parish benefice has come to be seen not just as an expedient born of the declining numbers of stipendiary clergy but as a realistic way in which to adapt the ancient structures of the Church of England.

Perhaps the greatest single problem arises from the belief that the Anglican parish system in rural areas is a static system. Chapter 5 has attempted to show the ways in which parishes have adapted and changed over the centuries. Whilst, in the late medieval period, there was almost certainly a resident priest in almost every parish, this situation did not recur until a short period in the last quarter of the nineteenth century and the years before the First World War. In the intervening centuries the parochial system changed in many ways, as it did before the late medieval period, and as it has done in recent years. The belief that it has been a single static system is not supported by a consideration of the Church's history. The rural church has always been in the process of change and development. In the future rural ministry will continue to be based upon holy places and sacred persons (on the church buildings and on the clergy) as it has been in the past. The way in which these are organized will depend in large measure on the impact of a number of changes which are not necessarily specific to rural areas; these will include changes in the nature of the Church itself; changes to the Church's structure; changes in the number of clergy and changes in the Church's finances; and, of equal importance, changes to the countryside itself (already considered in Chapter 6). Four areas of change can be identified.

First, until relatively recently, the dominant ethos of the Church of England arose from its rural ministry, and at parish level, the church was a community church which sought to embrace as many of the local community as was possible. It was a Church which had a firm centre, but which had low thresholds and boundaries; it was an inclusive Church rather than an exclusive Church and one that was frequently criticized for making few demands either doctrinally or organizationally. The Church of England's desire for inclusiveness rather than exclusiveness has meant that it has sought to define the few essentials of the faith but not to seek definition in inessential areas. At the same time, the clergyman was aware of offering a ministry to the whole parish rather than to just the worshipping congregation. The extent to which the modern country clergyman is willing to do this is one aspect of his ministry which will be prominently commented on by parishioners. In some places the Church's response to increasing cultural and religious pluralism has been a desire to define the Church more closely, both from the theological and the organizational point of view. In an age of cultural complexity and rapid social change, in which fewer generally agreed reference points remain, there has been a tendency for the Church to meet this erosion of old certainties with more assertive and exclusive statements. The Church has found it necessary to protect its own identity against the threat of corrosive secularism on the one hand and against the rise of non-Christian anthropocentric religious cults, characteristic of 'new age' religion, on the other. Much 'new age' religion is either implicitly or directly hostile to Christianity as it is itself a protest against the scientific and world-affirming approach to religion which has characterized Christianity from the Renaissance onwards.

The Anglican tradition of openness, tolerance, low thresholds and a desire to be the religious focus of the whole community, has been replaced in many places by a more exclusive, sharply defined and membership-orientated form of church life. Some writers have written recently of the dangers of Anglicanism being transformed into an urban sect with tight boundaries and a closely defined membership, who attempt to put a ring fence around the faith and keep it free from contamination that might come either from secularity or from other faiths. By contrast, the church in the typical village comprises a small core of practising Anglicans surrounded by a much larger body who look to the parish church with affection and feel that in some sense they belong to it; but it is a church from which they normally stay away. However, neither the Church of England nor they themselves are inclined to define them as not being members of the Church of England. Among the committed there are many whose grasp of the fundamental tenets of the Christian faith is at best uncertain, and there are among the 'nominals' and members of the fringe a number who have deep religious convictions. Much of the criticism of modern church practice arises from those on the fringe who feel that the Church of England is more ready to draw boundaries and more inclined to define belonging in terms of active participatory membership. Traditionally, Anglicanism has always been sensitive and sympathetic to that which others have called 'folk religion', but which is often an expression of that part of the gospel which emphasizes God's generosity and compassion for all people.

The *second* area of change, which is significantly affecting the rural church and will profoundly affect its future, concerns changes in the Church's structure. In George Herbert's time the Church was predominantly a local organization. Though parishes were set within a diocese and a parochial clergyman swore obedience to the diocesan bishop as his ordinary, in reality parishes operated as almost wholly independent units within large dioceses, whose bishop spent much of his time in London. To take an example from a slightly later period, although Parson Woodforde assiduously attended the annual archdeacon's visitation, he was in the presence of his bishop on only one occasion during his long ministry in Norfolk. The rise of the diocese, and beyond it, a sense of the Church of England as a national organization, are relatively recent phenomena; the former owes much to the educational and missionary societies of the nineteenth century, which were the first to create a diocesan network of local representatives. In the last years of the nineteenth century, Archbishop Benson wrote to Westcott: 'Diocesanism is a new force of dissent as virulent as congregationalism—and more.' It is only in this century, as the diocese became increasingly responsible for the financing of the Church's ministry, that the diocese became a significant structure in the life of the local church.

Today, there is a marked divergence between those who believe that the Church's survival is dependent upon a strong centralized organization within the Church to control ministry, finance and other matters, and those who believe that the Church should return to its essentially local nature and that much of what happens at national and at diocesan level could be devolved to the local church. There is a desire among some lay people to see the Church of England decentralized, particularly in matters of finance; and the devolution of financial control to the dioceses (as advocated in the report *Faith in the Countryside*) would return the Church to a situation with which George Herbert was familiar where the clergyman was paid from money derived from local sources. Democratic forms of government in the Church have a long history. In the diocese of Oxford under Bishop Wilberforce (and in the diocese of Lincoln under Bishop Wordsworth) a synodical style of government was pioneered in the teeth of much opposition from those who resisted a new model of church polity. The eventual legal implementation of synodical government in 1972 was an attempt to achieve a more democratic approach to church government, with the authority and power of bishops and clergy balanced by that of the House of Laity. There is little doubt that the trend towards lay control and decentralization of the Church (which has its roots in the Reformation) will continue to increase, not least because of its relationship to financial issues.

The *third* area of change which will substantially affect the rural church concerns the number of the stipendiary clergy. As has been seen, there was a considerable contraction in the number of clergy working in rural areas during the 1970s and 1980s. One clergyman commented that this was a change on a level of significance comparable with the Black Death. In rural areas, between 1885 and 1969, there was a 25% drop in the number of clergy; but the rate was already accelerating towards the latter years, and, in the period 1969 to 1991, there was a 26% decline. At the present time the number of ordinations remains relatively static at approximately 350 per year (men and women). The decline in the number of clergy (between 1992 and 1994 the overall picture will change by a decline of 170 men but an addition of 80 women) continues as a result of the relatively high number of retirements and the significant number of clergy withdrawing from ministry or taking early retirement (in 1991, this figure was nearly as high as the number of those ordained in that year). The Rural Church Project revealed that approximately a quarter of the clergy in rural areas are over 60 (compared with 15% in urban areas), and that approximately 20% of the clergy in rural areas are late ordinands (i.e. ordained after their fortieth year), as compared with 5% in urban areas. Together with this higher percentage of older and late entry clergy, a quarter of those ministering in rural areas have no previous rural experience.

The decline in the total number of clergy ministering in the Church of England (see pages 124–5) particularly affects rural areas. It is indicated that the number of ordinations, and the present age structure of the clergy, suggest that there will be a 10% decline in the number of stipendiary clergy in the next fifteen years. There is evidence to suggest that, if present policies continue, this will be translated into a 20% decline in most rural areas.

Without doubt, the recent decision of the Church of England to proceed to the ordination of women to the priesthood will have a major impact on rural areas. At present, whilst the number of male candidates for stipendiary ministry is in decline, there is an increase in the number of female candidates. At the same time, it is suggested that there will be a significant increase in the number of women who offer themselves for non-stipendiary ministry in rural areas. It is not easy to assess the future impact of the ordination of women to the priesthood on the countryside: on the one hand, many country parishes are still traditional in their liturgical and ministerial preferences, and do not see themselves agreeing to the appointment of a woman as their next incumbent; on the other hand, country people are above all else realistic and practical and, if faced with the possibility of a long vacancy at the vicarage, might afford an enthusiastic welcome to a woman priest. Such evidence as exists is at best contradictory: the survey undertaken by the Rural Church Project indicates that only 29% of churchgoers were happy about receiving the chalice from a lay person, whereas 91% of those questioned were prepared to accept Holy Communion celebrated by a woman.

The experience of other churches indicates that, in the main, women find their first ministerial opportunities in rural areas. Concern has been expressed in North American churches, where women principally minister in rural areas, and men appear to be appointed to the majority of urban posts. The setting up of ministerial teams will assist women in finding appointments alongside male colleagues (as has happened in other occupations). The larger benefices of the future (see pages 226−8) may prefer to have both a male and female member of staff, whose complimentary talents and abilities will strengthen the work of ministry in that area. Without doubt the appointment of women priests to stipendiary appointments in rural areas will change many established patterns and understandings. Not least, the male clergy spouse is unlikely to be prepared to accept the expectations formerly entertained (and in some cases demanded) of the vicar's wife.

Finance is the *fourth* factor likely to have a considerable impact upon the Church in the coming decades. There is increasing concern in some rural areas that the present financial arrangements under which the Church operates will not be sustainable in the long term. Over the years the situation has changed in a way that was graphically illustrated by one of those who presented evidence to the Archbishops' Rural Commission. He pointed out that a hundred years ago the clergyman was the main provider of charity and assistance in the parish, whilst, today, he is (indirectly) the main object for which money is raised. In every country parish a large sum of money (often equivalent to half of the total income of the parish) has to be sent to the diocese in order that the clergyman's stipend can be paid. It is noticeable in recent years that the number of parishes unable to meet their quota in full has risen in some dioceses. The pattern is uneven, but there are some dioceses where a significant proportion of the budgeted income is not received. It should be recalled that in every generation people have claimed that the financial arrangements of the Church cannot continue in their present state much longer, but there is cause for more serious concern today. This is principally because the sums are so much larger (the notional cost of a clergyman in post is approximately £25,000). Several dioceses have been forced to cut back on the number of full-time posts for financial reasons; the impact of these cuts is often felt first in rural areas.

At the same time, country parishes do seem able to continue to raise large sums of money for the maintenance of the church building. It is not uncommon to find small parishes, with a population of under three hundred, raising sums of money over a period of years equivalent to £500 for every person living in the parish. However, even in this area there is competition in fund-raising with national charities, and the increasingly active fund-raising carried out on behalf of the local school. It is particularly difficult to generalize in this area, but there is no doubt that there are many parishes in which finance is becoming an increasing problem, and it may well be that financial considerations will play a significant part in shaping the Church of the future.

The future of the rural church will not be the same in every place; just as parishes differ today, so there will be significant differences in the future, reflecting the impact of the changes noted above, as well as the history of the parishes and the personality and preferences of the clergy. However, at a simple level, it is possible to suggest *three scenarios of the future of the rural church* and the role of the clergyman, which may be found side by side in adjacent parishes.

The *first* scenario may be called the *centralist* scenario, for it is based on assumptions which stress the importance of maintaining and building up a strong centre and a strong central organization from which the life of the Church can radiate out into the more distant rural parishes. As has been seen above, many of the trends and tendencies within the Church in recent years have been in the direction of centralization. This is particularly noticeable in the area of finance and decision-making. Until relatively recently parishes operated as if they were individual entities (which in law they remain) within the framework of diocesan structures. The diocese itself made little impact on the life of a parish beyond the demand that the clergyman and churchwardens attend the archdeacon's visitation and an occasional visit to a confirmation held in one of the larger churches in the area. The payment of clergy was a local matter in that their income was derived from glebe and tithe. As has been seen, much of this changed in the early decades of the twentieth century, as the diocese became a much more significant structure in the life of a local parish and the payment of the clergy became a matter handled by the centre through the Church Commissioners and the Diocesan Board of Finance. Parishes were aware of themselves as members of a diocesan network to which they had to pay increasingly large contributions. Despite the Anglican tradition of dispersed authority and power, the growth of synodical government, and the attention that the Synod and its leaders have received in the media, have made the Church seem a more centralized organization, and conversely have made country parishes seem far removed from the centre of power and decision making within the Church.

Centralism, in any organization, is frequently regarded as a response to decline, for the pruning of the network, the limiting of the operational front, the concentration of resources in the most effective areas, are all responses to contraction and decline. It has been acknowledged, since the early decades of this century, that the level at which services and facilities can economically be offered in villages has steadily risen and the cost of acceptable minimum facilities has been increasing. Particularly in education and medicine, the only way of providing these facilities is by concentrating them on certain key or selected settlements. In this country, in the work of Harold Peake, who came to the forefront of rural planning affairs at the end of the First World War, and Henry Morris, who was Chief Education Officer for Cambridgeshire between 1922 and 1954, can be seen a determination to concentrate facilities and services in selected rural centres and for them to serve an extensive rural hinterland. In the United States and in Germany, W. Christaller and A. Lösch had developed theories and models of rural development, in the early decades of this century, which suggested that facilities and services could be provided where there was a 'critical threshold population' to create the necessary demand. Thus it was possible to create models of rural development based on hierarchies of settlements and needs, which took account of the fact that more specialized services required larger catchment areas.

The first country structure plans of the early 1970s reflected these insights (known as central place theory), for they uniformly proposed the selection and development of 'service centres' (variously known as capital, key or category A villages). Public investment, in the form of schools and council houses (still being built at that time), was directed to these selected settlements, which were also designated for residential and industrial development. By concentrating the provision of all but the most basic services in such centres it was suggested that a rural area was able to retain a degree of integrity and autonomy, and not become completely subordinate, in economic and social terms, to the neighbouring town. The key or selected settlement policy can be regarded as the principal agent of planned change in post-war rural Britain, although its implementation has not been without continued controversy.

Christaller's work was criticized for according little significance to topography (he developed his theories in the American Midwest), and more recently, commentators have suggested that the rigid implementation of this policy has been detrimental to the larger key villages, which have been greatly increased in size over too short a time span; and to the smaller settlements, which have experienced very strict control on their development, and in some cases have experienced population decline.

As the Church, in some ways, can be seen as being similar to other service providers, the logic of this argument has commended itself to some people in the rural church, who believe that the Church's future lies in concentrating its resources in the larger villages and market towns. One of the effects of the Pastoral Measure 1968 was to establish in every diocese a pastoral committee. In the early 1970s many of these committees produced strategy documents which were, in a real sense, the ecclesiastical equivalents of the country structure plans. These documents (Hereford 1971; Coventry 1972; Bath and Wells, and Worcester 1973; Exeter 1974) were in effect a management plan for the diocese, which in many cases involved the establishment of a management structure, the centralization of resources and the pruning of the extensive network of country churches; for the Pastoral Measure 1968 had introduced the possibility of declaring a church to be redundant as a regular place of worship. There were many who believed that the large number of rural churches, particularly in some of the remote areas, were one of the major hindrances to the effectiveness of the Church's ministry. In many dioceses, plans were adopted to prune, selectively, the Church's rural network, and lists were compiled of churches designated for redundancy. (However, it was found that when a rural church discovered that its name was on this list, this had a galvanizing effect on local church life.) Nevertheless, a significant number of rural churches have been declared redundant (between 1969 and 1984 the national total was 1,002). Eighty churches have been declared redundant in the Lincoln diocese, which, together with Norwich, has a very large number of medieval churches, many of them situated in small hamlets.

The second element in this centralist approach to the rural church concerned the rural dean and the rural deanery. Leslie Paul had placed much stress on the deanery as the basic area of the Church's operation, and had called rural deans 'bishops in little'. John Adair advocated the adoption of the deanery as the basic pastoral unit of the Church, saying: 'Central to my proposed policy is the concept of a team ministry based upon the deanery unit. The dean should be the leader of the ministry team in this area.' This accords with the work done by the Institute of Agricultural Economics in North Oxfordshire in the early 1940s, and its report is remarkable in that many of its central proposals anticipated those found in the report of John Tiller, *A Strategy for the Church's Ministry*, 1983. Although only seven of the 160 pages of this report are directly devoted to rural ministry, Tiller portrays a future which combines both centralist and localist elements. In his report, the stipendiary clergy would form a deanery team under the rural dean and be deployable throughout the deanery, but ministry at the local level would be the responsibility of a locally ordained ministry.

Such centralist theories, which depend upon the creation of strong intermediate units between the diocese and the parish (either the deanery or teams or groups), are often portrayed as clericalist and professionalist solutions to the problem of the rural church. In practice, the problems of patronage and freehold made it very difficult (certainly in the short term) to implement many of the recommendations found in the diocesan strategy documents of the mid 1970s. By contrast, in the Methodist Church a parallel policy was widely adopted; many small chapels were closed and ministry and membership were centralized in such market towns and key villages as Downham Market. The experience of this and other reorganizations was that, although a strong church was created in the market town, the membership of this church was not comparable with the aggregate membership of the small chapels that had been closed. Whilst it was possible to transfer ministry and money, it was found that membership was in many cases non-transferable.

In some dioceses, some aspects of the mid-1970s strategies have been implemented, but often in the face of much local opposition. In recent years, it has been noticeable that in the Church (and in other voluntary organizations), people's commitment to the organization has polarized to the larger scale unit (the diocese) and to the smaller unit (the parish). This is partly because these two structures coincide with people's pattern of belonging and commitments. They belong to the diocese, as the *unit of identification*, and, identify strongly with the person of the bishop, and, to a limited extent, with the diocese as an organization. At the same time, the local parish is the *unit of participation* in which they belong by direct personal involvement. In almost all organizations it is the intermediate units that have suffered in recent years, principally because they do not coincide with people's pattern of belonging. Although occasional clerical pleas for the widespread closure of rural churches can still be heard, it is now more widely acknowledged that the church is a local organization, and that its strength comes from people's loyalty to small scale and local organizations.

It is sometimes pointed out that people will travel many miles to shop and for recreational and other purposes, and, therefore, they should be willing to do the same in order to attend a central church which serves a large rural hinterland. However, the tradition of rural Anglicanism is that of a local, face-to-face, community, and such suggestions rarely receive a sympathetic response from parishioners. Others sometimes point to the fact that members of other denominations are willing to travel considerable distances to attend a Roman Catholic or a Baptist church, as a consequence of strong denominational loyalty. In the case of the Roman Catholic Church a more appropriate analogy is with church practice in rural France or rural Spain where the expectations and practices are similar to rural Anglicanism. That is to say that because Church membership is, in some part, an expression of local community life (in Anglican terms, the tradition of Hooker and George Herbert) people expect to attend worship within their own community. The acknowledgement of this tradition, to which much of the thinking in the 1970s and 1980s was a reaction, is now more widely held in rural dioceses, and the expectation that large numbers of rural churches would be closed is now less frequently heard.

Following the principles of central place theory which has dominated rural planning in recent decades, there have been a number of advocates of a new style of rural ministry based on the market towns. In practice, the centralist approach manifests itself in advocating the retreat of the rural church to the market towns or key villages, and the setting up of a collegiate style of ministry, sometimes called a minster ministry on the pattern of the Anglo-Saxon minsters (see pages 161–2). From the market town or key village a number of clergy serve a hinterland of small villages and hamlets. This style of ministry was advocated by a number of those who provided evidence for the Archbishops' Rural Commission *Faith in the Country-side* (see pages 1–2). However, as yet it has not been tried in many places, and those who seek to commend such a style often find it difficult to convince the smaller villages and hamlets that the Church is not in effect withdrawing from their communities.

The *second* scenario may be termed the *localist scenario*. As the number of clergy in a rural area has contracted, so the pattern of worship has been affected and, in most areas, a pattern of services has been established that is dictated by the capacity of the clergyman to circulate round the number of churches in his area. This is an essentially centralist solution and one that is being increasingly questioned and rejected in many areas by those who see the Church not as an organization run by professional personnel but as a community based local organization. In many places, in recent years, there has been a discernible rise in the strength of localism within the Church, coming, in part, as a reaction to the centralist policies of the 1970s and 1980s.

The maintenance of the church building has always been a local responsibility, and at no time has significant finance been available either nationally or at diocesan level for the maintenance of country churches. It is true to say that today more outside money is available than at any other time; partly government money available through English Heritage, and an increasing amount of money, though the proportions are much smaller, through the county Historic Churches Trusts, which now play a significant role in many dioceses, not simply as fund-raising organizations, but as a resource of knowledge and expertise, energy and enthusiasm for the care of rural churches. However, in every generation, the responsibility has essentially been a local one. Recently, local rural churches have been asked to take much greater responsibility for their own finances. Until quite recently, certainly within living memory, parochial church councils did not keep accounts that were much more sophisticated than the entries in the register of services. If there were costs these were sometimes met directly from the clergyman's pocket or from the church-wardens. More recently, as parishes have had to contribute to the diocesan budget and have had to pay the clergyman's expenses of office and the general expenses of running the church, so church finances have become much more sophisticated. Many quite small country churches operate on annual budgets of between £3,000 and £5,000 a year and within this is an annual provision for money set aside against major repair works on the church building. Through this area of financial responsibility the local church community has become increasingly aware of itself as an organization with significant responsibilities. The fact that many clergy minister for relatively short periods in the countryside and that each clergyman has come with his own different priorities and understandings of ministry, has led to an attitude in which the churchwardens and leading members of the congregation rightly see themselves as the local guardians of the life and future of that church.

At the same time, in recent years local churches have been encouraged to take greater responsibility for the ministry of the Church as the Church has recovered an understanding of ministry as being the function of the whole Church by virtue of baptism, and the laity have been encouraged to recover and rediscover their own priesthood. As the Church, particularly at the local level, is no longer seen as a professional organization but as an organization similar to other voluntary associational organizations, so its leadership is seen increasingly as a local function. As a consequence, leadership groups under a variety of names (sometimes called the ministry team) have developed in many parishes. These are served and guided by the clergyman, but effectively take increasing responsibility for the life of the local church. Lay people are involved in the leadership of worship, sometimes as readers but often simply as volunteers; at the same time, members of the congregation take an increasing responsibility for the leadership of various aspects of church life and for the general pastoral ministry.

As can be seen in the Tiller Report and other documents, such as the writing of Professor Robin Gill, there is a widespread belief that in future years the rural church will not be served by full-time stipendiary clergy but by non-stipendiary or locally ordained ministers, who will serve either in a spare time or a retirement capacity. It is widely believed that parishes would rather have their own man or woman as an authorized minister, even if that person was only available for a limited amount of time, rather than be joined together in a large clustering of parishes, served by a single stipendiary priest. However, the evidence is at best contradictory, and the researches of the Rural Church Project showed that rural people would rather have a fraction of a stipendiary clergyman than be served by a local ordained minister.

The widespread provision of locally ordained clergy would allow parishes to make their own arrangements about services, without having to fit in with a cluster of neighbouring parishes. There is much evidence that most rural parishes would prefer to have a morning service at around 10 a.m. and, where it is possible, to have a service at the same time every Sunday. Because a locally ordained clergyman would be serving a single small country parish, he would be more visible and more closely related to the community than is possible for a stipendiary clergyman living at some distance. Advocates of this form of ministry often quote examples from the Greek Orthodox Church and from missionary dioceses, where somebody from the village is chosen, sent away for training and ordination, and returns to his old job but is now able to act also as the priest within the local community. Local ministry has been taken up in a number of rural dioceses, especially Lincoln, where considerable emphasis is placed upon locating a local minister within a team.

There are strong forces within the Church at the moment which react against the centralism of previous decades. The widespread recruitment of local ministers would allow the maintenance of a parish system, in its present form, though many of the assumptions and understandings, which are part of that system, would be challenged by such a departure. Certainly, some are concerned that too strong an emphasis on localism would amount to a return to the parochialism of previous generations. Although some stipendiary clergy remain in their parishes for a long period of time, the average clergyman moves after a period of seven to ten years. By contrast, a non-stipendiary clergyman, ordained in mid life, could well remain in that parish for a further thirty to forty years. There are many questions around the issue of 'how local is local', and whether an entirely fixed and static concept of ministry is entirely compatible with traditional Anglican understandings. In some dioceses, non-stipendiary ministers are now being ordained only if they will agree to minister in other areas than their home parish if required, and, for a number of reasons, the need for the Church to retain some ability to deploy its clergy remains important.

In recent months, a number of dioceses have made statements to the effect that it is the policy of each diocese to provide 'a priest for every parish', and this is the classic expression of the localist scenario. While such a policy may be welcomed by some as bringing to an end the practice of joining parishes together, the Church may again discover, as it did in the late nineteenth century, that many country parishes are too small to operate as single churches in anything but a very restricted sense. As in all things, there is in the church a 'minimal critical size'. Whilst in George Herbert's time, when the church played a part in the lives of all those who lived in the community, clergy could minister in very small units, today larger populations are needed. It is sometimes said that in the modern countryside a total population of around 2,000 constitutes the minimal critical size. That is to say, in units significantly below this number, there is unlikely to be the breadth of support to provide sufficient lay leadership or to enable such things as children's work and youth work to prosper. If the Church's ministry in the countryside was fragmented into very small units, it would be difficult, without some further structure, to ensure the continuation of many of the activities currently found in multi-parish benefices.

Furthermore, the localist solution raises the question of how far small country parishes would cease to feel that they belonged, in any meaningful sense, to the Church as a diocesan, national and worldwide organization.

Some presentations of the localist scenario indicate that the withdrawal of stipendiary ministry from the countryside would lead to the flowering of a whole variety of local and non-stipendiary ministries. There is little in the current practice of the Church to encourage this view. In those places where there has been a significant development of local ministry, it has resulted from the fostering, encouragement and leadership of the stipendiary clergyman. His role in encouraging local ministry is critical.

Furthermore, local voluntary organizations are often the victims of high levels of conflict surrounding particular personalities. The role of the clergyman as 'the man from outside' who is able to provide guidance and leadership within a church community, but from outside, remains important. He is able to bring a wider perspective and vision to a small rural church and prevent it from being imprisoned in its own concerns. The man from outside can prevent the local church from becoming the redoubt of a particular group within the village or the fiefdom of a single family. In Methodism, one of the acknowledged problems of rural churches is that a single person can become so dominant that the church becomes known as 'Mr Smith's chapel'. The provision of ministry exclusively from within the local church is essentially an understanding of ministry which is more compatible with a gathered church. There is a sense in which a community church, which needs to keep itself open to all parts of a dispersed society, needs somebody from outside whose role it is to do this. It is for these reasons that many believe that the rural church of the future will contain a combination of localist and centralist understandings.

The *third* scenario is that of the *multi-parish benefice*, which includes some elements of both of the above. Here, a cluster of country parishes is placed together under the care of a stipendiary clergyman. This may be called a major benefice or is often called today a multi-parish benefice (but owes much to the ideas developed in the East Anglian group and team ministries of the 1960s and 1970s). The life of the Church is neither centralized into the market town nor dispersed into the many small settlements, but is balanced between the development of a ministry team or a community ministry at the centre of the multi-parish benefice, and the encouragement of local church life in the individual parishes. What is clear is that a clergyman serving in such a situation cannot continue to operate in the old style of rural ministry. When two or three parishes were put together, a clergyman was still expected to minister in a traditional way. It has to be appreciated, both by him and by the parishioners, that there is a significant difference between serving two or three parishes and serving a much larger pastoral unit. In order to appreciate that a threshold has been crossed, it is helpful to give such larger units a different name, such as a major parish or a multi-parish benefice, and it is necessary to regard them as a specialist form of ministry different in style from those of older forms of parish ministry. In Oxfordshire a quarter of the clergy serve such benefices, and they meet together regularly to share and develop understandings of this style of ministry.

Clearly, such multi-parish benefices represent a compromise between the centralist and localist tendencies noted above. As a consequence, in all such multi-parish benefices there is a degree of tension between the desire of some to centralize church life and the desire of others that it should remain essentially local. What makes multi-parish benefices different in character is the point at which this compromise is made. On the one hand, it is not hard to sympathize with the desire of the Lincolnshire clergyman, who, in 1984, presided at twenty-one annual general meetings of church and church related organizations, to have some degree of centralization. On the other hand, particularly at the major festivals of the Church, the parishioners wished to celebrate these events with their clergyman in their own church. In practice some compromise has to be achieved, that recognizes the limits of what a clergyman himself can do.

In many multi-parish benefices a ministerial team exists, by which the clergyman draws round him a number of people who together share in the work of ministry. Much of this has already been described in some detail in Chapter 7. By this means he is able to provide effective leadership of a group of people who together share the work of ministry throughout the multi-parish benefice. However, his role is central in drawing together this team, in providing the spiritual and other resources, and in providing the team with its leadership and its sense of direction. (Urban T. Holmes has written: 'All research of which I know into the life of a parish shows that . . . the priest in the community must be clearly identifiable and responsible if that congregation is to be healthy or even to survive.') It is he who provides the vision and the understanding that brings the team into being in the first place, and allows it to identify and achieve its goal. He must be willing to share his ministry with others, to recognize that it is primarily Christ's ministry in which he and others together share. It is his vision of this shared ministry and his willingness to work in this fashion that allows the team to come into being and to develop in this way. This cannot happen in every parish, and there will always be parishes in which this style of leadership may not be possible or appropriate.

It can be seen that the *centralist scenario* is essentially a clericalist solution in which the shape of the Church is determined by the availability of clergy. At a time of shortage it seems appropriate to some to conduct a policy of withdrawal and retrenchment and to focus the ministry on strong central points. By contrast, the *localist scenario* is essentially a lay solution to the problem, whereby the focus of church life is centred in the local congregation which is required to provide not only its own finance and leadership but also its own ministry. The *multi-parish benefice* represents neither a clericalist nor a lay solution to this dilemma but a proper relationship between the clergyman, as the full-time stipendiary priest, whose role it is to provide the vision and direction, the resources and leadership needed within the parishes and the laity. But he does not minister in isolation, nor can he comfortably refer to the parishes as 'my parishes' or 'my churches'; for he recognizes that all ministry is Christ's ministry, in which clergy and laity are called together to share, and that the churches are not his churches but places to which he has been called to serve within the long succession of rural clergy ministering in that place.

This book has sought, by returning to that formative period when George Herbert wrote *The Country Parson*, to restate the central Anglican understanding about the clergyman's role and ministry in the countryside and his life in the country parish. Then, as now, the pastoral strategy of the Church of England was based on the holy place and the sacred person, and, although the circumstances of rural ministry have changed considerably since Herbert's day, nonetheless the modern country clergyman finds much continuity between *The Country Parson* and his own experience. For generations, people have tended to look upon the life of a country clergyman as quiet and uneventful, slow-paced and un-demanding. Ashley Oxenden wrote in 1857 that: 'Ministry in the countryside is often looked upon as one of tranquil ease and unruffled calm and many a man, before ordination, has mapped out for himself a life of light burdens and few trials.' Far from being the Church's least demanding ministry, serving today in a multi-parish benefice covering four or more parishes requires an approach to ministry which is both energetic and disciplined. The experience of the Archbishops' Rural Commissioners was to find many country clergy who were unsure about what they were doing, and found serving a number of parishes, many with small congregations, to be a dispiriting experience, for the sense of not knowing what one ought to be doing saps the energy of even the most robust. Herbert's book, though written in very different circumstances, still provides *a mark to aim at* and a guide to those who minister in the countryside.

Whilst urban ministry is largely church based and is based on building up a strong church community in a particular place, almost as an alternative community, rural ministry is much more closely related to the local community itself. In the countryside the church building is usually used for worship alone and much of the country clergyman's life is spent within the community itself, where, unlike his urban counterpart, whose main aim is to create an alternative community, the country clergyman's role is to witness to God in the midst of the many activities of village life and to point the village towards God and his Kingdom. Rural ministry does not require people who are expert in anything, but individuals who can communicate the essential mystery of faith to others, and build up a team who share his vision of the Church in that place. The country clergyman must smell of heaven, as Esau smelt of the fields; he must communicate by his person something of the living reality of God, as he goes about his ministry in the villages that he serves, as did George Herbert in the mid-seventeenth-century Wiltshire countryside.

To minister to a cluster of small villages in the diversity of a modern rural community requires skills of a very high order, coupled with a patience and tolerance which do not degenerate to mere acceptance or apathy. To point a village towards God, to speak a word about the essential mystery of existence, to keep people mindful of God and his purposes, to live a life which is eloquent of that prayerful holiness and pastoral concern which in every generation has marked Anglican rural ministry at its best, is not likely to be easy. But the Church is not called to win the world for Christ; rather it is to help all to see that the world is already his and that the Kingdom is all about us.

To do this in the same place for many years and to accept with equanimity the trials and limitations of such a community is a demanding role. A clergyman in the contemporary countryside needs to have his spirituality firmly rooted in his knowledge of God and in the Church's life of prayer, and to have that quiet deep stability of faith which communicates itself to others. He may wear his faith lightly and unostentatiously, but he must believe in it implacably and communicate it to others.

Although the shape of the modern rural church will be that of a community ministry, the clergyman is still needed to be its representative, to be the leader of the praying community, to be its principal pastor and teacher, not in the sense of a man who does everything for a passive congregation, but as a man who motivates and enables people to be the Church in the local situation. Such a man, as he goes about the village, must project the deep joy and excitement of Christian believing if he is to communicate it to others. He must be patient and willing to accept disappointments and rebuffs but, as George Herbert knew, there is no greater joy, no more profound privilege.

Bibliography

All books are published in the United Kingdom, unless otherwise stated.

I (chapter 1)

The Country Parson and the Anglican Pastoral Tradition

Archbishops' Commission on Rural Areas, Report: *Faith in the Countryside* (1990).

Archbishop of Canterbury's Commission, *Faith in the City; a call for action by church and nation: A report of the Archbishop of Canterbury's Commission on Urban Priority Areas* (1985).

Church, R. W., *The Oxford Movement* (1891).

Crockford Prefaces, *The Editor Looks Back* (1947).

Davies, D., Watkins C., and Winter, M., *Church and Religion in Rural England* (1991).

Forder, C., *The Parish Priest at Work* (1947).

Russell, Anthony, *The Clerical Profession* (1980).

Russell, Anthony, *The Country Parish* (1986).

II (chapter 2)

The Role of the Clergyman

Battiscombe, G., *John Keble: a study in limitation* (1963).

Blizzard, S. W., 'The Minister's Dilemma', *Christian Century* (25 April 1956), p. 508.

Blizzard, S. W., 'Role Conflicts of the Urban Protestant Parish Minister', *City Church VII: 4* (September 1956), p. 13.

Blizzard, S. W., 'The Protestant Minister's Integrating Roles', *Religious Education* (July–August 1958), p. 1.

Blizzard, S. W., 'The Parish Minister's Self-Image and Variability in Community Culture', *Pastoral Psychology* (October 1959).

Blizzard, S. W., 'The Parish Minister's Self-Image of his Master Role', *Pastoral Psychology* (December 1958).

Card, T., *Priesthood and Ministry* (1988).

Cecil, Lord D., ed., *The Oxford Book of Christian Verse* (1940).

Fichter, J. H., *Religion as an Occupation* (South Bend, Indiana, 1961).

Gilbert, A. D., *The Making of Post-Christian Britain* (1980).

Jackson, M. A., *The Sociology of Religion: theory and practice* (1974).

Jones, C., Wainwright, G., and Yarnold, E. SJ, eds, *The Study of Spirituality* (1986).

Martin, B., *A Sociology of Contemporary Cultural Change* (1981).

Martin, D., *A Sociology of English Religion* (1967).

Martin, D., *The Religious and the Secular: studies in secularization* (1969).

Martin, D., *A General Theory of Secularization* (1978).

Martin, D., *Breaking the Image* (1980).

Martin, D., and Martin, B., *Religious and Cultural Change in Britain* (1987).

Milton Yinger, J., *Religion, Society and the Individual* (New York, 1957).

Newsome, D., *The Parting of Friends: a study of the Wilberforces and Henry Manning* (1966).

Ranson, S., Bryman, A. and Hinings, B., *Clergy, Ministers and Priests* (1977).

Thomas, L., 'Parish Priests in Search of a Role', *Church Times* (14 April 1989).

Thomas, T., ed., *The British: their religious beliefs and practices* (1988).

Tonnies, F., *Gemeinschaft und Gesellschaft* (1887), tr. C. P. Loomis, *Community and Association* (1955).

Towler, R., 'The Changing Status of the Ministry', *Crucible* (May 1968).

Towler, R., and Coxon, A. P. M., *The Fate of the Anglican Clergy: a sociological study* (1979).

Wilson, B. R., 'The Paul Report Examined', *Theology* 98 (1965), p. 89.

Wilson, B. R., *Religion in Secular Society: a sociological comment* (1966).

Wilson, B. R., *Religious sects* (1970).

Wilson, B. R., *Contemporary Transformations in Religion* (1976).

Wilson, B. R., *Religion in Sociological Perspective* (1982).

Yeo, S., *Religion and Voluntary Organizations in Crisis* (1976).

III   (chapters 3 and 4)

George Herbert and *The Country Parson*

Addleshaw, G. W. O., *The High Church Tradition* (1941).

Addleshaw, G. W. O., and Etchells, F., *The Architectural setting of Anglican Worship* (1948).

Andrewes, L., *Preces Privatae*, tr. F. E. Brightman (1903).

Arnold, D., *Praying with John Donne and George Herbert* (1991).

Aubrey, J., *Brief Lives*, ed. O. Lawson Dick (1972).

Auden, W. H., ed., *Herbert: poems and prose* (1973).

Avis, P., *Anglicanism and the Christian Church: theological resources in historical perspective* (1989).

Beeching, H. C., *George Herbert's The Country Parson* (1898).

Blackstone, B., *The Ferrar Papers* (1938).

Blythe, R., *Divine Landscapes* (1986).

Bodington, C., *Books of Devotion*, Oxford Library of Practical Theology (1903).

Bottrall, M., *George Herbert* (1954).

Brown, D., ed., *Selected poems of George Herbert* (1960).

Bourne, E. C. E., *The Anglicanism of William Laud* (1947).

Carey, J., *John Donne: life, mind and art* (1981).

Chadwick, O., 'The Fisherman and His God: Izaak Walton', Drawbridge Lecture, King's College, London (1984).

Chadwick, O., *The Reformation* (1964).

Charles, A., *A Life of George Herbert* (Cornell University Press, 1977).

Chute, M., *Two Gentle Men: the lives of George Herbert and Robert Herrick* (1960).

Cropper, M., *Flame touches Flame* (1949).

Cuming, G., *The Godly Order; texts and studies relating to the Book of Common Prayer* (1983).

Davies, G., *The Early Stuarts 1603 – 1660* (1937).

Dircks, W. H., ed., *Autobiography of Edward, Lord Herbert of Cherbury* (1888).

Dugmore, C. W., Parker, T. M., Ratcliffe, E. C., and Cuming, G. J., *The English Prayer Book 1549 – 1662* (1963).

Edwards, D., *Christian England (vol 2): From the Reformation to the Eighteenth Century* (1983).

Eliot, T. S., *For Lancelot Andrewes; essays on style and order* (1929).

Etchells, R., *A Selection of Poems by George Herbert* (1988).

Fincham, K., *Prelate as Pastor; The Episcopate of James I* (1990).

Frere, W. H., *The English Church in the reign of Elizabeth and James I* (1904).

Gardner, H., *Religion and Literature* (1971).

Harrison, A. W., *Arminianism* (1936).

Higham, F., *Faith of our Fathers; the men and movements of the seventeenth century* (1939).

Higham, F., *Lancelot Andrewes* (1952).

Higham, F., *Catholic and Reformed: a Study of the Anglican Church 1559 – 1662* (1962).

Hill, C., *Society and Puritanism in pre-revolutionary England* (1964).

Hooker, R., *Works* ed. J. Keble (1845).

Hutchinson, F. E., ed., *The Works of George Herbert* (1941).

Hutton, W. H., *The English Church from the accession of Charles I to the death of Anne* (1903).

Hyde, A. G., *George Herbert and his times* (1906).

Lacey May, G., *Wings of an Eagle: an anthology of Caroline preachers* (1955).

Lamont, W., and Oldfield, S., *Politics, Religion and Literature in the Seventeenth Century* (1975).

Lossky, N., *Lancelot Andrewes The Preacher (1555 – 1626); the origins of the mystical theology of the Church of England* (1986), tr. A. Louth (1991).

Martin, H., ed., *The Country Parson and Selected Poems by George Herbert* (1956).

Mason, K., *George Herbert: priest and poet* (1980).

Maycock, A. L., *Nicholas Ferrar of Little Gidding* (1938).

McAdoo, H. R., *The Spirit of Anglicanism; a survey of Anglican theological method in the seventeenth century* (1965).

Moorman, J. R. H., *The Anglican Spiritual Tradition* (1983).

More, P. L. and Cross, F. L., *Anglicanism: the thought and practice of the Church of England, illustrated from the religious literature of the seventeenth century* (1951).

Moxley, C., *Apostles of Love* (1991).
Mulward, P., *The Religious Controversies of the Jacobean Age* (1978).
Novarr, D., *The Making of Walton's Lives* (1959).
Palmer, G. H., *The English Works of George Herbert* 3rd edn. (1915).
Pollard, A., ed., *Richard Hooker: Ecclesiastical Polity* (1990).
Powell, A., *John Aubrey and his Friends* (1948).
Procter, F., and Frere, W. H., *A New History of The Book of Common Prayer* (1965).
Purcell, W., *Anglican Spirituality: a continuing tradition* (1988).
Reidy, M. F., *Bishop Lancelot Andrewes: Jacobean Court Preacher* (Chicago, 1955).
Ridley, J., *Thomas Cranmer* (1962).
Scarisbrick, J. J., *The Reformation and the English People* (1984).
Stone, L., *The Causes of the English Revolution 1529 – 1642* (1972).
Stranks, C. J., *Anglican Devotion* (1961).
Summers, J. H., *George Herbert: his religion and art* (1954).
Sykes, N., *The English Religious Tradition* (1953).
Thomas, R. S., ed., *A Choice of George Herbert's Verse* (1967).
Tobin, J., ed., *George Herbert: the Complete English Poems* (1991).
Trevor-Roper, H., *Archbishop Laud* (1940). (with new preface, 1962).
Trevor-Roper, H., *Catholics, Anglicans and Puritans: seventeenth century essays* (1987).
Tuve, R., *A Reading of George Herbert* (1952).
Tyacke, N., *Anti-Calvinists: the rise of English Arminianism 1590 – 1640* (1987).
Van de Weyer, R., and Saunders, P., *Lament and Love; the vision of George Herbert* (1989).
Vedler, H., *The Poetry of George Herbert* (Cambridge, Mass., 1975).
Walton, I., *The Lives of John Donne; Sir Henry Wotton, Richard Hooker; George Herbert and Robert Sanderson*, ed. S. B. Carter (1951).
Walton, I., *The Compleat Angler* (1953) (with part II by Charles Cotton, first published in 1676; Oxford University Press World Classics edition 1982).
Welsby, P. A., *George Abbot: the unwanted Archbishop* (1962).
White Singleton, M., *God's Courtier* (1987).
Wignall, P., ed., *The Anglican Spirit* (1982).
Willey, B., *The Seventeenth Century Background* (1934).
Woodhouse, H. F., *The Doctrine of the Church in Anglican Theology 1547 – 1603* (1954).

IV (chapter 5)

The Changed Church

Abbey, C. J., and Overton, J. H., *The English Church in the Eighteenth Century*, 2 vols (1878).
ACCM, *The Place of Auxiliary Ministry, Ordained and Lay* (1973).
Adair, J., *The Becoming Church* (1977).
Adamson, J. W., *English Education 1789 – 1902* (1930).

Addison, W., *The English Country Parson* (1947).
Allen, R., *Voluntary Clergy* (1923).
Allen, R., *The Case for Voluntary Clergy* (1930).
Ashby, M. K., *The Changing English Village 1066 – 1914* (1974).
Best, G. F. A., *Temporal Pillars* (1964).
Beveridge, W. E., *Managing the Church* (1971).
Brander, M., *The Country Divine* (1981).
Carpenter, E., *Cantuar: The Archbishops and their Office* (1971).
Carr-Saunders, A. M., and Wilson, P. A., *The Professions* (1933).
Chadwick, O., *The Victorian Church*, 2 vols (1966, 1970).
Chadwick, O., *The Secularization of the European Mind in the Nineteenth Century* (1975).
Chadwick, O., 'Classical Anglicanism and Lancelot Andrewes', Southwell Lecture (1986).
Christmas, F. E., *The Parson in English Literature* (1950).
Church Assembly, *The Church in Country Parishes* (1940).
Currie, R., Gilbert, A., and Horsley, L., *Churches and Church Goers: Patterns of Church Growth in the British Isles since 1700* (1977).
Diocese of Coventry, *Auxiliary Pastoral Ministry, a report by John Moses and Anthony Russell* (1976).
Diocese of Lichfield, *On Patterns of Ministry* (1980).
Ditchfield, P. J., *The Parish Clerk* (1907).
Ditchfield, P. J., *Old Time Parson* (1908).
Dunbabin, J. P. D., *Rural Discontent in Nineteenth Century Britain* (1974).
Edwards, D. L., *Religion and Change* (1974).
Fendall, C. P., and Critchley, E. A., *The Diary of Benjamin Newton 1816 – 1818* (1933).
Francis Brown, C. K., *A History of the English Clergy 1800 – 1900* (1953).
Gibbs, J. A., *A Cotswold Village* (1898).
Gilbert, A. D., *Religion and Society in Industrial England: Church, Chapel and Social Change 1740 – 1914* (1976).
Goldner, F., et al. 'Priests and Church: the professionalisation of an organisation', *American Behavioural Scientist* no.14 (1972), pp. 507 – 24.
Haggard, H. R., *A Farmer's Year* (1899).
Hammond, P., *The Parson and the Victorian parish* (1971).
Handy, C., *Understanding Organisations* (1976).
Hastings, A., *A History of English Christianity 1920 – 1985* (1986).
Heeney, B., *A Different Kind of Gentleman* (Connecticut, 1976).
Henson, H. H., *Anglicanism* (1921).
Henson, H. H., *The Church of England* (1939).
Holloway, R., ed., *The Anglican Tradition* (1984).
Horn, P., *Labouring Life in the Victorian Countryside* (1976).
Horn, P., *Education in Rural England 1800 – 1914* (1978).
Inglis, K. S., *Churches and the Working Class in Victorian England* (1963).
Jackson, J. A., ed. *Professions and Professionalization* (1970).
Jarvis, P., 'The Ministry: Occupation, Profession or Status?', *Expository Times* (June 1975).

Bibliography

Jarvis, P., 'The Parish Ministry as a Semi-Profession', *The Sociological Review* 23 (1975).

Kitson Clark, G., *The Making of Victorian England* (1962).

Kitson Clark, G., *Churchmen and the Condition of England 1832 – 1885* (1973).

Laslett, P., *The World we have Lost* (1965).

Lathe, A., ed., *The Group: 21 years of the Hempnall Group of Parishes in Norfolk* (1986).

Lloyd, R., *The Church of England 1900 – 1965* (1965).

Macaulay, T. B., *History of England*, ed. C. H. Firth, 6 vols (1913).

MacDermott, K. H., *The Old Church Gallery Minstrels* (1948).

MacFarlane, A., *The Origins of English Individualism* (1978).

Marsh, P. T., *The Victorian Church in Decline* (1967).

McClatchey, D., *Oxfordshire Clergy 1777 – 1869* (1960).

McLeod, H., *Class and Religion in Late Victorian England* (1974).

McLeod, H., *Religion and the Working Class in Nineteenth Century Britain* (1984).

Mingay, G. E., *English Landed Society in the Eighteenth Century* (1962).

Mingay, G. E., *Rural Life in Victorian England* (1977).

Moorman, J. R. H., *A History of the Church of England* (1953).

Morley Report, *Partners in Ministry* (1967).

Morsley, C., *News from the English Countryside 1850 – 1950* (1983).

Neill, S., *Anglicanism* (1958).

Newsome, D. H., *The Parting of Friends* (1966).

Norman, E. R., *Church and Society in England 1770 – 1970* (1976).

Obelkevich, J., *Religion and Society in South Lindsey 1825 – 1877* (1976).

Ollard, S. L., *A Short History of the Oxford Movement* (1915).

Overton, J. H., and Relton, F., *The English Church 1714 – 1800* (1906).

Owen, D., *English Philanthropy 1660 – 1960* (1965).

Oxley, J. W., *Poor Relief in England and Wales 1601 – 1834* (1974).

Paul, L., *The Deployment and Payment of the Clergy* (1964).

Paul, L., *A Church by Daylight: a reappraisal of the Church of England and its future* (1973).

Peacock, A. J., *Bread and Blood: A Study of the Agrarian Riots in East Anglia 1816* (1965).

Quinault, R., and Stevenson, J., *Popular Protest and Social Order 1790 – 1820* (1974).

Quinlan, M. J., *Victorian Prelude: A History of English Manners 1700 – 1830* (1941).

Ramsey, A. M., *The Anglican Spirit*, ed. D. Coleman (1991).

Reader, W. J., *Professional Men: the Rise of the Professional Classes in the Nineteenth Century* (1966).

Rowell, G., *The Vision Glorious: themes and personalities of the Catholic Revival in Anglicanism* (1983).

Rowell, G., ed., *Tradition Renewed: the Oxford Movement Conference Papers* (1986).

Rudge, P. F., *Ministry and Management: Studies in ecclesiastical administration* (1968).

Russell, Anthony, ed., *Groups and Teams in the Countryside* (1980).
Smith, A., *The Established Church and Popular Religion* (1970).
Smith, A. C., *The South Ormsby Experiment* (1980).
Soloway, R. A., *Prelates and People: Ecclesiastical social thought in England 1783 – 1852* (1969).
Sykes, N., *Church and State in England in the Eighteenth Century* (1934).
Sykes, S., and Booty, J., *The Study of Anglicanism* (1988).
Thompson, F. M. L., *English Landed Society in the Nineteenth Century* (1962).
Thompson, K., *Bureaucracy and Church Reform* (1970).
Tiller, J., *A Strategy for the Church's Ministry* (1983).
Tindal Hart, A., and Carpenter, E., *The Nineteenth Century Country Parson* (1954).
Tindal Hart, A., *The Eighteenth Century Country Parson* (1955).
Tindal Hart, A., *The Country Priest in English History* (1959).
Trevelyan, G. M., *English Social History* (1944).
Trollope, A., *Clergymen of the Church of England* (1866).
Virgin, P., *The Church in an Age of Negligence; ecclesiastical structure and the problems of Church Reform 1700 – 1840* (1989).
Ward, W. R., *Religion and Society in England 1710 – 1850* (1992).
Warne, A., *Church and Society in Eighteenth Century Devon* (1969).
Welsby, P. A., *A History of the Church of England 1945 – 1980* (1984).
West, F., *The Country Parish Today and Tomorrow* (1960).
West, F., *Sparrow of the Spirit* (1961).
Wickham, E. R., *Church and people in an Industrial City* (1957).
Wilkinson, A., *The Church of England and the First World War* (1978).
Willey, B., *Nineteenth Century Studies* (1949).
Wolf, W. J., ed., *The Spirit of Anglicanism* (1982).
Young, C. M., *Victorian England* (1953).

V   (chapter 6)

The Changed Countryside

Agricultural Economics Research Institute, Oxford, *Country Planning: A Study of Rural Problems* [in north Oxfordshire] (1944).
Ambrose, P., *The Quiet Revolution* (1974).
Arkleton Trust, *Popular Images and the Reality of Deprivation in Rural Areas*, Brian McLaughlin (1990).
Arkleton Trust, *Rural Poverty and Deprivation in Europe – from analysis to action*, James Hunter (1990).
Ashton, J. and Long, W. H., eds, *The Remoter Rural Areas of Britain* (1972).
Association of District Councils, *Rural Recovery: Strategy for Survival* (1978).
Association of District Councils, *Rural Deprivation* (1979).
Baker, W. P., *The English Village* (1953).
Barrell, J., *The Idea of Landscape and the Sense of Place* (1972).
Beckinsale, R., and Beckinsale, M., *The English Heartland* (1980).

238   *Bibliography*

Bell, C., and Newby, H., *Community Studies: an introduction to the sociology of local communities* (1971).

Bell, C., and Newby, H., eds, *Sociology of Communities; a selection of readings* (1974).

Beresford, T., *We Plough the Fields: British Farming Today* (1975).

Best, R. H., and Rogers, A. W., *The Urban Countryside* (1973).

Blunden J. and Curry, N., eds., *A Future of our Countryside* (1989).

Blythe, R., *Akenfield: Portrait of an English Village* (1969).

Bonham Carter, V., *The English Village* (1951).

Bonham Carter, V., *The Survival of the English Countryside* (1971).

Bracey, H. E., *English Rural Life: village activities, organisations and institutions* (1959).

Broady, M., ed., *Marginal Regions: essays on social planning* (1973).

Champion, T. and Watkin, C., eds., *People in the Countryside: Studies of Social Change in Rural Britain* (1911).

Cherry, G. E., ed., *Rural Planning Problems* (1976).

Chisholm, M., *Rural Settlement and Land Use* (1962).

Christaller, W., *Die Zentralen Orte in Suddeutschland*, tr. C. W. Baskin, *Central Places in Southern Germany* (1966).

Clark, D., *Rural Housing Initiatives* (1981).

Clark, K., *Civilization: a personal view* (1964).

Clark, K., *Ruskin Today* (1964).

Cloke, P., *Key settlements in Rural Areas* (1979).

Clout, H. D., *Rural Geography: an introductory survey* (1972).

Cohen, A. P., *Belonging; identity and social organization in British rural culture* (1982).

Constable, M., ed., *No Place in the Country: A Report on second homes in England and Wales* (1973).

Crichton, R. M., *Commuters' village: a study of Community and Commuters in the Berkshire village of Stratfield Mortimer* (1964).

Darley, G., *Villages of Vision* (1978).

Davidson, J., and Wibberley, G. P., *Planning and the Rural Environment* (1977).

Donaldson, J. G. S., and Donaldson, F., *Farming in Britain Today* (1969).

Emmett, I., *A North Wales Village; a social anthropological study* (1964).

Ernle, Lord, *English Farming, Past and Present* (6th edn. 1961).

Faber, R., *The Myth of the Rural Idyll* (1983).

Fairbrother, N., *New Lives, New Landscapes* (1970).

Frankenberg, R., *Village on the Border; a social study of religion, politics and football in a North Wales community* (1957).

Frankenberg, R., *Communities in Britain* (1966).

Franklin, S. H., *Rural Societies* (1971).

Galeiki, B., *Basic Concepts of Rural Sociology* (1972).

Gilg, A., *Countryside Planning: the first three decades 1945–1976* (1978).

Green, R., *Country Planning: the future of rural regions* (1971).

Haggard, H. R., *Rural England* (1902).

Havinden, M. A., *Estate Villages: a study of the Berkshire villages of Ardington and Lockinge* (1966).

Higgs, J., ed., *People in the Countryside* (1966).

Horn, P., *The Rural World 1780–1850: social change in the English countryside* (1980).

Jennings, P., *The Living Village* (1972).

Jones, G., *Rural Life* (1973).

Knoepflmacher, U. C., and Tennyson, G. B., eds., *Nature and the Victorian Imagination* (1977).

Kroeber, K., *Romantic Landscape Vision: Constable and Wordsworth* (Wisconsin, 1975).

Lerner, L., *The Uses of Nostalgia: Studies in pastoral poetry* (1972).

Lewis, G. L., *Rural Communities: a social geography* (1979).

Littlejohn, J., *Westrigg; the sociology of a Cheviot parish* (1964).

Lively, P., *The Presence of the Past* (1975).

Lowe, P., et al., *Countryside Conflicts: the politics of farming, forestry and conservation* (1986).

Lowenthal, D., *The Past is a Foreign Country* (1985).

Malmse, E., *English Landscaping and Literature* (1966).

Marsh, J., *Back to the Land: the pastoral impulse in Victorian England from 1880 to 1914* (1982).

Martin, E. W., ed., *Country Life in England* (1966).

Massingham, H. J., *The English Countryman* (1942).

Mills, D. R., ed., *English Rural Communities; the impact of a specialized economy* (1973).

Mingay, G. E., *Enclosure and the Small Farmer in the Age of Industrial Revolution* (1968).

Mitford, M. R., *Our Village* (1824; 1912).

Moreau, R. E., *The Departed Village* (1968).

Morgan, D. H., *Harvesters and Harvesting 1840–1900; a study of the rural proletariat* (1982).

Muir, R., *The English Village* (1980).

Newby, H., *The Deferential Worker; a study of farm workers in East Anglia* (1977).

Newby, H., *Green and Pleasant Land? Social Change in rural England* (1979).

Newby, H., *The Countryside in Question* (1988).

Orwin, C. S., and Wheetam, E. H., *History of British Agriculture 1846–1914* (1964).

Packington, H., *English Villages and Hamlets* (1934).

Pahl, R. E., *Urbs in Rure: London School of Economics Geographical Paper No. 2* (1965).

Parker, R., *The Common Stream* (1975).

Perry, P. J., *British Agriculture 1875–1914* (1973).

Quennell, P., *John Ruskin; the portrait of a prophet* (1949).

Ravillious, J., and Ravillious, R., *The Heart of the Countryside* (1980).

Rees, A. D., *Life in a Welsh Countryside: a second study of Llanfihangel yng Ngwynfa* (1950).

Robin, J., *Elmdon: community and change in a north-west Essex village 1861–1964* (1980).

Royal Agricultural Society of England, *The State of Agriculture in the*

United Kingdom: Report prepared by a group under chairmanship of Sir Derek Barber (1991).

Saville, J., *Rural Depopulation in England and Wales 1851 – 1951* (1957).

Seebohm, F., *The English Village Community* (1883).

Sharp, T., *The Anatomy of the Village* (1946).

Shepard, P., *Man in the Landscape; a historical view of the esthetics of nature* (New York, 1967).

Slater, G., *The English Peasantry* (1907).

Stacey, M., *Tradition and Change: a study of Banbury* (1960).

Tate, W. E., *The English Village Community and the Enclosure Movement* (1967).

Thomas, F. C., *The Changing Village* (1938).

Thorburn, A., *Planning Villages* (1971).

Thorns, D., *Suburbia* (1973).

Unwins, R., *The Rural Muses* (1954).

Walker, A., *Rural Poverty: Poverty, deprivation and planning in rural areas* (1978).

Warren, C. H., *England is a Village* (1940).

White, D., 'Dying Villages', *New Society* 19 (1972), pp. 108 – 9.

Williams, M., *Thomas Hardy and Rural England* (1972).

Williams, R., *The Country and The City* (1975).

Williams, W. M., *A West Country Village: Ashworth —Family, Kinship and Land* (1963).

Williams, W. M., *The Sociology of an English Village: Gosforth* (1969).

Young, F. B., *Portrait of a Village* (1937).

VI (chapters 7,8 and 9)

The Country Clergyman Today and the Future of the Rural Church

ACCM, *A Supporting Ministry* (1968).

ACCM, *Ordained Ministry Today* (1969).

ACCM, *Call to Order, vocation and ministry in the Church of England* (1989).

ACCM Occasional Paper No. 22, *Education for the Church; Ministry* (1987).

ACCM Occasional Paper No. 24, *Guidelines for Local Non-Stipendiary Ministry* (1987).

Adair, J., *Training for Leadership* (1968).

Archbishops' Council on Evangelism, *A Workbook on Rural Evangelism* (1977).

Arthur Rank Centre, *Evangelism in the Countryside: Papers of a Conference of Bishops* (18 January 1991).

Avis, P., *Authority, Leadership and Conflict in the Church* (1992).

Baelz, P. and Jacobs, W., eds., *Ministers of the Kingdom: exploration in non-stipendiary ministry* (1985).

Beeson, T., ed., *Partnership in Ministry* (1964).

Bell, G. K. A., *The Modern Parson* (1928).

Biersdorf, J., *Creating an Intentional Ministry* (New York, 1976).

Bishops' Regulations for the Selection and Training of Candidates for Auxiliary Pastoral Ministry (1970).

Board of Mission and Unity, *The Priesthood of the Ordained Ministry* (1986).

Bradley, I., *Marching to the Promised Land* (1992).

Brothers, J., 'Social Change and the Role of the Priest', *Social Compass 10*: 6 (1963), p. 477.

Browning, W., *A Handbook of the Ministry* (1985).

Burrick, R. J., 'The Ecclesiastical Minister and Marriage, *Social Compass 12*: 1 – 2 (1965), p. 93.

Calvert, I., ed., *Second Workbook in Rural Evangelism* (1984).

Carr, W., *Brief Encounters* (1985).

Carr, W., *The Priestlike Task* (1985).

Carr, W., *The Pastor as Theologian: the integration of pastoral ministry, theology and discipleship* (1989).

Carr, W., ed., *Say One for Me: the Church of England in the next decade* (1992).

Christian Action, *The Church in Urban Society* (1991).

CIO Publication, *All are Called: Towards a Theology of the Laity* (1985).

Clark, J., *Mission in Rural Communities* (1978).

Clark, S. B., *Unordained Elders and Renewal Communities* (New York, 1976).

Coates, C. H., and Kustler, R. C., 'Role Dilemmas of Protestant Clergymen in the Metropolitan Community', *Review of Religious Research 6*: 3 (1964 – 5), p. 147.

Coates, M. A., *Clergy Stress: the hidden conflicts in ministry* (1989).

Coleman, P., 'A Local Temple', *Theology 88* (1985), p. 424.

Croft, P., 'Rural Deaneries', *Prism Pamphlet 5* (1962).

Croft, P., 'Making the Deanery Work', *Parish and People* (1991).

Dalby, M., *The Gospel and the Priest* (1974).

de Haas, P., *The Church as an Institution: critical studies in the relation between theology and sociology* (New York, 1974).

de Waal, E., *Seeking God: the way of St Benedict* (1984).

de Waal, V., *What is the Church?* (1969).

Diocese of Hereford, *The People, the Land and the Church* (1987).

Diocese of Lincoln, *Exploring Local Ministry: Diocese of Lincoln Local Ministry Scheme Preparatory Course for Parishes* (1990).

Dorey, T., *Rural Ministries: Report of Oxford Institute for Church and Society* (1979).

Doubtfire, B., et al., *Working with Faith in the Countryside: change and challenge for churches in small communities* (1991).

Down, M., 'The Shape of the Rural Church', *Theology 87* (1984), pp. 164 – 72.

Dudley, C. S., *Making the Small Church Effective* (Abingdon, USA, 1978).

Dudley, C. S., and Walrath, D. A., *Developing Your Small Church: Potential* (Valley Forge, Pennsylvania, 1988).

Dulles, A., *Models of the Church* (1974).

Dunstan, G. R., ed., *The Sacred Ministry* (1970).

Eaton, D., 'Ministry in Surrey Villages', *New Fire 8* (1984), pp. 203 – 8.

Ecclestone, G., ed., *The Parish Church?* (1988).

Faith in the Countryside: shortened version ed. M. Burrell (1991).

Ferris, P., *The Church of England* (1963).

Fletcher, J. H., 'A Comparative view of the Parish Priest', *Archives de Sociologie des Religions* 8: 16 (1963), p. 44.

Francis, L. J., *Rural Anglicanism: a future for young Christians?* (1985).

Fuller, J. and Vaughan, P. H., eds, *Working for the Kingdom; the story of ministers in secular employment* (1986).

General Synod, *A Rural Strategy for the Church of England: Proposals for an Archbishops Commission on Rural Areas* (1986).

Gill, R., 'Theology of the Non-Stipendiary Ministry', *Theology* 80 (1977), pp. 410–413.

Gill, R., *Prophecy and Praxis* (1981).

Gill, R., *Beyond Decline: a challenge to the churches* (1988).

Glasse, J. D., *Profession: Minister; confronting the identity crisis of the Parish Clergy* (New York, 1968).

Gore, C., *The Church and the Ministry* (2nd edn. 1889).

Green, S. V., 'Blue-print for the Rural Deanery', *Prism* (September 1961), p. 14f.

Greenwood, R., *Reclaiming the Church* (1988).

Guiver, G., *Company of Voices: Daily Prayer and the People of God* (1988).

Guiver, G., *Faith in Momentum* (1990).

Gustafson, J. M., 'The Clergy in the United States', *Social Compass* 12: 1–2 (1965) p. 35.

Habgood, J. S., *Church and Nation in a Secular Age* (1983).

Hacking, R., *On the Boundary: a vision for non-stipendiary ministry* (1990).

Hall, R. H., 'Professionalization and Bureaucratization', *American Sociological Review* 33 (1968), pp. 92–104.

Hanson, A. T., *Church, Sacraments and Ministry* (1975).

Hanson, A. T., *The Pioneer Ministry* (1961).

Hanson, R. P. C., *Christian Priesthood Examined* (1979).

Hanson, A. T., and Hanson, R. P. C., *The Identity of the Church* (1987).

Hardy, C., and Stamp, G., *The Rural Deanery and its Future* (St George's House, 1981).

Harrison, P. M., *Authority and Power in the Free Church Tradition* (1960).

Harvey, A. E., *Priest or President?* (1975).

Henson, H. H., *Church and Parson in England* (1927).

Hocking, M., *A Handbook of Pastoral Work* (1977).

Hodge, M., *Non-Stipendiary Ministry in the Church of England* (1983).

Hollings, M., *Living Priesthood* (1977).

Holmes, U. T., III. *The Priest in Community* (New York, 1978).

Hopkins, S., *The Rural Ministry* (1970).

Hume, B., *Light in the Lord: reflections on priesthood* (1991).

James, E., *The Nature and Function of Priesthood* (1955).

James, E., *Odd Man Out?* (1961).

James, E., ed., *Stewards of the Mysteries of God* (1979).

Jay, E., *The Church; its changing image through twenty centuries* vol II (1978).

Kung, H., *Why Priests?* (1972).

Lambeth Essays on Ministry (1968).

Lash, N. and Rhymer, J., eds., *The Christian Priesthood* (1970).

Lemaire, A., *Ministry in the Church* (Eng. edn. 1977).

Luke, R. H., *The Commission of the Church in the Countryside* (1982).

Macquarrie, J., *Theology, Church and Ministry* (1986).

Madsen, P. O., *The Small Church: valid, vital and victorious* (Valley Forge, Pennsylvania, 1975).

Manson, T. W., *Ministry and Priesthood, Christ's and Ours* (1958).

Martineau, R., *The Office and Work of a Priest* (1992).

Mason, K., *Priesthood and Society* (1992).

Mathieson, M. B., *The Shepherds of the Delectable Mountains: the study of the Washington County Mission Program* (Ohio, 1979).

McAdoo, H. R., *Anglican Heritage: theology and spirituality* (1991).

Methodist Conference Report, *The Ministry of the People of God* (1986).

Metz, J. B., *The Emergent Church: The Future of Christianity in a Post-Bourgeois Society* (1981).

Ministry Co-Ordinating Group, *The Church's Ministry – a Survey* (Report 1980).

Ministry Co-ordinating Group, *Team and Group Ministries* (1985).

Ministry Co-ordinating Group, *The Ordained Ministry: Numbers, Cost and Deployment: A discussion paper* (1988).

Moberly, R. C., *Ministerial Priesthood* (1899).

Mobery, D. O., *The Church as a Social Institution* (New Jersey, 1962).

Moody, C., *Eccentric Ministry: pastoral care and leadership in the parish* (1992).

Moore, C., Wilson, A. N., and Stamp, G., *The Church in Crisis* (1986).

Morgan, E. R., *The Church in Country Parishes* (1940).

Mueller, E. W., and Ekola, G. C., *The Silent Struggle for mid-America: The Church in Town and Country Today* (Minneapolis, 1963).

Neagele, K. D., 'Clergy, Psychiatrists and Teachers: a study in idea and socialization', *Canadian Journal of Economical Political Science* 22 (1956), p. 46.

Newton, L., *Life and Death in the Country Parish*, Board of Mission and Unity (1981).

Niebuhr, H. R., *The Purpose of the Church and its Ministry* (New York, 1956).

Nott, P., *Moving Forward* I and II (1989 and 1991).

Parsons, T., 'The Professions and the Social Structure', *Social Forces* 17 (1939) pp. 457–67.

Paton, D. M., *Reform of the Ministry: a study in the work of Roland Allen* (1968).

Paul, L., Russell, A. and Reading, L., eds., *Rural Society and the Church: Report of the Hereford Conference 1976* (1977).

Perham, M. F., *Liturgy Pastoral and Parochial* (1984).

Pickering, W. S. F., *Anglo –Catholicism; a study of religious ambiguity* (1989).

Poulton, J., *Fresh Air; a vision for the future of the rural church* (1985).

Quinley, H. E., *The Prophetic Clergy* (New York 1974).

Ramsey, A. M., *The Christian Priest Today* (1972).

Report of the Lincoln Consultation on Rural Society, ed. I. Beckwith (1979).

Report of the Oxford Diocesan Board of Social Responsibility. *The Rural Face of the Diocese* (1981).

Richardson, J., ed., *Ten Rural Churches* (1987).

Robinson, A. W., *The Personal Life of the Clergy* (1902); republished as *The Personal Life of the Christian* with preface by John Robinson 1980).

Rural Theology Association, *Occasional Papers*.

Rural Theology Association, *The Rural Church: Towards 2000*, ed. M. Wilson (1989).

Russell, A., *Christian Unity in the Village*, BCC (1986).

Sanford, J. A., *Ministry Burnout* (New York, 1982).

Saumarez Smith, W. H., *An Honorary Ministry*, ACCM Occasional Paper no.8 (1977).

Schillebeeckx, E., *Ministry* (1981).

Sedgewick, P., ed., *A Rural Life Reader* (1984).

Smith, A. C., *Deaneries – Dead or Alive* (1963).

Stamp, G., 'Does the Deanery make a Difference', *Crucible* (July 1982).

Stark, R., Foster, B. D., Glock, C. Y., and Quinley, H. E., *Wayward Shepherds* (New York, 1971).

Stewart, C. W., *Person and Profession: career development in the ministry* (New York, 1974).

Strudwick, V., 'Local Ordained Ministry: Yesterday's case for Tomorrow's Church', *Theology* 84 (May 1981), pp. 170 – 176.

Sykes, S. W., *The Integrity of Anglicanism* (1978).

Sykes, S. W., *The Identity of Christianity* (1984).

The Place of Auxiliary Ministry Ordained and Lay CIO, (1973).

Thompson, K. A., 'Religious organisations', *People and Organisations*, eds G. Salaman and K. A. Thompson (1973).

Thung, M. A., *The Precious Organisation: sociological exploration of the church's mission and structure* (Moulton, 1976).

Thurian, M., *Priesthood and Ministry* (1983).

Tomorrow's Church Group, *Kingdom and Ministry; a workbook on lay ministry* (1979).

Turner, H. J. M., *Ordination and Vocation: Yesterday and Today* (1990).

Van de Weyer, R., *Wickwyn* (1986).

Van de Weyer, R., *The Little Gidding Way* (1988).

Van de Weyer, R., *Little Gidding* (1989).

Van de Weyer, R., *The Country Church: a guide for the renewal of rural Christianity* (1991).

Van de Weyer, R., *The Country Church* (1992).

Vaughan, P. H., *Non-Stipendiary Ministry in the Church of England: a history of the development of an idea* (San Fransisco, 1990).

Vere Hodge, F., *Handbook for the newly Ordained* (1986).

Walker, P., *The Anglican Church Today: rediscovering the Middle Way* (1986).

Weston, N., *Taking on Faith in the Countryside – some comments on the pastoral aspects of the report of the ACORA* (1991).

Whale, J., *The Future of Anglicanism* (1988).

Wignall, P., *Taking Custody of the Future* (1982).

Williams, C., *The Church* (1969).

Index

248

Index

St Bees 18
Salisbury 93-5, 127, 132
Salisbury Cathedral 48, 50, 66, 133
Sanderson, Robert (Bishop of
  Lincoln) 27
Savoy Conference 98
schools 113-14
second home ownership 155
Sheffield Report 124
South Ormsby Group 125
Southampton, Earl of 40
Stanley, Edward (Dean of
  Westminster) 102
stress 205-6
Sunday school 2
Sidney, Sir Philip 28

Taylor, Jeremy (Bishop of Connor,
  Down and Dromore) 72, 189
Temple, The (Herbert) 24, 25, 45,
  50, 51
Tennyson, Lord Alfred 143
Theodore, Archbishop 161
theologians 181
Thomas, Edward 144
Thomas, Ken (Bishop of Bath and
  Wells) 26
Thorndike, Herbert 39
Tiller, John 122, 125, 224
Tillotson, John (Archbishop of
  Canterbury) 106
Tindal Hart, A. 101

tithe 119-20
*Treatise of Temperance and
  Sobrietie* (Herbert) 91
Trinity College, Cambridge 35-7
Trollope, Anthony 202
Turner, John 138, 142

Ussher, James (Archbishop of
  Armagh) 69

village shop and Post Office 153
Virginia Company 28
visiting 178-9

Walton, Izaak 22, 26, 27, 29, 30,
  35, 41, 45, 47, 48, 55, 64, 84, 99
Waterperry 98
Westminster Abbey 43; School 32
Whitgift, John (Archbishop of
  Canterbury) 57
Wilberforce, Samuel (Bishop of
  Oxford and Winchester) 113, 213
William of Orange, and Mary 99
Williams, John (Bishop of Lincoln)
  29, 34, 42, 43
Wilton House, 30, 50, 81
Woodforde, James 101, 105, 107
Woodnoth, Arthur 45, 46, 47, 49
Wootton, Sir Henry 27
Wordsworth, William 138, 140

Yonge, Charlotte 101